DOWN THE RIDGELINE

It was 2030 hours. The attack on the right had been sustained. The ridge was dark and almost quiet. Firing had dwindled to a halt. From behind the Japanese lines came the vague sounds of movement that could mean only one thing: They were regrouping there, and being resupplied.

A strange gray mist crept over the ridge, drifting into the ravines. It was reported to division. "What is it, gas?" demanded Jerry Thomas.

"Negative. The Japs have kicked out a few smoke shells."

The division D-3 looked at his watch: 2130. The sound of a sudden fusillade came in clearly over the still-open phone.

"They're at us again, Jerry. Hold your hat."

The Kawaguchis had launched their second assault of the night. All down the ridgeline they came, yelling screaming, cursing. They hit the wire—the dying and dead serving as their carpet . . . .

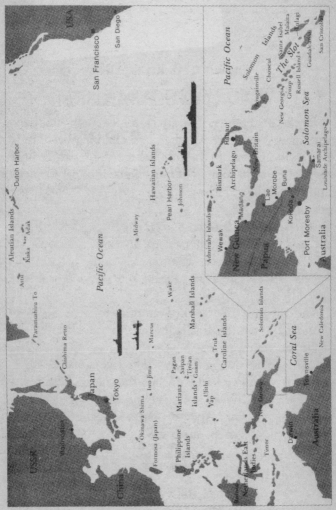

VICTORY AT GUADALCANAL
ROBERT EDWARD LEE

ZEBRA BOOKS
KENSINGTON PUBLISHING CORP.

ZEBRA BOOKS

are published by

KENSINGTON PUBLISHING CORP.
475 Park Avenue South
New York, N.Y. 10016

CONTENTS

ACKNOWLEDGMENTS

The author wishes to express his appreciation for the assistance provided him by Headquarters, United States Marine Corps, and the eminent historian, Col. Verle E. Ludwig USMC (Ret.). The author's special gratitude is due Mrs. Billie Farris, Assistant to the Commandant, United States Marine Corps (Ret.), who for several years gave generously of her time and knowledge; to Lt. Col. Robert A. Miller USMC (Ret.) and Maj. C. Allen Smith USA (Ret.) for their comments and encouragement; and to Rain Blockley, for her gracious empathy, sensitivity, and understanding as the editor of this book.

Introduction

GUADALCANAL AND STALINGRAD

On February 2, 1943, in the bitter cold of a Russian winter, Field Marshal Friedrich von Paulus surrendered the pitiful remnants of the once-mighty German Sixth Army to his Russian besiegers in front of Stalingrad. On hand to receive the surrender was a Russian army commissar whose star, as a result, was destined to rise in the Soviet hierarchy. His name was Nikita Khrushchev. The date marked the end of the bloodiest siege in the annals of warfare. It had cost the lives of two million soldiers and civilians.

Seven days later, half a world away in the steaming jungles of the South Pacific, another siege was lifted, this one with diametrically opposite results. On February 9, Guadalcanal was declared "secure." American marines and soldiers had held it against an attack by Japanese imperial forces for six months and two days, the longest single battle in American history.

Thus, within a week, two epic struggles ended, shaping the destiny of World War II. One fortress had held, the other had fallen.

Hitler had charged von Paulus with the holding of Fortress Stalingrad "to the last man." As a carrot, the führer had dangled an item before his fortress-keeper which he felt would ensure compliance. The object was a marshal's baton, cherished above all to a Wehrmacht officer. The baton was duly airlifted to the commander of the beleaguered garrison. Hitler rubbed his hands gleefully. It was a masterstroke of genius, he confided to Herman Goering, then visiting him at Wolf's Lair. "No marshal in all of German history," he told Goering, "has ever surrendered."

Von Paulus was to disappoint him. The fall of Stalingrad marked the turning point of the war in Europe. The Germans had lost the initiative.

The results of Guadalcanal offer a parallel in history. General Alexander A. Vandegrift, the marine commander, underlines that parallel in simple, undramatic prose. In a one-page foreword to the official Marine Corps report on the Campaign, Vandegrift wrote:

> We struck at Guadalcanal to halt the advance of the Japanese. We did not now know strong he was, nor did we know his plans. We knew only that he was moving down the island chain and that he had to be stopped.
>
> We were as well trained and as well armed as time and our peacetime experience allowed us to be. We needed combat to tell us how effective our training, our doctrines, and our weapons had been.
>
> We tested them against the enemy, and we found that they worked. From that moment in 1942, the tide turned, and the Japanese never again advanced.

PROLOGUE TO INVASION

The operation that was to put the U.S. Marines ashore on Guadalcanal began on the afternoon of December 16, 1941, just nine days after Pearl Harbor. Secretary of the Navy Frank Knox had returned to Washington from a hurried trip to the Hawaiian base, shocked by what he saw, depressed at the enormous damage to the U.S. Pacific Fleet and its installations.

On the long flight home he had jotted down his thoughts; by the time the plane reached Washington, those thoughts were included in a long memorandum to the president. Perhaps the most vital item in the memorandum was his recommendation that the post of Commander in Chief, United States Fleet, be revived and that Adm. Ernest J. King be named to that post.

Admiral King, then sixty-three, was Commander in Chief, Atlantic. There was no overall navy boss. But Knox knew that Roosevelt admired King and liked him personally. If there was any chance of putting across this concept of centralized command, Knox knew that King would get the approval from "The Boss." He had the report delivered to the White House late Monday night.

And on Saturday, December 20, the Navy had a "COMINCH," Ernest J. King, a man so tough he "shaved with a blowtorch," or so gossip in the wardrooms had it—a man with a singleness of purpose in whom the offensive spirit dominated—a man who could "wheedle the mighty," if need be, to promote his objectives.

King wasted no time. One of his first directives was a

11

dispatch to Adm. Chester W. Nimitz, who had assumed command of the Pacific Fleet and the title CINCPAC—Commander in Chief, Pacific—less than two weeks before.

> Cover and hold the Hawaii-Midway line. Protect the communications with the continental United States and maintain the security of sea lanes between the West Coast and Australia, at all costs.

It was a big order. But even then, as the Arcadia conference was underway, outlining the concept of grand strategy to be used against the Axis powers, King was thinking beyond his first directive.

Arcadia brought together Roosevelt and Churchill and their top military planners. Out of the conference came a document entitled ABC-1. Gen. George C. Marshall, the U.S. Army chief of staff, Gen. Alan Brooke, chief of the Imperial General Staff, and King were to be the principal executors.

ABC-1 called for the concentration of Allied effort on "Bolero" the code name for the buildup of an attack on Fortress Europe. Every ship, every ounce of war materiel, every bomb, and every unit not urgently needed elsewhere were to go to Bolero. With that dictate, the war in the Pacific was relegated to the backwaters of overall strategy.

To this King had to agree. Indeed, he knew that to disagree would have meant his dismissal; so he gave lip service to the strategy while pursuing his own ends. Early in January, General Marshall became aware of that duplicity, as did General Brooke, who was to write that nothing anyone could say "had much effect in weaning King away from the Pacific. The European war was just a great nuisance that kept him from waging his Pacific war undisturbed.''

That Roosevelt was aware of this friction between his high-level commanders is undeniable. FDR thrived on intrigue and divergent points of view in his command echelons, both politically and militarily. He encouraged dissent among his subordinates, particularly if that dissent was supportive in some way of his larger strategies.

And FDR had a larger concern: a mandate from the American people, born of frustration, over how to "get at those Japs." It was a gut mandate. And FDR, ever attuned to the pulse of public opinion, was about to concede to its call.

Thus, behind Marshall's back and in contravention of ABC-1, there began a quiet conspiracy between the president and his naval commander. Within a week the first gambit was played. There on General Marshall's desk was a letter from King outlining the continuing disasters which had fallen Sir Archibald Wavell in the Australian-British-Dutch-American command in the Far East. Hong Kong, Malaya, and Jolo in the Sulus and Sarawak had fallen or were about to. The series of disasters, King wrote, made it imperative that the Japanese initiative be stemmed. He recommended that certain specific islands of the central and southwestern Pacific be seized.

The grim-visaged Marshall ignored the letter. To the chief of staff the matter was not germane under the directives of ABC-1. Two weeks went by as the conspirators fidgeted. Direct action, apparently, was needed. Intimating that he had heard about the letter through the grapevine, Roosevelt gently prodded Marshall. "Just find out what King has in mind."

On March 2, King's plan of operation reached Marshall's desk. Three days later, with objections from Marshall attached, the paper reached the president. King's plan was succinct and to the point: Hold Hawaii, support Australia, drive northwest from New Hebrides. Essentially the plan envisaged a step-by-step advance up the ladder of the islands, from Efate as the southern anchor to Rabaul on New Britain in the north. And although it was not mentioned, Guadalcanal in the Solomons chain was almost in the middle.

The proposal, and the knowledge that King had gone through the back door to the president, exasperated Secretary of War Henry L. Stimson and Marshall, who lamented the fact to his British counterpart, General Brooke. Together they drew up a report which described the King proposal as "diversionary and dangerously dispersive." They reiterated the ABC-1 directive and called attention to the "drain on slender military resources" that would result from the proposed use of land forces in the vast Pacific area.

Their arguments fell on deaf ears. The president was searching for a tool to placate an aroused public, and the naval commander in chief was a man whose favorite admonition had always been "make the best of what you have." Somewhere from within "the great arsenal of democracy" the means had to be found, scrounged, or diverted to make a stand in the Pacific.

The Great Conspiracy had worked.

Orders were sent out, reluctantly, to put the machinery in motion. The Americal Division of the army, under Maj. Gen. Alexander M. Patch, was put ashore on New Caledonia. The Marine Corps contributed its 4th Defense Battalion, a seacoast and antiaircraft artillery organization, to the new command. Units were reassigned, commands were shuffled, and down in the Carolinas, the 1st Marine Division stepped up training, its mission as yet undetermined.

1

AUGUST 7, 1942

Task Force 62 was forty nautical miles from touchdown and the sky was beginning to lighten. Talking died down, the jokes became more infrequent, and off to the northeast, the misty outline of Tulagi began emerging.

Two hours earlier, the task force had broken into two columns, fifteen transports heading toward Guadalcanal, eight toward Tulagi.

Aboard the U.S.S. *McCawley*, flagship of Task Force 62, Rear Adm. Richmond K. Turner was on the bridge, noting the maneuver as the two columns separated. Following the "Wacky Mac" toward Guadalcanal came the *Fuller, American Legion, Bellatrix, Barnett, Elliott, Libra, Hunter Liggett, Alchiba, Fomalhaut, Betelgeuse, Crescent City, President Hayes, President Adams,* and *Alhena.* They were known as 62.1, or Transport Group X-Ray, at the moment of breakoff.

They were soon hull-down to the other contingent, 62.2 or Transport Group Yoke. The Tulagi-bound fleet consisted of *Neville, Zeilin, Heywood, President Jackson, Calhoun, Gregory, Little,* and *McKean.*

The task force carried 18,722 marines of the 1st

Marine Division, the first major combat unit to be committed to the offensive by the U.S. in World War II.

The strategic missions of Groups X-Ray and Yoke were identical, their tactical orders simple. Seize and invest the two islands. Destroy the Japanese forces which had, for the past four months, been feverishly at work developing air and sea bases from which new thrusts toward Australia were to be mounted.

There was a good deal more tension on the bridge than there was on deck or in the holds. And the quiet of the final approach, the absence of any signs of the enemy, had caused a tautness brought on by apprehension.

"I can't believe it," the watch officer on the *McCawley* said to Adm. Rich Turner. "I wonder if the Japs can be that dumb. Either they're very dumb . . . or it's a trick."

Intelligence had hinted that the Japanese expected an attack upon their positions sometime in July or early August. Whether this was merely a shrewd guess by the Japanese high command or whether it was based on hard information was unknown to American intelligence. Fact or rumor, the possibility had been passed down through command.

Suddenly, at 0614 hours, a yellow-green flash was observed from the dull gray shape of the cruiser operating off the starboard flank of the convoy. The troops followed the course of the salvo arcing its way toward shore in a red line. A second later the *crump* of the eight-inch battery was heard.

Other cruisers of the covering forces soon joined in, the concussion of their fire shaking the decks of the transports. Shoreward, the salvos reached home, sending geysers of red flame high into the predawn darkness and a steady *crump, crump, crump* back toward the fleet.

Then planes appeared on the horizon. "Ours or theirs?" was the question whispered throughout the plodding ships.

In the lifting fire of the cruisers there came the answer as the dive-bombers came in first, swooping low over the beaches and strafing as they finished their passes. The carrier fleet of Vice Adm. Frank Jack Fletcher, comprised of the *Wasp*, the *Saratoga*, and the *Enterprise*, was sending its birds to battle.

The three carriers, part of Task Force 61, had steamed to within fifty miles of Guadalcanal during the night. The gallant old *Saratoga* had as its mission the bombardment of Beach Red on Guadalcanal. The *Wasp* was assigned to soften up the landing beaches at Tulagi, and the *Enterprise*—"Big E" to the fleet—was delegated to provide air cover for the operation.

All the pieces were in place for an attack on an island few had ever heard about.

Just as the eastern skies were beginning to lighten, the thousand-man garrison of Tulagi was startled by flashes of light to the south. Lt. Maruyama Juntaro, on his way to breakfast, thought it might be heat lightning, although there were no clouds hanging overhead.

A few seconds later, other flashes blinked green and white against the horizon. And then it came, the rolling sounds of cannonade, the unmistakable rumble of naval gunfire, the orchestration of five- and eight-inch batteries fired in salvo.

The lieutenant put his head down and hightailed it across the cricket field toward the officers' mess. In the darkness, he ran headlong into another racing figure, knocking him down. The other figure was Sergeant Raizo Tanabe, one of the lieutenant's men.

"What is it, Lieutenant?" Tanabe asked.

The whistle, whoosh, and crump of a five-incher passing overhead made the question academic. New flashes from the harbor below added confirmation.

"It's the Americans. They've come."

Juntaro motioned to Tanabe to follow him, and the two went off at the double towards the base communication shack which their unit was assigned to protect. As they ran, the cannonading redoubled, searching shots whirling overhead in the same direction they were following.

A few minutes later, fire from the American ships slackened somewhat, but a new dimension was added: the droning sound of approaching aircraft. Juntaro pointed, and his sergeant nodded back in grim acknowledgment of the impending air attack. For several days the base has been subjected to an occasional high-level dusting by American B-17 Fortresses based, the Japanese thought, in Australia. Those attacks had done little actual damage to the Tulagi installations, and Japanese intelligence, Juntaro was told, had written them off as mere nuisance raids. The droning of the engines now overhead sounded somehow more purposeful.

Meanwhile, inside the radio shack, the interceptor radios began squawking a strange gibberish as American radio silence was broken at the tactical level.

It was the between-plane talk of pilots of Flight 101 assessing the targets below them in Tulagi Bay and plotting their destruction.

They had taken off a short while ago from the decks of the carrier *Wasp*, which was then steaming in company with the *Saratoga* and the *Enterprise* some sixty-five nautical miles west of the landing beaches on Tulagi. They arrived on time and on target. In their wake was Flight 102—fifteen dive-bombers—for whom 101 was to provide fighter cover.

As Lieutenant Juntaro and Sergeant Tanabe neared the radio transmitter, the dive-bombers were striking with considerable effect. They screamed down, one behind the other, dropping their deadly eggs and pulling back to climb into the darkness of the western skies. Geysers of flame shot up after each pullout. The harbor and its docks rocked with explosions.

Following the dive-bombers came Flight 101, passing over the target area to strafe, pull out, and head for home. One of the strafers, a stubby-winged Grumman, passed over the radio shack, squeezing off a final burst that hemstitched the walls of the small building. The lieutenant hit the dirt a split second after his sergeant took cover.

It was 0620.

Juntaro hammered at the door. A frozen-faced communications specialist let them in. "He was somewhat distraught," Juntaro recorded, "and I sought to calm him down." The lieutenant assured the man that he would stay to protect the installation against attack. "He returned inside a much more composed man, answering the headquarters telephone which had been ringing since my arrival. . . . I was pleased with my part in assisting a fellow officer to regain his proper composure and spirit. It is not given to us all, the true Bushido, and those who are blessed with more than our share should give gratefully of its strength to others less fortunate."

Aboard the *Wasp*, Adm. Frank Jack Fletcher paced carrier flag plot nervously. The big clock on the wall read 0625. There was a crackle on the intercom, then the encoded message:

Commander Wasp Air Group to commander Wasp. All flying boats in the target area set afire by bombardment. Returning to base.

The announcement drew a spontaneous cheer from the assembled officers and ratings within earshot. Even Frank Jack Fletcher let his face slip a little.

At the same moment, a worried officer at the radio station serving Vice Adm. Gunichi Mikawa in Rabaul began decoding the news of the American strike.

Enemy surface force of twenty ships has entered Tulagi. While making landing preparations, the enemy is bombarding the shore. Shellfire is searching inland, and . . . .

Blam! A close hit by one of the searching five-inchers silenced the Tulagi station. There was a frantic scrambling to repair the damage done by the blast.

In the intervening minutes of silence, Admiral Mikawa was notified of the initial interrupted message from his beleaguered garrison. He was on hand a few minutes later when the jury-rigged auxiliary unit at

Tulagi reopened communications.

> This is not a feint. Repeat: not a feint. Landing of enemy troops has begun.

It was nearing 0700, and the intelligence pouring in from the Tulagi and Guadalcanal radio stations continued to affirm that the Americans were, indeed, landing in force. Mikawa gathered his staff about him, his eyes blazing. What he had feared had come to pass.

He had taken over the Rabaul-Guadalcanal-Tulagi area on July 26 from Adm. Shikeyoshi Inoue in a ceremony at Truk, as eager to assume his new command as Inoue appeared content to be relieved of it. At the staff conference there, Mikawa had discovered the huge vacuum that existed in the eastern New Guinea-Solomons area. But when his misgivings were aired during the conference, Fourth Fleet officers dismissed them out of hand. There was nothing to worry about, Mikawa was told. The Americans had shown no inclination to assume the offensive in this or other theaters. U.S. forces in the Pacific would remain on the defensive; what offensive capabilities the Americans now had, it was argued, were unquestionably committed to the support of Great Britain and the mounting of a "Second Front" in Europe. The Yanks in the Pacific were still reeling from the shocks of defeat at Pearl Harbor and Bataan.

His main concern, Mikawa was told, was to shape up his command, which included the Seventeenth Army, for the continued push from Buna in New Guinea over the Owen Stanley Mountains for an attack on Port Moresby, gateway to Australia. The Eighth Fleet was to capture other bases in the eastern New Guinea sector, such as Milne Bay. Then, the briefing continued, Japanese forces will move from Kokoda down the Owen Stanley range toward the main objective. When Port Moresby falls, it was concluded, the line of assault toward Australia will be unobstructed.

His anxieties relieved, Mikawa had been piped aboard his flagship, the heavy cruiser *Chokai*, happy to be away from the gold-braided echelons of high staff with their know-it-all condescension toward line officers. He would shape up his command, as directed.

On the morning of July 30 the *Chokai* entered Simpson Harbor, Rabaul. As his car approached headquarters on the ride up from the docks, his admiral's flag was broken out sharply; it was the only sharp performance Mikawa was presented with. He quickly commandeered materials for planning and communications rooms and set about the business of running a war.

These eight days following his arrival at Simpson Harbor proved to be the most hectic period of Mikawa's long and distinguished naval career. First there was the report of Lieutenant Okamura from Guadalcanal; he was ramrodding the construction of the airfield there, and the runways were nearing completion. A request on July 31 that fighter planes be dispatched to the new field was rejected when, on the same day, a supply convoy to Buna was broken up and dispersed. Losses were minimal, but it was there on the eastern corner of New Guinea, Mikawa pointed out on the planning map, that the Yanks were concentrating their efforts. Perhaps the intelligence officers at Truk were correct.

The next big convoy for Buna was scheduled for

August 8. This one would have better protection.

Commander Toshikazu Ohmae, the admiral's operations officer, looked at his chief admiringly. The hard decisions of command came easily to the soft-spoken, strangely gentle man standing with pointer in hand. At fifty-three, Mikawa had commanded the support forces of the Pearl Harbor striking forces—had been, in fact, second in command under Vice Adm. Chuichi Nagumo. After Pearl Harbor his force of battleships and cruisers had prowled over more than a third of the world's surface, delivering sledgehammer blows to Allied shipping and naval forces from Ceylon to the Marianas.

Mikawa was credited with the innovation—later used by both British and American naval strategists—of linking up modern battleships with carriers in task forces, each choosing its own target area and roaming at will, wreaking havoc wherever it appeared.

In its rampage across the Pacific and Indian Oceans, the Japanese battleship-carrier juggernaut sank five enemy battleships, one aircraft tender, one cruiser, one destroyer, and many thousand tons of merchant shipping. It damaged three battleships, three cruisers, and a destroyer; and it destroyed hundreds of aircraft. The task forces returned to home waters on April 2, 1942, after five months at sea without damage to a single ship of their own. No armada in naval history had wreaked such destruction.

Returning to his home in the Tokyo suburb of Setagaya, Mikawa missed the Coral Sea engagement; but he was aboard when Admiral Yamamoto assembled 350 ships and 100,000 men—the largest concentration of power assembled in the Pacific—for the blow that was to be the knockout punch to the American navy, the attack on Midway.

So it was an admiral who had tasted both the bitter and the sweet who sat at Simpson Harbor and pondered the latest U.S. Navy move. Lingering doubts about the fallibility of Truk and its bright young staffers flickered through his mind.

Tulagi had reported B-17s coming over daily. On August 1, ten of the Flying Forts made their appearance. The Guadalcanal garrison reported that native laborers working on the nearly completed strip had laid down their shovels and headed into the bush. Three more Flying Forts appeared over the Guadalcanal airfield the next day.

Search planes dispatched on August 6 returned to base reporting heavy overcast to the south of Guadalcanal but no ships in sight. It was the consensus that night that renewed and increased enemy activity in the Tulagi-Guadalcanal area was but a feint, meant to divert Japanese efforts to support the Buna reinforcement convoy scheduled for August 8. Mikawa had reluctantly approved the operations report and gone to bed.

At 0635 on August 7, there was a timid knock at his door.

"Admiral?"

Commander Ohmae waited with a dispatch clutched in his hand. He knew the admiral was a light sleeper. There was the briefest stirring from within and in a moment Mikawa met him at the door.

"Bad news?"

Ohmae studied the admiral's ascetic face for a sign of indecision or alarm. There was none. "I'm afraid so, sir."

In silence Mikawa studied the message. "This is marked 0625," he said without expression.

"Yes, sir. We have lost communication with Tulagi. We are attempting to get through."

"Get me Nakajima." He handed the message back to his operations officer. "I'll be down in a minute." The admiral closed the door and Ohmae raced away to locate Commander Tadashi Nakajima, a veteran of the China campaign and now commander of the fighter wing at Rabaul.

Five minutes later, Nakajima was ushered into command plot. The admiral looked up. His briefing was clear and concise. "I want you to take every Zero that will fly and get on down there."

The fighter commander turned pale as the extent of his assigned mission became clear. "But sir, that is impossible!" He pointed at the map. "It is six hundred miles to the target and six hundred miles back. Even if we refueled at Buka," he designated the small island dot, "it would be the longest fighter mission we have ever flown."

"I realize that. But it can be done."

"Only with my best pilots. The new ones would be lost."

"Then, Commander, take your eighteen best pilots and your eighteen best Zeros and see that they get through."

Nakajima stiffened to attention. "Yes sir!"

The admiral was touched. The tough mask relaxed into a hint of a smile. "You'll make it, commander," he said softly. "I must know how many carriers the Americans have. It is vital. That is your mission. Find the carriers."

Commander Ohmae came in as Nakajima saluted and left the room. "I have the updated reports on planes available for immediate missions, sir."

"How does it look?" Mikawa adjusted his glasses and sat down behind a cluttered desk as his operations officer put down a sheaf of papers.

"We have sixty-eight aircraft of all types, sir."

Mikawa thumbed through the documents. The Tainan Air Group, under Nakajima, showed a strength of twenty-four Zeros. The 2d Air Group had sixteen torpedo planes and fifteen of the navy-converted Zero fighters known to the American side as Hamps. At Vunakunau Airfield was the 4th Air Group, with thirty-two dive-bombers. That totalled eighty-seven aircraft, sixty-eight of which were combat-ready.

Mikawa shook his head. It was not much muscle to throw at three carriers, if indeed they were in the landing area. And he had a gut feeling they were.

"How about the reinforcement group from Tinian, when are they due in?"

"We have just contacted them, Admiral. They are sending seven from the Misawa Air Group, due in this morning, with the remaining seventeen aircraft scheduled in for tomorrow."

"Good. Now for the operational order." He gestured toward the door through which Nakajima had just departed. "I have ordered the commander of the Tainan Air Group to take his eighteen best pilots and find the enemy carriers. That's our primary mission, understand? Find the carrier fleet."

Ohmae made the proper notations on his clipboard.

"Secondary mission: punish the landing forces. I assume that all the floatplanes of the Yokahama Air

Group at Tulagi will have been destroyed."

The operations chief nodded glumly. "I think we can assume the worst, sir."

"Yes. Now we go to work. Find the carriers. Punish the landing forces! Put every ship in the air that will fly." He paused, rising to go to the window that looked out over Simpson Harbor and the four air fields that circled it. His thoughts, Ohmae knew, had shifted from aircraft to battlewagons. "Get out a message to the *Chokai*. I've got a job to do."

The shortwave radio in the next room came through, static crackling over the sound of human voices. "We have picked up the Tulagi station again, sir. They're back on the air."

The admiral took the decoded message handed him.

Landing of enemy troops has commenced. The troop strength is overwhelming. We will defend to the last man, praying for everlasting victory. Shells are now falling near the radio installation.

The radio went silent at 0800. On Tulagi, Lieutenant Juntaro's primary mission, the defense of the radio shack, had ended.

As eighteen Zeros lined up at the Rabaul airstrip, Nakajima's chosen fighter pilots listened in silence in the briefing room and checked chronometers. "Takeoff," Nakajima concluded, "is 0900."

Far to the south, the thirty-one-minute concert of fire from the five- and eight-inch batteries of the supporting cruiser-destroyer force had lifted. To the marines aboard it had been an awesome display, thousands of rounds and tons of steel being hurled ashore. Finally, like firecrackers at a Fourth of July show, the pyrotechnics came fitfully to a halt, one last round sputtering off here to be answered by yet another final round there.

And then there was silence.

A gentle, almost unbelievably blue sea lapped against the dull grey hulls of the fifteen ships of the transport division of Group X-Ray, lying off Beach Red, Guadalcanal. The only sound was the rattle of winches as the first landing craft were swung oversides.

On shore, the dust and debris settled slowly to reveal the topless trunks of giant coconut trees. Cordite fumes from the naval barrage began drifting seaward in the slight offshore breeze. Hundreds of giant land crabs that had survived the bombardment scuttled away from the beach.

On deck, the attack battalions assigned to the first wave began a well-rehearsed move towards the landing nets now being dropped overside. Their chaplain, Father Reardon, bowed his head in prayer as they clambered down.

"This is it." The words echoed many times that morning. And to many of those in the first wave, making their way topside from the holds, up the steaming companionways, it was a moment of almost welcome relief.

Pvt. Russell Miller revealed that emotion to his buddies of Company B, 2d Marine Regiment, as he looked down the thirty feet of net that stretched to the bobbing Higgins boat. He watched each man going over the side, loaded down by extra bandoliers of ammo, ammo boxes, rifle, pack, and rations. Helmets were worn with the V-chinstraps unfastened in case a man hit the drink instead of the boat.

"It's a strange feeling," Miller said. "That thing looks like a cork down there." And then he was over the side. As the craft filled, Miller's face became lost in the crowd. But fate had him marked. He was to become the first Marine to be killed in action ashore.

Below decks, those awaiting their turn at the nets continued their shipboard activities of the past seven days. The acey-deucey and showdown games speeded up as the losers demanded "one more hand." The crap game in Hold D continued unabated until one last "break it up, break it up," sent the high rollers hurrying for their packs.

Dr. Malcolm V. Pratt, the medical officer, was amazed by their coolness. Awaiting his turn, a private from North Dakota continued to whet a razor-sharp bayonet. A few service Bibles appeared here and there. On the fourth-tier bunk one lad checked his rifle clip one final time as he informed his buddy down below: "This one's got Tojo's name on it."

"Mebbe so," came the retort. "I hope you squeeze 'em off better'n you did on the range."

All along the companionways, the heat and smell of bodies packed so closely became almost unbearable. But as they inched up the ladders, rifles and packs banging away, a new look, a new consideration was noted in the words and action of the crewmen.

"Here, let me help you, Mac," as the gear stuck to ladders. There were countless pats on the fanny from those less vocal.

And suddenly, the holds were cleared.

2

"WHERE ARE THE JAPS?"

Aboard the U.S.S. *McCawley*, apprehension was as thick as the wardroom coffee. Staff members huddled around Gen. Archer Vandegrift on the flying bridge, worried eyes scanning the skies to the north. The one unanswered question running through the entire invasion fleet at 8 A.M. on Friday, August 7, 1942 was, "Where in the hell are the Japs?"

It was an impressive armada that had been gathered there within striking range of Beach Red. Over the horizon to the southeast steamed the carrier force of Frank Jack Fletcher: *Saratoga*, commanded by Capt. Dewitt C. Ramsey; *Enterprise*, Capt. Arthur C. Davis; and *Wasp*, Capt. Forrest P. Sherman.

Off to the flank of this force, steaming southwest, came the magnificent battleship *North Carolina*, newest and most powerful ship in the U.S. Fleet, with Capt. George H. Fort on the bridge.

Six heavy cruisers—*Atlanta, Minneapolis, New Orleans, Portland, Salt Lake City,* and *San Francisco*—were on station around the flattops, darting now and then at flank speed as the fleet changed course. Maneuvering between the heavier vessels came sixteen lean destroyers of the screening force, their principal mission to guard against the "Long Lance" torpedoes of the Japanese submarine service.

The flattops had been busy. Besides the floatplanes destroyed, the Japanese destroyer *Yuzuki* had been sunk off Tulagi, and several smaller craft sent to the bottom.

Yuzuki had been a companion vessel to the cruiser-minesweeper *Okinoshima* in the small flotilla of vessels that supplied the Tulagi-Guadalcanal garrison from Rabaul. The *Okinoshima* survived the dive-bombing and strafing attack by planes from the *Wasp* that morning, but she had been badly hit in the furious melee over Sealark Channel. "I got me a big one, right on the stack," the pilot's message crackled back to *Wasp* operations. Nonetheless, the *Okinoshima* battled her way north towards Malaita, taking refuge in the uncharted coves of Santa Isabel Island as she limped toward Rabaul.

Archer Vandegrift, the U.S. ground-forces commander, stood on the starboard wing of the *McCawley*'s bridge, alone with his thoughts. And the "Wacky Mac" provided a fitting companion. Slab-sided, ugly by every standard of marine architecture, the *McCawley* somehow epitomized the man who stood there looking for all the world like the Straw Man in the Wizard of Oz. But unlike Dorothy's companions, Archer Vandegrift needed no search for courage, extra heart, or brains; nature had fully endowed him with those qualities. The right man, in some strange and inexplicable fashion, was in the right place at the right moment in history.

Nonetheless, the past twenty-eight days had been a nightmare for Vandegrift. Accurate maps of the island he was about to invade were nonexistent and, outside the occasional pages of the *National Geographic* magazine, little had been written of Guadalcanal's rugged terrain. Along its central backbone ran a range of mountains on an east-west axis, with peaks rising to eight thousand feet. Massive rain forests circled its ninety-mile length and extended across its twenty-five-mile girth.

Those few maps that were available had been drawn from naval hydrographic charts which, if adequate for the skipper of an occasional copra schooner, were hardly the thing to use to direct artillery fire. They were accurate to the edge of the reefs; Vandegrift's marines had to cross those reefs.

There had been an effort at photo reconnaissance by a few tired B-17s operating out of Australia. But the results were poor and, more often than not, misleading.

Then, too, there had been the so-called "terrain sketches" made from memory by former residents, Australian officials, and natives. Many were helpful, but too often these sketches further complicated matters. A footnote on an operational map, produced just two weeks before the landing, emphasized the severe handicap under which staff was asked to conduct its planning:

This map was reproduced from a special sketch map drawn from information supplied by a man thoroughly familiar with the terrain shown. It is drawn from this person's memory. It is not to be

33

construed as an accurate map.

The footnote was prophetic. The map not only misspelled the central topographical feature, which was Mount Austen; it also misplaced it by several miles.

In the attempts to identify recognizable landmarks, there was on most of these primitive maps a reference to a "little grassy knoll," a patch of *kunai* grass that thrust its head above the surrounding rain forest. But in the tangle of jungle growth, it would soon fail as a landmark.

Vandegrift turned to more optimistic thoughts. For seven days, it seemed to him, the marines had lucked out. Not one ship of the vast armada had been detected. And now all the pieces were in place. To the west, the carrier fleet steamed slowly on its assigned station, its planes in action under the watchful eye of Adm. Leigh Noyes.

The transports of Task Force 62 were unloading on schedule. Feverish as was the action aboard, it was left to the destroyer screen to provide the most vivid picture of action stations as eleven slim greyhounds of the sea were unleashed to prowl the flanks at both ends of Sealark Channel. The screen included *Selfridge*, *Mugford*, *Henley*, *Hull*, *Dewey*, *Elliott*, *Southard*, *Hopkins*, *Trevor*, *Zane*, and *Hovey*. Inside the destroyer screen, plodding more slowly on assigned grids, were the cruisers, divided into three battle squadrons to guard against action from all directions. All three were under the command of Rear Adm. Victor Alexander Charles Crutchley, RN, his flag flying from the yardarm of H.M.S. *Australia*. With him, to the joint forces assembled, had come the Aussie heavy

34

cruiser *Canberra* and the light cruiser *Hobart*.

It was an imposing screening force, and its commander radiated vigor and confidence. A tall man of jovial countenance, Crutchley sported a full red beard set off to its most dazzling brilliance on occasions when he wore summer whites with attendant gold braid and shoulder boards. His appearance on the bridge on invasion morning was a bit more subdued. But nothing could take away the dash, the bronze skin, or the hirsute elegance. At forty-nine, Crutchley's charm was an undeniable as his courage. He had won the Victoria Cross in World War I at Jutland, and the *Croix de Guerre* just for good measure.

On his way north from Fiji, he had bent his tall frame over an Operation's desk to scribble out a battle order that left no doubt whatever as to its intent.

> It will be my aim to meet the enemy seaward of the area between Savo Island and Sealark Channel, and the force engaging him shall at all times remain interposed between the enemy and this area.

A secondary paragraph, it was noted later, made a reasonable but disastrous assumption.

> It is expected that our extensive air reconnaissance will give warning of the approach of enemy surface forces.

Far to the north, at Rabaul, Admiral Mikawa's moves to meet the invasion threat had already been observed, as Crutchley had so confidently predicted. A lone Flying Fort banked lazily for home as it sent out a radio message of the gathering storm. It was the first warning of the approach of enemy forces Crutchley's commanders received.

Meanwhile, the final decision had been made aboard the *McCawley* for the landing of troops. Admiral Turner returned to the bridge and walked over to his troop commander. Sweat from the tropic heat had liberally stained the back of Vandegrift's combat jacket. The two men nodded their heads in agreement; they shook hands.

"Yes, Admiral, 0910 looks okay. Let's make it 0910," Vandegrift said softly.

That settled the question of H-Hour for the marines' landing on Beach Red, but it left another question wide open. Where were the Japanese?

In the half hour since "Land the landing forces" had been sounded, several divisions of assorted landing craft had already begun churning about, mostly in clockwise circles.

A floatplane from the cruiser *Astoria*, launched by catapult a few minutes earlier, buzzed the *McCawley*'s bridge, where Vandegrift stood in conference with Admiral Turner. They waved and followed her course as she banked toward land and the mouth of the Tenaru River; then they returned to watching the deck alive with movement—troops going over the side at the waist, and farther aft a battery of four 105 howitzers being unlashed for second-wave delivery. The tarps had already been removed from barrels and trails, and gun crews clustered around, wiping off the last speck of dust and moisture. Here and there below, Higgins boats coughed and sputtered, the Navy coxswains in their sterns working frantically to get them started again.

General Vandegrift had noted earlier, during the staging period in the Fijis, that many of the landing craft were not in the best condition. In one ship alone, twelve of the precious boats were found to be inoperable. The newer stuff had been consigned to the European theatre. What was left, in the main, were tired old training vessels dredged up from Kaneohe Bay, Quantico, and Parris Island, veterans of a thousand practice landing operations, many of them worn out and far from combat-ready.

Reports from the *Astoria*'s floatplane, directing cruiser fire on Red Beach, were more than encouraging, far more so than Vandegrift had hoped for. "I'm over the landing beach," the pilot communicated, "and I spot no Nips. Repeat, no Nips in sight. You've done a good job on the coconut trees."

The coconut trees and the Tenaru River had been on everybody's mind and had figured in every assessment in the intelligence planning since Fiji.

Lt. Evard Snell, the battalion S-2 on author Richard Tregaskis's ship during the approach, had talked to him about the landing that was about to take place.

"Our division intelligence figures that only one in three boats will reach shore safely in the first wave," he said. Three out of four marines in the several waves hitting the beach, he estimated, would make it. Snell's memorandum, which became a textbook for the troops aboard, stated:

> From our landing point, our forces will have to cross a stream about twenty feet wide and four hundred yards south of the beach. The name of the stream is the Ilu and it runs westward and

37

parallel to the shore into the Tenaru River. Actually, it's a backwater of the Tenaru and except in the rainy season is still and stagnant. Its banks are steep, boggy, and from five to six feet high. The bottom is silted. One method of crossing would be to cut down the banks and throw the excavated material into the stream, filling it up. If necessary, this crossing could be topped with trunks of coconut trees.

On the south bank of the Ilu is high grass averaging four feet in height which affords possible positions for machine guns, riflemen, etc., with a field of fire extending across the stream toward the beach.''

There had been many inward groans as this memo had been gone over, in great detail, with the troops now loading into their battered Higgins boats. It went on:

Another river which our forces will have to cross is the Tenaru. The banks of the Tenaru average eight to ten feet in height and are covered with grass and thick brush affording possible positions for riflemen and machine guns. Just beyond the west bank of the Tenaru are deep holes, six feet deep and one hundred feet long, which have been scooped out by the river during floods, thus forming natural concealed positions. After fording the Tenaru our forces will advance across the Tenaru Plantation. This consists of coconut trees planted regularly in groups of four, in diamond formation. The result is that lanes of observation radiate in all directions. Most of these lanes are twenty-seven feet wide. Now they are beginning to be overgrown, but nevertheless afford good observation and fields of fire.

On leaving Tenaru Plantation our forces will emerge onto a grassy plain. Here is grass, if it has not been burned by the Japs, that is about four feet high. Although the ground is mostly firm, after about a half mile it becomes swampy in patches and wooded at the headwaters of Alligator Creek. At this season these headwaters are usually dried up and easily crossed. The woods, however, are dense, with a visibility of hardly five yards. There are no roads or paths.

To the platoon leaders who assembled daily for the briefing sessions, this sounded like a rugged assignment: a tough terrain and a tough foe. Small wonder that the report from the aerial observers, as the landing craft filled, moved off, and circled around the transports, was received with relief.

East of the Tenaru River, mistakenly called Alligator Creek in those pre-invasion briefings, was the Japanese airstrip. That was the big apple, the brass ring, the rationale for the entire Operation Watchtower. From the banks of the river, through the waving *kunai* grass, you could just see the construction huts along the nearly completed runway, poking up their unpainted roofs about a mile off.

News from Tulagi that invasion morning was also good. His uniform stained with sweat in ever-widening circles, Vandegrift raised a clenched fist in delight over reports from across Sealark Channel, where Tulagi was taking a pasting from Flights 101 and 102 off the *Wasp*.

H-Hour for the attack on Tulagi had been set for 0800, one hour prior to the landing on Guadalcanal. And now, from Red Beach, seventeen miles across Sealark Channel, Brig. Gen. William J. Rupertus was on the line requesting Vandegrift's permission to go in early. It was 0740.

Rupertus was assistant division commander in charge of the Tulagi operation. Part of the plan was to send a force to nearby Florida Island. Aussie intelligence indicated that there were Japanese about. And Rupertus was worried about his flanks.

"I know I'm jumping the gun, General. But we're all ready to go and I'd feel better about it."

"Take off," came back the reply.

Semaphores blinked. A slowly circling line of landing craft straightened out, forming two parallel columns. There was only the slightest pause as they formed up; then the Navy coxswains throttled forward to full throttle and the little Higgins boats headed shoreward.

On board, four thousand yards and ten minutes away from the beach, were 252 marines of Company B, 2d Marine Regiment, 1st Marine Division, reinforced by an attached heavy-weapons platoon of machine guns and 81mm mortars. They were under the command of Capt. Edgar J. Crane and would be the first of the invasion forces to wade ashore.

Keeping ahead of schedule was vital. The timetable was tight, the high navy command sensitive, even skittish, at the thought of becoming "sitting ducks in an open roadstead," as one operations officer termed it. The lessons of Pearl Harbor were still being brooded over, eight months after the fact.

Vandegrift had no doubt reviewed the danger signals many times since the final invasion conference aboard the *Saratoga* eight days before in the Fiji harbor. At this conference, Vice Adm. Robert Lee Ghormley, the theater commander, had been absent.

In an amazing, and what was to prove nearly fatal, delegation of authority, Ghormley had waived his command responsibility and sent his chief of staff, Rear Adm. Daniel J. Callaghan; he'd elected to stay in his headquarters in Wellington, thousands of miles away from the scene of action, more concerned with his duties as theater commander, it seems, than he was with the troops and ships committed to battle in America's first major invasion.

Vice Admiral Fletcher presided at the July 26 council of war. At fifty-seven, Frank Jack had more combat experience with the Japanese than anybody else aboard. He had been in command of carrier forces at Midway and in the Coral Sea. Sitting to the right of Fletcher was Callaghan, representing the theater commander. A second notable absentee was Admiral Crutchley, the red-bearded Australian commander of the cruiser forces. His ship had not arrived by the time of the meeting.

Fletcher was brief. He handed out the operations order and suggested that each man read it, and that was that. There were not enough copies to go around, it seemed, so troop and division commanders huddled in pairs around the table. Callaghan, apparently, was not given a copy—or, if he was handed one, he failed to take it back with him for delivery to Robert Lee Ghormley. At any rate, the South Pacific Theater commander, the nominal head of the assembled task force, did not get to see the order until a month after the landing.

Turner was stunned by what he read. Beetle-browed and craggy of face, the fifty-seven-year-old commander of Task Force 62, the transport fleet, expostulated over the five points of the operations order. "You can't do this to us," was the repetitive theme of his protests.

Vandegrift, too, saw inherent danger in the orders. Frank Jack Fletcher waved them off. There were only four carriers in the Pacific, he pointed out, and three of them were here. He would not risk them beyond forty-eight hours after H-Hour on D-Day, and that was that.

The five orders were ominous and implicit:

1. The seaborne operation, troop transport, supplies, and surface and air support would be withdrawn in their entirety after four days.
2. Surface ships might have to leave sooner.
3. Transports must complete off-loading on the first day.
4. The so-called "floating reserve" would not be available at all. (The reserve was originally to be formed of units of the 2d Marine Division, recently shipped out of San Diego. Vandegrift had counted on their support, but the theater commander, through Fletcher, felt that a new Japanese threat from the Gilbert Islands was a possibility that could not be overlooked. Thus the reserve was being denied and withheld for deployment to Ndeni, far out of support range.)
5. In any event, because of commitments which had not been fulfilled by higher headquarters,

and because the theater in general was weaker in men and materiel than had been originally planned, the carrier-based aircraft support would have to be even further shortened.

The conference had a sobering effect on those present, particularly on Vandegrift. But now, standing on the *McCawley*'s wing bridge, the commanding general eyed the landing procedure with more satisfaction. There was not a single pessimistic bone in Vandegrift's body. There had been good signs and hopeful auguries. He was ahead of schedule. A slow smile lightened his face. He turned to an aide. "Goddammit, I think we'll make it."

3

H-HOUR

Guadalcanal, seen from the air, was like a travel poster, or so thought the young pilot whose Curtiss SOC had been catapulted from the cruiser *Astoria* a few minutes before. At 0859, eleven minutes before the first troops were to hit the beach, he radioed back a reassuring message: "No enemy activity of any kind observed on Red Beach." His single-float biplane, its struts and wires singing in the wind, had flown the entire length of the landing area at treetop altitude.

Mission completed, he banked lazily and pulled back the stick. The panorama was breathtaking. The rising sun glinted on the undulating high timberline, pointing delicate emerald fingers down the spines of dozens of sharp ridges which reached for the sea. Off to the east were Mount Austen and the "grassy knoll," both constant points of reference in the many flight briefings. They seemed like old friends. Far below him in the bay came line after line of wooden Higgins boats heading for shore. It was the first wave, and the young pilot found himself repeating the Twenty-Third Psalm aloud for the marines who packed those boats to the gunwales.

Now he was over the transport area where the second wave was forming. Still other landing craft circled round and round their mother ships, awaiting their turn at the nets and booms; jeeps and 105s dangled oversides.

It would not be difficult, he concluded, for the navy coxswains, perched on the stern of landing craft to hit their assigned sector at just the right point. There was no surf to speak of, just a constant creaming of gentle waves against a curving beach. A few minutes earlier, two catapult planes had planted smoke bombs at the east and west boundaries of the assigned landing area; curling black plumes had already climbed over a thousand feet into an unbelievably blue sky.

Aboard the *McCawley*, there was still tension in the air, but it was now relaxed somewhat by tight-lipped smiles and an occasional playful punch on the arm, indicating that the "first act" had been played out well.

Additional reports were mildly disquieting. Aerial observers reported "a concentration of Jap vehicles near the airfield." But then came a subsequent "It looks like they're taking it on the lam. . . . There goes one, two, three of 'em. They're heading into the jungle."

At 0900 the big charge began, destroyers moving up on the flanks of landing craft which were now churning full-speed for shore. Cruisers on the covering force stood in for close support, their eight-inch turrets leveled to point-blank range.

Japs, or no Japs, Beach Red was in for a hell of a pasting. Father Reardon of the 5th Marine Regiment offered a silent prayer. In his landing craft, Lt. James

V. Donoghue, a platoon leader assigned to B Company of the 5th with a section of heavy machine guns, was more concerned for the temporal welfare of his troops. The former Notre Dame football player hoisted his beefy frame and gesticulated. "Get your damned heads down, all of you!"

With a menacing roar, the final shore bombardment began. To the men in Higgins boats, the salvos sounded like freight trains passing overhead. At such close range, their firing was followed only seconds later by the *crump* of their blast ashore. Within a minute, the pop of the destroyers' five-inchers were drowned by the heavier calibers. For three minutes, sheets of yellow fire blanketed the decks of the big ships. Ashore, black and grey geysers, studded with sparkling orange and red flames, hid the landscape.

Those in the first wave remained for the moment unaware of the silence that followed, so deafened were they by the bombardment at close range. From his command boat circling in the wake of the first wave, Col. Leroy P. Hunt noted with some amazement that squad leaders seemed to be shouting in a land of the deaf: mouths opened, but no words came forth. The commander of the 5th Marines, Hunt—who had anticipated this very event but had forgotten about it in the awful din—smiled at his companions huddled around him. One of them was Richard Tregaskis, who remembered that a smile from Colonel Hunt was the prearranged signal for a successful landing of wave one and the go-ahead sign for the second wave.

At 0919, only nine minutes behind schedule, the assault boats hit the beach. Colonel Hunt, peering shoreward, could not see Captain Kaempfer's A

Company men nor Captain Hawkins's B Company land and disappear at high port into the bush fifteen yards behind the beach. But in a few seconds, the sound of small-arms fire broke out, and here and there came the "burst of six" from the muzzles of Lieutenant Donoghue's water-cooled Browning machine guns and the unmistakable thump of the mortar section's 60mm mortars.

There was no answering fire. The *Astoria*'s observation pilot had been right: there were no Japanese—at least not as far inland as the marines' first phase.

The order of battle ashore was simple. The force under Colonel Hunt would land battalions abreast, 1st Battalion on the right, 3d Battalion on the left. They would move inland to a distance of approximately five hundred yards, dig in, hold, and protect the beachhead.

At H-Hour plus fifty minutes, the 1st Marine Regiment, under the command of Col. Clifton B. Cates, would land a column of battalions, 2d Battalion leading, followed by 3d and 1st. They would quickly form up in the shallow perimeter and launch an attack on azimuth 260, almost due west. Their mission: the grassy knoll.

The support group, consisting of Headquarters and advance party of the 11th Marines, would land over the original beachhead with the division artillery.

As the landing beaches were only about a mile in width, the beachhead proved to be a pretty congested piece of real estate. One correspondent, noting the planned madhouse at the water's edge as jeeps, 105s, ammo boxes, medical supplies, and assorted flotsam of war started piling up, recorded drily that it looked like

Times Square on New Year's Eve.

To the military eye, however, there was a reassuring order emerging from the apparent chaos. Working parties had formed up, stripped to the waist, to unload bigger barges of their burdens: generators, engineering machinery, tractors, and the like. A light tank left its tender and cranked off into the bush. In a badly mangled thatch hut, knocked askew by the shore bombardment, men propped up the roof, squared away the debris, hooked up the portable generator, and calmly began their radio transmissions. All up and down the beach, signs went up at prearranged rendezvous points: "Headquarters, Pioneer Section," "Beach Master," "B Co. Supply."

By 0938, the command boat of the 5th Marine Regiment, the spearhead force, had thumped ashore. Colonel Hunt took a cursory look around before heading inland to set up his command post.

By mid-morning, Col. Clifton B. Cates had moved ashore with an entire regiment, the celebrated 1st Marines, 1st Division, battalions 1, 2, and 3. They passed through the shallow perimeter on the specified azimuth and took up positions astride the Tenaru River: 2d Battalion, under Lt. Col. Edwin A. Pollock, upstream and on the right bank; 3d Battalion, under Lt. Col. William McKelvy, Jr., downstream and on the left bank. First Battalion, with Lt. Col. Lenard Cresswell in command, was held in reserve amid the coconut groves, about a thousand yards to the east of the Tenaru.

There was still no sign of the enemy. And no one had been able to find the Grassy Knoll.

By noon, part of the mystery had been cleared up.

Floatplanes from the cruiser *Quincy* had gone in low, buzzing the troops and setting for all time the exact position of that elusive knoll. It was eight miles away from where it was supposed to be. It might as well have been, in that trackless jungle, eight thousand miles away.

At that point Cates asked General Vandegrift for a re-examination of his regiment's objective. "OK, Cliff, continue to snoop and poop. I'm coming in and we'll see about it then." At 1515 Vandegrift moved his command post ashore, shaking hands at the ship's ladder with Admiral Turner. Saluting the quarterdeck, Vandegrift left, carrying a last message from his engineers that they had just completed a rough bridge of dunnage and timber across the once-feared Tenaru.

It was heartening news, and the 1st Battalion of the 5th Marines, then within the perimeter, was ordered up to secure the right bank of the river where the bridge crossed, near its mouth.

The marines ashore were learning their lessons fast, from the commanding general to the lowliest private. Those who had viewed Guadalcanal as a beautiful sight from the air, as had *Astoria*'s pilot, and those who had viewed it from the sea, as had the troops now ashore, were in for a surprise. Beneath the surface beauty was a crawling ugliness: an infestation of things that stung, sucked, and bit. Big crocs slithered along the festering creek banks. Giant webs, strong as light tackle and spun by spiders as big as a mess kit, clung to the face. There were, patrols quickly learned, a "slew of critters" in the thick bush that were unidentifiable except by an entomologist, and some that were easily recognized, including scorpions, centipedes, and swarms of flies, mosquitoes, and gnats. Patrolling by stealth became a practical impossibility: in the trees were carrion birds and bats whose noise upon sighting the point man would have awakened the dead.

As the men in one of Colonel Cates's patrols pushed on down the tangled path assigned them, they heard the *thump, thump, thump* of bombs striking the Japanese airfield about a thousand yards away. Carrier bombers were working over the now-abandoned field. Tomorrow, Vandegrift outlined from his new command post ashore, the marines would push on to capture it. Now nightfall was approaching. It was best to dig in, perimeter defense. And watch out for night attack.

Intelligence had revised its earlier figures as to enemy strength. The Japanese garrison was now pegged at around two thousand, only a quarter of what had been predicted in the pre-invasion reports.

Over on Tulagi, across the bay, things had been going well, too. General Rupertus had reported details of several sharp firefights and noted that the marines were moving inland to objective lines on schedule. He was told to dig in.

And so the insect repellent came out, and such wire as could be brought forward was strung. The heavy machine guns and the light .30s sought final protective lines that would intersect on the wire. The 81mm mortar crews staked out the "dead spots" and the 60mms targeted around them. Back in the landing area, the 105s registered all along the probable routes of counterattack. Entrenching tools were unlimbered throughout the fleet landing force. In the jungle, the men had been told, there are no flanks, no rears. Each unit is an enclave unto itself in which all-around defense must be maintained.

It had all been rehearsed in training. Now, for the first time, it would be put to the test. They dug in for the night, as Vandegrift had ordered.

Mikawa, on the other side, was intent on attacking the American foe. He felt sure there must be two or possibly three carriers lurking in the wings. If this were so, he would reassemble his cruiser force and strike at night. Yes, that would be the tactic employed. Ohmae was kept jumping. The orders poured forth.

And then, as happens in nearly every military operation, there came a time of painful waiting. The hours of the morning passed slowly, with only fragmentary reports filtering back, many of them confusing and contradictory. One thing was emerging for a certainty: none of the sixty-eight planes dispatched to the battle zone, including Commander Nakajima's eighteen Zeros, had sighted an American flattop.

Enemy carrier planes, however, were in plentiful evidence, Mikawa deduced. They were taking their toll of the Japanese air groups that had been sent out to punish the landing forces. By 1100 hours, all doubt had been removed that the American effort was a major one, not a feint.

That much was confirmed in the late afternoon hours by a crestfallen Nakajima, who reported failure of his primary mission to his admiral. The flight had been long; Tainan Air Group was straggling back to base, distraught and fatigued.

Mikawa was sympathetic. "There will be another day, Commander. How many planes did you lose?"

"I cannot yet be sure, sir. I think six."

"But you are sure that what you ran into was carrier-based?"

"Yes sir. I estimate there were sixty to seventy over the area. Our first debriefings confirm that figure."

Mikawa led the downcast fighter pilot to the door and patted his shoulder gently. "Get some sleep. You'll need it tomorrow."

No word had been received from Seventeenth Army command regarding his request for immediate reinforcements. Wise to high command echelons, he had expected none. Mikawa snorted. He would send what he could scrape up from his own base troops. The search by Commander Ohmae located 410 men, including office "pinkies," clerks, and security people, and they were hustled aboard the transport *Meiyo Maru*, armed with a few machine guns and rifles, and sent southward with two escort vessels.*

Meanwhile the destroyer *Yunagi* had been sent at flank speed to intercept the *Chokai* and her companion ships—Mikawa not realizing that they had anticipated his order—and the cruisers *Tenryu* and *Yubari* were also ordered to make ready for sea.

What was left to be done was to obtain approval for the proposed night attack. The telegraph to the Naval General Staff buzzed away. In Tokyo the chief of General Staff, Adm. Osami Nagano, was aghast. Such a proposal, he told his solemn-faced, gold-braided aides, was madness. It would be absurd to send a

---

*Next evening the *Meiyo Maru* was caught in the crosshairs of a periscope of the American submarine S-38, commanded by Comdr. H. G. Munson; and two fish, which did happen to explode, sent her to the bottom. Left with nothing to escort, the supply ship *Soya* and the minelayer *Tsugaru* returned to base.

disorganized group of ships down the channel to attack in the dead of night against forces whose composite strength and capabilities were as yet unidentified. Ridiculous—particularly the paragraph which specified that Mikawa himself would lead the charge. Insane. No.

But Nagano was failing to take into account the power of Bushido, the true code of the samurai. As he listened to what turned out to be a joint lecture from his subordinates about the virtues of attack, he reconsidered. And finally relented.

At 1630 hours the *Chokai* was back in Simpson Harbor, her turbines throttled back, her anchors still up. By then, intelligence reports from returning search planes were in Mikawa's possession. Large fires had been noted at both Tulagi and Guadalcanal. One transport was believed afire. The reports said that three heavy cruisers were in the area, and that thirteen transports off Tulagi and twenty-seven off Guadalcanal were being off-loaded. There were an estimated sixty to seventy fighter craft overhead. The carriers? Not sighted. But there must be at least three lurking around.

They were not Mikawa's immediate problem as he was piped over the side and his red-and-white admiral's pennant was hoisted aloft. In a night attack, they would not interfere with his plans. On the return? Well, that was something to consider on another day.

The turbines shook in answer to "flank speed" from the telegraph atop the *Chokai*'s bridge. Signal flags were run up and the fleet moved out into the roadstead.

A samurai warrior was off to battle.

4

D-DAY PLUS ONE

Dawn's brief passage on August 8, 1942, was noted by a single slash of pink which brocaded the black night over the island of Malaita, forty miles to the east of the 'Canal. There hadn't been much sleep on the perimeter of Guadalcanal that night. Sporadic small-arms fire had hemstitched the shadows. Unblooded troops of all wars possess a characteristic common denominator: itchy trigger-fingers.

The 105s of the regimental artillery had done some registering. They had been unlashed from the decks of the transports and swung oversides by chugging donkey-engines the previous afternoon. Now they were emplaced and ready.

With first light, probing began all along the front. Eyes puffy from the sting of insects peered across small clearings and fields of waving *kunai* grass for a sight of the enemy. Lips swollen from the suck of white leeches and the bite of a thousand other "night critters" opened and closed to the slow, painful ritual of the morning meal.

On Beach Red, there was chaos in the making as supplies began backing up. The ships had moved closer to shore and the tons of supplies needed were being off-loaded faster than the fatigued beach parties could find a place for them. It was one of the two major problems Vandegrift faced as the sun moved higher.

The other lay across the channel. It had been twenty-four hours since Captain Crane and his 252 officers and men had stormed ashore on Florida Island near Haleta to protect the flank of the Tulagi operation. They had been unopposed. As at Guadalcanal, the Japanese defenders had hightailed it out.

But unlike Guadalcanal, this area offered no jungle fastness to which they could retreat. Tulagi, Gavutu, and Tanambogo, the three islands to be assaulted, were too small.

Admiral Turner's Operation Plan A 3-42, issued at the rehearsals at Koro Island on July 30, gave an intelligence estimate of enemy forces as 1,850. It was pretty close to accurate. As the first waves of the Tulagi operation approached the selected landing beach, the advance information regarding the treacherous coral reefs also proved itself out. Not a single landing craft hit the beach; all of them were caught on coral, thirty to one hundred yards offshore. The assault troops waded in with water up to their armpits.

The Japanese had expected landings on the eastern and southeastern shores of Tulagi, where better landing beaches were available; but high ground so dominated those shores as to make an assault there a precarious operation in the face of determined resistance. So the men of the 1st Marine Raider Battalion, commanded by Lt. Col. Merritt "Red Mike" Edson, made an end run, and the Japanese retreated to Hill 280 on the southeastern third of the island.

The Raiders drove swiftly across the slim island to a point two-thirds up the boot. By then they had reached Phase Line A, with their left anchored on Carpenter's Wharf. Thanks to fine intelligence, they had taken the enemy line of defense "in reverse," a classic military maneuver. The 2d Battalion, 5th Marines, meanwhile, had wheeled left to overrun the more lightly defended northwestern end of the island, only four thousand yards in length and one thousand yards at its widest part. The Japanese fought skillfully from caves and crevices, and the Raiders learned quickly that it took field expedients, like grenades tied to bamboo poles, to silence pockets of resistance.

By mid-afternoon, the marines had driven the length of the island and had closed the door of escape. Organized resistance had ceased. And Red Mike Edson, flushed by success and proud of his handpicked Raiders, took up residency in the white colonial headquarters building alongside the cricket field.

During the morning and early afternoon, Edson's communications with General Rupertus had been spotty. Now, Rupertus was able to report to General Vandegrift the good tidings: "We've got 'em holed up in Hill 280. The rest of Tulagi is secure."

"Dig in," came back the order from headquarters. The marines on both sides of Sealark Channel complied. The brief tropic twilight faded into darkness. Below them, in Tulagi Harbor, the flames of D-Day still burned brightly. Oil tanks, shore installations: the effect of cruiser bombardment and carrier strikes was still evident.

But there was another, more ominous fire. It lit up the residency with its intensity, as Red Mike and his commanders joined in a critique of the day's operation and made plans for the morrow, for the final assault on Hill 280.

"It's the *Elliott*," said Maj. Robert S. Brown, the Raider operations officer. "She took one, she's beached, and she'll burn all night."

To the superstitious, the bombing and burning of the *George F. Elliott* by Admiral Mikawa's planes carried ominous overtones. Launched in 1918 as the *City of Los Angeles*, she was one of the oldest transports of the invasion fleet.

That night the marines on Tulagi took the war's first *banzai* attack. From here and there in the dark, in twos and fours, in small groups and squads, the Japanese came out of their caves. From the redoubt caves on Hill 280, they poured forth.

It was noisy, unsubtle, incredible. They slapped bamboo sticks together as if somehow the very noise and act might lend them encouragement. "Hey, Babe Ruth," came a strident shout. "Here we come. We kill you, Yank."

"We drink American-boy blood."

"For the emperor. You die, Yank, for the emperor."

Others howled threats in Japanese—threats, they had been told during indoctrination, that would strike fear in the Americans so that they "would scatter like leaves before the *kamikaze*."

They fired as they ran. Five times that night they crashed against the entrenched marines, punching holes in the southern flank positions and closing with knives. Five times they were repulsed, each time the rifle and machine-gun fire taking a frightening toll, grenades and mortars crashing and thumping along the wire as the Japanese fell back and regrouped. In the end, toward daybreak, they were at last driven off. Sheer courage, the marines were to learn, had found its penultimate limits.

As dawn broke, the futility of the *banzai* matched the words of *Umi Yukaba*. There were, as the anthem relates, corpses in the field—more than 750 of them, clustered in a macabre circle of death around the marine positions. Only a few among the Kure Special Landing Force, which had raised the flag of the Rising Sun a hundred days ago, had believed in any other destiny. A mere twenty were taken prisoner. In America's first land offensive of the war, the proportion of dead to wounded gave mute testimony to the savagery one might expect in battles soon to come.

The marines had 338 casualties, including 144 Americans killed. It was a higher ratio of killed to wounded than in any battle or skirmish in American history—higher than at Sharpsburg or at "bloody Shiloh" in the Civil War. It was a statistic pondered the next morning as one of the Raider first-sergeants filled out the killed-in-action column of his morning report. "I wonder," he mused, "how the folks back home will take it."

As the sun rose across the International Date Line, it was Saturday a third of a world away. The bell on the wire-service printer at the *New York Times* finished a routine paragraph to a news story. The printer chattered "more to come," then a coded garble and the time of day. Four bells rang out, the warning for a high priority message. The printer chattered, then a new word emerged for the first time. "Dateline:

SOLOMONS . . .'' The folks back home were about to hear.

Front-page stories throughout the nation that day, while being pushed back by the fast-developing Pacific bulletin, concerned themselves with war in other places.

"Nazis Close In On Maikop . . . Black Sea Trap Tightened," read one of them. "The steel net that the Germans are throwing around Krasnodar and Russia's Black Sea ports is tightening." In the Middle East, reports out of Cairo told of U.S. Air Corps planes sinking a ten-thousand-ton enemy transport and cooperating with RAF planes in the "smashing of harbor and repair-shop facilities behind the Alamein front."

The offensive in the Pacific would not prove popular with two of America's allies, word had it. The Russians, of course, had been clamoring all along for the establishment of a Second Front which they hoped would relieve the pressure of the Nazi juggernaut, still seemingly unstoppable. The British, too, had their back to the wall. Their Eighth Army had been chased across the desert to the edge of Egypt, with Rommel and his Afrika Korps poised at El Alamein for a final thrust which the Desert Fox hoped would cut the Suez Canal and the British lifeline to India.

The struggle for the sinews of war as produced by the "great arsenal of democracy" was taking place on three fronts. Churchill had changed commanders to trap a Desert Fox; he cajoled and wheedled as only the master cajoler-wheedler was capable of doing. And on this date in history, he was "on the spot" in Cairo, hard by the ancient Pyramids, breathing new life into a demoralized Eighth Army.

Far to the north in the brooding Kremlin, Marshal Stalin, cold and forbidding, was demanding a Second Front. Not later, but now. His logic seemed unanswerable. How else could the immense pressure of Hitler's Panzer assault be eased?

And far off in the Pacific, a Third Front was being launched. It was the stepchild of two great forces: American public opinion and the American presidency.

The Japanese admiral and the American general most concerned with the events being chronicled in the world press on August 8 were, at 2000 hours that evening, only about a hundred nautical miles apart as darkness shrouded the Solomons. They were worlds apart, philosophically; and yet, action and counter-action of the past thirty-six hours had given the two men one common denominator, a very singular human emotion: the agony of frustration.

Red-faced with anger, General Vandegrift emerged from a thirty-minute conference with Admiral Turner. His remarks to his staff, as he descended the *McCawley*'s ladder into the waiting launch, were scarcely intelligible.

"They're leaving us bare-assed. Plain ol' bare-assed!"

Turner had wasted no words. Task Force 62, the entire transport fleet, would pull up anchor and sail out tomorrow morning at 0900.

"But what about the four days?"

"Forget the four days. We've got until 0900 tomorrow. Anything that doesn't get off the ships by then stays in the hold.''

There were immediate protests. There were reminders of the Fiji conference at which Frank Jack Fletcher had presided.

''These are Frank Jack's orders.''

There was no appeal. By 0900 on the morrow, the marines now ashore at Tulagi and Guadalcanal would be completely isolated from any base of supply. What was worse, tons of supplies, even troops themselves, would not be able to be off-loaded in the time remaining.

The navy brass was on edge. In the council of war aboard the *McCawley*, the marine commander's protest carried little weight. And the one man to whom an appeal might logically have been made was a thousand miles away, out of touch, out of mind: Adm. Robert Lee Ghormley, the theater commander, the court of last resort. Ghormley had made his final delegation of command in absentia, at the Fiji conference, before Operation Watchtower was launched.

On Guadalcanal, aside from the ever-growing snafu in the landing and storing of supplies, progress had been excellent. In the thirty-six hours since H-Hour, the 1st and 5th Marine Regiments had crossed the Tenaru River and pressed on one thousand yards across the *kunai* grass to the airfield. The original bombardment and the subsequent landings had disturbed Japanese troops and construction workers at their breakfast. Rice and tea were still on the tables of the Japanese mess halls when the first marine scouts pressed into the hastily abandoned buildings surrounding the airstrip. There were even a few unopened bottles of *sake* sitting around on the wooden tables.

"Hey, lookie what we got here, men!" There were toasts, drunk in derision, to the emperor whose troops had fled into the bush.

It had been estimated that the Japanese garrison on Guadalcanal consisted of one infantry regiment—about three thousand men—and two thousand laborers working on the construction of airfield and dock facilities. Curiously, even captured enemy documents failed to pinpoint the exact number of troops on hand when the marines landed. It was clear, however, that no unit comparable in fighting quality to Tulagi's Kure Special Landing Force existed here. And the Japanese force, mostly workers, had just plain skedaddled.

Observation planes from the the *Astoria* and carrier planes from the *Saratoga* had reported trucks and troops scurrying westward down the coast past the Matanikau River and Kokumbona and into the jungle. What the marine units found as they probed west was a nearly completed airstrip with machine shops, an ice plant, and a peculiarly constructed pagoda-like administration building and flight tower, almost ready for occupancy. Down by Lunga Point and Kokumbona there were storage sheds and docks piled high with equipment and materials.

It was a good haul, cheaply acquired.

Included were large quantities of ammunition, engineering materials, electrical apparatus, radio equipment and, most important, rice by the ton. The rice store would later prove to be the most valuable of them all.

Staff reports indicated that the Lunga Point facilities had been developed to a remarkable state. Since July 4, the reports stated, the Japanese had built a near-ready installation. "I figure two weeks will get everything in shape to make it operational," an engineering officer had written. Bridging material, power plants, semi-permanent camps, two radio stations, and wharfs jutting out into Sealark Channel were either completed or very nearly so.

Vandegrift had pointed out these facts to Admiral Turner during the conference, but to no avail. "With those docks in our hands, Admiral, maybe we won't need four days to unload. Give me two days. Even one." The admiral had shaken his head.

"Why, my engineers tell me we can patch up the runways on the airfield in a day, and we can have land-based aircraft on the field, if that's what's worrying you." The answer was still negative.

"It's like talking to yourself," Vandegrift related sadly to his staff on the boat ride back to shore. "We give 'em a thirty-six-hundred-foot runway, complete, and it's not good enough."

Down towards Savo Island, to the west, the marine officers knew, lay the cause for the navy's alarm. There, in the dark of early evening, flames clearly visible, lay the transport AP 13, the *George F. Elliott*. She was still burning, her civilian crew long since having abandoned the blazing hulk. The plane that hit her had been shot down in flight, but the pilot had somehow guided his faltering bird to crash on the *Elliott*'s decks.

The word *kamikaze* had not yet been added to the glossary of U.S. war terms. But the "Divine Wind" philosophy's implementation had begun among the Japanese pilots of the 2d and 4th Air Groups stationed at Rabaul and Vunakunau airfields on invasion morning. Mikawa's peremptory orders to them had been terse and succinct: "Punish the landing forces." They had flown down the Slot—the six hundred miles of water surrounding the Solomons chain from Rabaul to Guadalcanal—for the first time.

American carrier planes, circling overhead, had their first glimpses of the Japanese Hamps, Vals, and Bettys that made up the enemy striking force. Approximately forty twin-engine torpedo planes had participated in the attack. In debriefing sessions the Yanks claimed sixteen "meatballs."

Two ships had been lost. The destroyer *Jarvis* was badly damaged and limped out of the area under her own power, beating her way to the southeast. She was never seen or heard from again. All hands went down with her.

The *Elliott* proved tougher, and thereby created a greater tragedy. Cruisers of the supporting force had hammered her throughout the afternoon with 5- and 8-inch battery fire. She would not sink. Even a final torpedo attack failed to send her under, and she drifted toward Savo, finally beaching herself there. Included in her cargo had been an important share of the materiel for the 2d Battalion, First Marines—supplies that would be even more precious now that the decision had been made to send the fleet out on the morrow.

As the *Elliott* burned into the night, a Japanese portable radio transmitter crackled on nearby Cape Esperance. The operator reported the *Elliott*'s position. And her plight. Approximately one hundred miles to the north, in the radio shack of the cruiser *Chokai*, that message was received. It was delivered to Admiral Mikawa at 2011 hours.

Earlier, Mikawa had received flight intelligence from Rabaul on the results of the forty-plane mission that had brought an end to the *Elliott*. Twelve of the twin-engine torpedo bombers had been shot down by anti-aircraft fire and fighter planes. It was believed the American planes were carrier-based, possibly from as many as three carriers.

The admiral ground his teeth. He had the bad news. Now for the good news: "Our debriefing indicated," he read, "that the Americans lost seven aircraft during the raid." The damage inflicted on the invasion fleet? Insignificant. Paltry. Unacceptable! Mikawa towered in his rage. His staff stood about, tight-lipped and silent. "It is well," he confided to his executive officer, "that I am on the way myself to do the job that must be done."

At 2015 hours, silence descended upon *Chokai*, and the admiral disappeared into his quarters for prayers and meditation, a quiet man seeking spiritual guidance and strength for the task at hand.

Stretched out behind the flagship were the *Aoba*, *Kinugasa*, *Furutaka*, *Kako*, *Tenryu*, *Yubani*, and *Yunaki*; in all, eight powerful vessels. They were less than one hundred nautical miles from a place soon to be christened "Iron Bottom Bay."

Arrayed against them was the Allied Screening Force commanded by Rear Adm. Victor A. C. Crutchley, RN, holder of the Victoria Cross.

To and fro across Sealark Channel plodded the vessels of his command, eight cruisers and eight destroyers patrolling on a geometric pattern between Cape Esperance—the northwest tip of Guadalcanal—and Tulagi. Savo Island stood in the middle, and because of this it was designated the patrolling boundary between the force's southern and northern squadrons.

To the south were posted the cruisers *Canberra* and *Chicago*, with destroyers *Bagley* and *Patterson*. In the northern squadron were the *Vincennes, Quincy*, and *Astoria*, with DDs *Helm* and *Wilson*. Inside the channel, guarding the twenty-two remaining transports, were stationed the *San Juan* and the *Hobart* as well as the ten-thousand-ton heavy cruiser *Australia*, flagship of the fleet.

Far to the north of the assembled armada were two picket ships, the destroyers *Blue* and *Ralph Talbot*, chosen for their mission because each possessed that magnificent new device called radar. The state of the art was in its infancy, but as America's most guarded secret weapon it enabled the U.S. Navy to spot its enemy in the dead of night. There were troublesome dead spots, of course. But research and technology would correct those in due time.

Right now, little time remained. With night glasses trained, and with the best eyes in all Nippon behind them, Mikawa's fleet was bearing down, spoiling for a fight.

It was the kind of fight, Mikawa felt, that he was best prepared to handle. Moreover, he had a fair idea of the approximate strength of the Yank screening force. He knew that there were two or three carriers lurking within easy supporting distance. And three carriers, he surmised, would mean at least five heavy cruisers. Perhaps even a battleship. That would put the U.S. forces available at, say, three flattops, one battleship, and thirteen cruisers, plus assorted destroyers. He had eight cruisers. It shaped up as the naval mismatch of the war.

Except for one vital element: surprise. Perhaps another: darkness. A ferret uses both against the mastiff guarding the chicken. And now, at flank speed, the ferret would reach the henhouse in less than four hours.

5

THE BONZO BOYS

Admiral Mikawa had never met Capt. Martin Clemens, but he knew Clemens's work only too well. In the final hours of his journey down the Slot, Clemens and his men caused the Japanese admiral a certain amount of apprehension.

Captain Clemens, His Britannic Majesty's civil representative in the Solomon Islands, had recruited carefully and well in those hundred days since the Japanese invasion. Known on the rolls of the Australian defense establishment as "coastwatchers"—and among themselves as the "Bonzo Boys"—his experienced and dedicated men had spent most of their lives in the area and now volunteered to "keep an eye on the Nippers" from secret radio transmission stations along the islands of the Slot.

As darkness settled on August 8, Paul Mason, tall and angular, had retired to a thatch hut where he'd reflected on a busy day—the busiest, in fact, since he'd opened his station at Buin. At each station there were six to a dozen natives to assist. Paul Mason had ten, and they had been at their posts since dawn's first light on invasion morning. A flight of "meatballs" had arisen from the four fields around Rabaul; by 11 A.M. they were in formation over Buin.

Bonzo Boy Mason had heard the drone of their propellers. He rushed out of his palmetto hut on Malabite Hill and raised his binoculars. He counted eighteen in the flight. They looked like Kates, he thought, studying the silhouettes. Kates, he knew, carried the Long Lance torpedo.

Identification of planes flying at ten thousand feet is an inexact science, at best. The cloud cover over Buin on invasion morning had been heavy, and Mason's silhouette charts of Japanese aircraft were of prewar date. What he saw were eighteen Bettys of the Japanese 4th Air Group, which had taken off half an hour after Commander Nakajima's Zeros.

Nakajima's Zekes had not charted their course over Buin, and the reports of two eighteen-plane flights, one bomber and one fighter, had caused considerable anxiety at the other end of the intelligence line. Mason was not concerned with that part of the job. He was there to call 'em as he saw 'em, and he did exactly that.

He ran back to his hut. The native boy began cranking the double-handed generator. Mason switched on and picked up the mike.

The message from Buin flashed over the Bonzo network. Details of speed, flight pattern, number of aircraft, projected armament, and estimated time of arrival were duly computed and passed on to all vessels. The messages were even relayed to Pearl Harbor, where a backup communications system augmented the fleet information.

Twenty-five minutes later, the bullhorn aboard the

Australian cruiser *Canberra* crackled with this announcement: "Now hear this: This ship will be attacked at thirteen hundred hours by eighteen torpedo bombers."

The announcement was in bored overtones, something like the voice one hears at the supermarket over the store intercom, announcing a special sale. More emphasis, however, was given to the follow-up message. "All hands," the bullhorn crackled, "will pipe to dinner at eleven hundred hours." It was "fair dinkum," the Aussies reasoned, to advance luncheon by one hour because of the projected attack, rather than postpone it by two.

At 1130 hours, Nakajima's Zekes made their appearance high over the invasion fleet, tiny silver dots in the sky, their throttled-back motors making scarcely a hum in the blue. They were conserving fuel for the reception committee they knew would be on hand to greet them.

The deck watch on the *Canberra* observed them pass over to the south and east and out of sight. Admiral Crutchley, standing on the bridge, lowered his glasses. "I would guess they were looking for the carriers," he said to the watch commander. "We'll have more visitors soon. Signal 'Prepare for evasive action.' "

At 1300 hours, right on schedule, the attacking planes appeared over Sealark Channel to find ships of the fleet already squirming in giant S-turns, antiaircraft weapons at the ready. In the melee that followed, ack-ack shot down two of the twin-engine Jap-97 planes, most of their deadly eggs splashing harmlessly. The destroyer *Mugford* took a 250-pounder amidships and suffered twenty casualties, the first inflicted on navy personnel.

Two hours later, the Japanese mounted a second air attack on the fleet, with ten Aichi-99 dive-bombers swarming into the transport area. Their approach, too, had been previously announced by the Bonzo Boys. Two more enemy planes hit the drink in this attack, with no casualties to the defenders.

It was the intelligence report on these two strikes which had so infuriated Mikawa. And now, sitting before his small shrine aboard the *Chokai*, he went over the sobering details of the day's air action. He had little to show: two destroyers hit, one only lightly, and one transport beached and burning. Sixty-eight planes carrying the imperial red circle had gone aloft from Kavieng and Rabaul. A total of twenty-six had failed to return. In daylight action for August 7 and 8, he had sustained a combat loss of forty percent.

The admiral was not the only one who was counting that night. Back from his conference aboard the *McCawley*, General Vandegrift was on the beach, conferring with the beachmaster and the division supply officer. They were telling the general just how "bare-assed" he really was.

Lt. Col. Randolph Pate, the D-4 in charge of supplies, had a clipboard in hand. He was rifling through the attached papers. "We've got fourteen units of Class I and Class II supplies ashore," he told the worried general. "At least, I think we've got that much." He was talking about the categories of ammunition and food.

"Fourteen units? Why God damn it, Colonel, that's hardly enough for a two-week maneuver. And here we're stuck way off to hell and gone. . . .'' Vandegrift's voice almost cracked with his distress. He thumbed through Pate's pile of documents by the dim light of an issue Coleman lantern. The mosquitoes bore in. ''Fuckin' navy!'' For a quiet Virginia gentleman it was quite a mouthful, Pate thought.

As if in response to this derogation, the blinkers on the heavy cruiser *Australia* chattered out a message to the transports now anchored close in to Beach Red. Admiral Crutchley's flagship lay off Kukum, herding the frantically busy transports like a giant sheepdog.

The admiral had been pleased with the deployment of his screening force. He scanned the situation map with satisfaction. His radar picketships *Blue* and *Talbot* were well advanced, protecting both the left and right approaches to the channel around Savo. Plugging up the left approaches were the *Canberra* and *Chicago* with the destroyers *Patterson* and *Bagley*. And down here, the *Vincennes, Quincy*, and *Astoria*, with destroyers *Helm* and *Wilson*, were putting the old stopper in the right. And should the Nips elect to come around to his rear, he had the *San Juan*, the *Hobart*, and the *Australia* with seven DDs to cover that direction. There was still no news of any vessels approaching from the north. Yes, he signalled Turner, he'd be ready to pull out at 0900 in the morning.

His red bush emphasizing a jocular, confident mien, Crutchley rested his case. To the hero of Jutland, all that needed doing had been done. This was, admittedly, a different war, a different foe.

Off to the southeast, steaming in slow parallelograms, was Task Force 61, the carrier force, its planes on deck battened down, its elevators idle. An intership conference was going on down there, too.

"He's as mad as hell," reported Admiral Turner to his boss Frank Jack Fletcher in reference to his recent explosive meeting with Vandegrift aboard the Wacky Mac.

"He'll just have to stay mad," Fletcher's coded message shot back. "We pull out starting at 0600."

"Vandegrift wanted to know if you've heard from Ghormley or checked it out with him?"

"Negative."

The on-the-spot deputy to the theater commander did not think that necessary, or even advisable. And he gave two major reasons that affected his decision. The wireless crackled:

"First, there's fuel. We're short. Second, there's the plane situation. Noyes [Rear Admiral Leigh Noyes] reports twenty-one of ninety-nine planes on three carriers lost or inoperational."

The report on the loss to U.S. carrier planes, had he known of it, would have provided a measure of soothing salve to the conscience of Admiral Mikawa, who was then less than three hours away from Savo Island.

He would have been perplexed, however, at the status of the fuel logs of the invasion fleet. The reported "shortage" has over the years continued to baffle naval researchers searching for a more logical explanation for the withdrawal. Official fleet logs show that at 2100 hours on August 8, there was a minimum of seventeen days of fuel in the bunkers of the three carriers present for duty. The battleship *North Carolina* had eighteen days. The cruiser force had an average of eleven days. Most of the destroyer screen had more than seven days' fuel on hand. The transports were not as well off. But the same official records disclose that none had less than four days' supply on hand, of which very little was being consumed during the unloading operations.

Back in Auckland, the theater commander received a routine report from his deputy without much comment. "Fletcher is the man in charge," Ghormley said. If the withdrawal had not been prompted by Japanese aerial attacks nor by "an impulse of the moment," as Vandegrift charged to Turner, Ghormley might well have reflected on the reason why his ground-forces commander had not sooner been informed of the proposed withdrawal.

This, in itself, remains one of the unsolved mysteries of the war. Its taproots were probably linked with the Pearl Harbor hysteria that still gripped some echelons of high navy command—that, and a lack of reconnaissance in depth.

Far more ominous, in every respect, was the Japanese naval force then slashing down the Slot and approaching Santa Isabel Island, to the north of Savo. It had been sighted eleven hours earlier by a solitary American observation plane which had shadowed it for a solid hour. The plane had reported the position of the ships at once—noting meticulously their estimated speed, direction, and composition—until, short of gas, it had banked for home.

The Marine Corps' official monograph on the Guadalcanal landings poses the mystery of Mikawa's undiscovered approach as well as any:

The results of the aerial observation were reported

74

at once, but through some mixup in the communications chain which has never been satisfactorily explained, the screening force of United States and Australian ships apparently was not apprised of the potential danger which the enemy task force presented.

Mikawa, who had noted the shadowing aircraft overhead, could hardly have wished for anything as fortuitous as "a mixup in the communications chain." Crutchley's force became two flotillas of sitting ducks, one on each side of Savo Island. Battle stations were only half-manned throughout the fleet.

On his bridge in starched whites and gold braid, Mikawa looked up at the skies with approval. He called for his rain slicker and was helped into it by a silent orderly. A tropical storm had come up to further darken the already pitch-black night. Heat lightning flickered across the southern skies. The muzzles of the *Chokai*'s 8-inchers pointed back at it.

On the stern, a young Japanese flier climbed aboard the floatplane nestled on its catapult. A crewman patted his helmet twice and closed the canopy. The pilot adjusted his goggles and waved a hand to those who stood by in silence.

Soon he would be shot aloft.

He knew in his heart that he had two chances of being recovered: slim and none. But he was proud of his role. It was important that the admiral should know, firsthand, whether AP 13 still burned.

Three months earlier the U.S. destroyer *Blue* had been fitted out with that new electronic marvel, air-search radar. That was why she had been stationed as the forward picket ship of the screening force. But now, at the stroke of midnight, as Mikawa's Task Force approached, her sophisticated equipment inexplicably failed. No telltale blips were recorded on her screen.

Aboard the *Chokai*, it was a tense moment. Keen Japanese eyes, especially trained in night observation, picked up the *Blue*: she was on a collision course with the Japanese column. Mikawa gripped the splinter screen on the *Chokai*'s bridge. His fingers were "like an eagle's claw," recorded an aide. "The knuckles were as white as bleached bones." Nothing could be heard in the night save the swishing sound of the bow wave.

And then, suddenly, the American destroyer changed course, away from the *Chokai*. Comdr. Nordmark Williams, in command of the *Blue*, had ordered the helm put over for another reach in her plotted parallelogram. The fortunes of war sometimes hold mysterious rewards for the unwary: one or two seconds later, *Blue* would have been incinerated by the heat of the Japanese salvo.

From the bridge of the *Chokai* there was a sigh. "Hold all fire," came the order. "Proceed on course." Thirty-four 8-inch guns revolved in their turrets, away from the picket ship. Fingers on the firing mechanisms eased. Mikawa slipped by the sleeping watchdog at twenty-six knots.

He now had all the information he needed. His catapult plane had made a thorough reconnaissance. The transport *Elliott* was still beached and burning near Tulagi. Japanese ground observers near Cape Esperance had added their intelligence via shortwave. "Can see five capital ships in the area," came the report. "One, perhaps, is a battleship."

Mikawa retired to operations to make the final plot. He would use Savo Island as his pivot, swinging to the left. The observation plane had reported two flotillas, one on each side of Savo. He would deal with the south fleet first.

Mikawa marched his calipers across the chart, stiff-legged and sharp. The results showed him he would start his end run around Savo at 0130 hours. The admiral consulted his chronometer: that was one hour and twenty-six minutes from now.

His eyes were getting old, he thought as he stepped back out on the deck, and they were certainly not trained to the dark. But out there, past the *Chokai*'s white wake, he knew his column was in order. There were the *Aoba*, *Kinugasa*, *Furutaka*, *Kako*, *Tenryu*, *Yubari*, and *Yunagi*. And on their bridges, comrades he could trust. He went over the list in his mind, ticking off the names: Hayakawa, Hisamune, Sawa, Araki, Takahashi, Asano, Ban, Shimazui, and Okada. And if anything should happen to him, there were Goto and Matsuyama, rear admirals junior to himself, but fully capable of command.

One hour to go. He would spend part of that precious time in further meditation.

In the last hour before the first sea battle off Savo Island, what the American and Australian forces appeared to need most was not meditation, but mediation; mediation of widely divergent strategical and tactical concepts as they affected Operation Watchtower.

Tragically, there was no one to mediate.

* * *

Admiral Frank Jack Fletcher was executing one last loop off the northern tip of San Cristobol Island. Within the hour he would be taking his battleship, his three carriers, his six heavy cruisers, and his sixteen destroyers out of the area to the southeast.

There went the deputy commander. The overall commander had never been on the scene.

A veritable torrent of raw information had been pouring into Fletcher's headquarters all day concerning the presence in the Slot of Japanese warships, headed south into the combat area. A B-17 long-range reconnaisance plane out of General MacArthur's command had been first to note their presence, reporting "five Jap cruisers headed south from Kavieng." Later, the U.S. submarine S-38 had shadowed the gathering Japanese fleet, Lieutenant Commander Munson noting carefully that it was "heading southeasterly, now in position west of Cape St. George." From Milne Bay, on the eastern tip of New Guinea, two separate flights of Lockheed Hudson bombers had sighted Mikawa's ships, one at 1026 hours, the other shortly after 1100. Both had reported the fleet sailing "at high speed, maybe thirty knots."

Simple navigation means—projected course, estimated speed, and a set of calipers—would place that fleet only ten or twelve hours away from the invasion beaches. Word spread all over the American ships.

In his messages to Admiral Noyes, Fletcher queried his carrier commander sharply:

"Do you think we've been detected?"

"Negative."

"Did that last flight carry torpedoes?"

"Affirmative."

"How many torpedoes?"

And so it went. A distressing preoccupation with torpedoes, the feared Long Lance. If there was such a thing as a "secret weapon" at this stage in the war in the Pacific, it was the Japanese torpedo. The oxygen-fueled Long Lance traveled wakelessly at fifty knots, carrying more than a half ton of warhead. And when it hit, it exploded without fail.

Behind in radar research, the Japanese had also pursued night battle tactics with ferocity. They had perfected a unique and powerful night marine glass, and they had combed the provinces and the fleet for men with exceptional eyesight. As a result of training and indoctrination, the Imperial Navy was equipped as no other navy in the world was for night fighting at close quarters.

In this moment of stress, Frank Jack Fletcher was more concerned with his three carriers and their fate than he was with the twenty thousand marines on Guadalcanal and Tulagi; more concerned than he was for the twenty-two remaining transports. Certainly more concerned than he was for the screening fleet of red-bearded Admiral Crutchley.

He was, foremost, a carrier leader. He had three of the remaining four U.S. carriers in the Pacific. And those were all there were. He could not bring himself to accept their possible loss, even though the odds favored his fleet, to gamble on the success that might accrue from their remaining. At 1800 hours on August 8 he ended his personal Gethsemane by sending a dispatch to Vice Admiral Ghormley.

Admiral Turner intercepted the message; it was the first word he had that the carrier force would, in fact, be withdrawn. He had no illusions about the request being denied. The message read:

Fighter plane strength reduced from 99 to 78. In view of the large number of enemy torpedo planes and bombers in this area, I recommend the immediate withdrawal of my carriers. Request tankers sent forward immediately as fuel running low.

Fuel running low? It would scarcely hold water, that argument. What spooked Admiral Fletcher were the twin-engine Bettys carrying that awesome Long Lance—even though seventeen had been shot down, mostly by fleet actions, that very day.

Those statistics were not relevant to him. What was, it would seem, was the memory, the terrible memory, of the Coral Sea battle and the sight of the gallant *Lexington* attempting to dodge eleven aerial torpedoes, their wakes streaking toward her thin sides at the same moment. She dodged nine of them, but two got home. And the Big Lex was gone.

Memories, too, of Midway, and the *Yorktown* aflame from severe bomb damage. Her crew, fighting gallantly, had appeared to have that bomb damage under control. But then submarines had lurked ever closer, like sharks following a trail of blood, and again the Long Lance had delivered the *coup de grâce*.

In the staff conference leading up to the withdrawal order, many of Fletcher's senior officers had disagreed, pointing out that the landing operation was paramount in the strategic planning. It was put forth, strongly, that any risk to the carriers should be accepted.

It was further argued that if the reported Japanese fleet should continue down the Slot, seeking night action, then carrier-based planes could surely badly damage that fleet, perhaps sink it all, during tomorrow's early hours. What great help, what a magnificent opportunity it would be for America's first invasion effort!

It was all in vain. Even before Ghormley could acknowledge Fletcher's message, the fleet was underway at flank speed.

At midnight, August 8, Capt. Frederick Riefkohl was the senior officer present for duty with the Allied Screening Force guarding the Savo Island approaches. The only trouble was that he didn't know it. Nobody had bothered to tell him.

A mantle of command had fallen on the skipper of the heavy cruiser *Vincennes* some three hours earlier, as the "Vinnie Maru" led the *Quincy* and the *Astoria* in routine box patrol north of Savo. To the south of the island, the same formation was maintained by cruisers *Australia*, *Canberra*, and *Chicago*, with Admiral Crutchley in overall command from his bridge on the *Australia*.

Or so thought Riefkohl, blissfully unaware that the *Australia* had pulled out of the line and headed back toward the invasion beaches off Guadalcanal, leaving *Chicago* and *Canberra* to continue the patrol guarding the southern entrance bounded by Savo Island on the right and Cape Esperance on the left.

The *Australia*'s withdrawal was prompted by a message from Turner to Crutchley at 2030 hours.

Crutchley from Turner: Come on board as soon as possible. Will send boat as you approach.

Whether Admiral Turner actually wanted the *Australia* pulled out of line, thus greatly weakening the southern approaches, or whether he just wanted Crutchley to take his admiral's gig and make the ten-mile journey to the Wacky Mac, has never been fully ascertained. But Crutchley must have felt that the part of the transmission reading "will send boat as you approach" indicated Turner wanted him to come in the *Australia*.

In doing so, he left a confused chain of command—certainly a broken one. The withdrawal of the *Australia* automatically placed Capt. Howard "Ping" Bode, skipper of the *Chicago*, in direct command of the so-called "southern" force; it put "Fearless Freddie" Riefkohl, as senior officer present, in charge of the whole screening force. Bode was favored by this message from Comdr. G.C.O. Gatacre, Crutchley's Operations Officer:

Take charge of patrol. Am closing CTF 62 and may or may not rejoin you later. Crutchley.

And Reifkohl? "Fearless Freddie," as his ship's company fondly called him, had gone in to dinner at about the time he had become the titular though unannounced commander of the Allied Screening Force.

It was approaching midnight when the destroyer *Ralph Talbot*, in answer to her helm, made a ninety-degree turn according to her plotted schedule of search. The picket ship was ten miles northwest of the *Vincennes*.

Earlier in the evening, Lt. Comdr. Joseph W. Callahan had been handed an intercept: "Jap forces headed for Savo." The message carried no emanation point. Callahan had read the message and "guessed Admiral Turner knew about it, too."

Seconds after the turn, a low-flying plane buzzed directly over the *Talbot*. Lt. (jg.) Russ Walton, who had the dog watch, saw it from the bridge, as did the other men on deck. A few moments later, the *Talbot* sent a TBS: "Warning, warning. Unidentified plane headed yours." The message did not specify the type of plane. It had been too dark for that.

The *Talbot* was some twenty-five nautical miles from Admiral Turner's flagship *McCawley*, anchored off Kukum. When the Wacky Mac failed to acknowledge, Comdr. Frank Walker, in the destroyer *Patterson*, replied: "Will try to get your message through." The *Patterson*, with the *Canberra* and the *Chicago* behind her, was nearer the command ship.

Captain Riefkohl, leaning on the bridge of the *Vincennes*, also received the warning. He discussed it with his executive officer, Comdr. William Mullan.

"I guess it's one of ours, Bill."

It seems that the whole fleet, or at least all those who were not below sleeping the sleep of the exhausted, either saw or heard Mikawa's reconnaissance plane. Even the *Blue*, whose radar had not spotted those eight ships slipping by, now picked up the bogey headed toward Savo.

Everybody waited. Riefkohl turned to go below.

"Yeah, must be ours . . ." Off the stern of the *Vincennes*, its captain noted, the *Elliott* was still burning brightly. ". . . or Turner would have signaled us by now."

For the moment, however, Turner and Crutchley were just leaving the admiral's cabin on the Wacky Mac, their conference over. Vandegrift had left earlier. He thought Turner and Crutchley looked "beat." In truth, all three of them were just that. Their supply of adrenalin had been fully used up in the past forty-eight hours, and the effect could hardly fail to show on middle-aged faces.

The warning message reached the *McCawley* at twelve minutes past midnight, the logs showed. There was still time to sound general quarters throughout the task force. But Turner himself never received it.

It was a fitting prelude to disaster.

The grandfather clock, standing tall in the corner of what had been a reception room, tolled once as the sound of jeep tires crunched up the gravelled driveway of the old British Residency in Tulagi. It was 0100 hours on 9 August, and rain muffled the sound of approaching footsteps on the wide wooden porch of the handsome house which now served as headquarters for Brigadier General Rupertus.

The assistant division commander stood at the doorway to receive his thoroughly drenched chief. The two shook hands solemnly and Rupertus silently led the way down a long hallway to a small paneled office, motioning his guest to be seated.

"It's been one helluva day, general," Vandegrift opened, "but I wanted to give you a complete update

. . . just in case." He paused, pulling rumpled notes from a soaked combat jacket. The ride across Sealark Channel in an open LCM had been long and wet and the cumulative fatigue was beginning to show. A mess orderly slipped in quietly with two steaming mugs of "navy joe" and Archer Vandegrift huddled over his as if to draw strength from it.

He looked up at his deputy. "I just left a conference with Admiral Turner," he said slowly, shaking his head, "and what I have to tell you isn't good. I don't mean our job. We've done just about everything we've been sent to do. But this . . ." he slapped a pile of soggy notes in his lap, "this is pretty grim stuff."

He ticked off the details of the conference, and told how his appeal to Admiral Fletcher for one more day of fleet support had been denied. "As far as I know, the carrier force has already sailed." The transports, he related, were still unloading, but "the stuff is piling up on the beach and we can't move it inland fast enough to make room for more." Turner had given priority to the off-loading of ammunition and rations. "But we have to face the fact, Bill, that they'll never get our stuff off by 0600. Hell, that's only five hours from now and then they'll be gone."

"Has the 2d Battalion been off-loaded?" Rupertus asked.

"Negative. Their essential gear is way down in the holds and when the transports sail, they sail with them."

"Damn!" Rupertus grimaced. Not only ammo and rations but troops and materiel. "Did Turner give you any indication when we'd get it back?"

"None."

"How about air support?"

Vandegrift grinned for the first time. Rupertus thought the grin was brought on by the visceral relief of "laying it all out on the table."

"What air support? We won't have a Piper Cub between us in a few hours."

For half an hour, the two went over the notes, point by point. Then the far-off drone of a single-engine plane could be heard above the pelting rain as the squall renewed its strength. The two looked at each other inquiringly.

Outside the small room where the two generals huddled, a staff officer stood by the window, looking seaward toward the still-burning hulk of the *George F. Elliott*. A sudden flash of brilliance lit up the darkness high over the ship. It hung there.

"God Almighty damn!" the staff officer swore softly to himself. There was an immediate scurry to join him at the window. Off the in the far distance another light exploded and drifted slowly down. Then another. And another. A greenish pallor highlighted the features of those who gathered by the window. "What do you make of it, Sarge?" a smallish clerk-typist whispered to his section chief.

"Parachute flares, Corporal. Theirs, not ours."

What the flares portended was soon apparent, as bright flashes of a different hue began winking over the surface of the distant sea. The tempo increased so that an ever-widening area blinked and flashed, disclosing the dark forms of surface ships.

New and more ominous flashes erupted. Then to the Residency came the unmistakable rumble of large caliber guns.

One staffer noted the grandfather clock, its brass pendulum unhurriedly marking the time. It was 0133 hours . . . and counting.

The ferret was in the hen house.

6

IRON BOTTOM BAY

The passage between Cape Esperance, on the tip of Guadalcanal, and Savo Island is just seven miles wide. It was into this narrow channel that Admiral Gunichi Mikawa flung his battle column at 0133 hours on Sunday morning, August 9.

There was little finesse in his movement. The square-jawed samurai warrior had figured the odds, measured his opponents, and cast the die. He had on his side that priceless military ingredient: surprise. He had been spotted, he had been shadowed, he had been watched and reported. Yet the superior "weight of metal" against his chances of success had been thrown away, dissipated, eroded, by a combination of factors: fear, doubt, and misunderstanding. Mikawa, peering into the darkness of the tiny channel, was again to prove the military maxim that a poor plan, vigorously executed, will prevail every time over a superior plan whose execution is faulty.

There was deathly quiet on the bridge of the *Chokai*. All eyes were riveted on the small man who stood on the starboard wing, immaculately turned out, his arm held aloft. The arm chopped down. For a split second, the quiet held. Then there was bedlam.

"Tora, Tora, Tora!"

It was the signal. Its message swept down the line of the seven warships following the *Chokai* into battle. "Attack, attack, attack." Like a giant flying wedge the Japanese fleet poured through the narrow opening into Sealark Channel, hell-bent for election, all turbines at maximum revs.

The destroyer *Patterson*, patrolling off the port bow of the southern force cruiser flotilla, saw their shadowy shapes first. "Strange ships, repeat, strange ships, entering the harbor," she flashed. The alarm klaxon wailed throughout the ship, and half the crew scrambled sleepily to General Quarters.

Suddenly, there could be no more doubt. The clouds above and the sea below turned an eerie green as floatplanes, launched earlier from Japanese catapults, dropped parachute flares.

Silhouetted sharply against a leaden sea, the Australian cruiser *Canberra* was spotted by the *Chokai*'s gun and torpedo crews first, barely two miles away. The enemy had penetrated to point-blank range. Capt. Frank Getting had just reached the bridge when the *Chokai*'s salvo whistled home. A split second later, 8-inchers from the *Aoba* and *Furutaka* followed. The gallant *Canberra* shuddered under the impact.

From her bridge, Lt. Comdr. E. J. Wright, the principal fire-control officer, sought vainly to unmask her main batteries. "Port thirty-five degrees," he ordered the helm.

Another bridge officer, Comdr. J. S. Mesley, shouted down the voice tube to plot. "Enemy report, two unknown ships. Bearing three hundred. One mile.'' There was no answer. Plot had been obliterated.

Captain Getting reached the bridge. ''Hard astarboard!'' It was his final command. A full salvo struck the bridge. Shortly afterwards, two of the dreaded Long Lances thudded into the side of the stricken cruiser. The *Canberra* was finished. She had never got off a round; she had sustained twenty-eight hits from 8- and 4.7-inch battery fire, plus two fish.

The *Chicago*, about a half mile astern, was next as the Japanese fleet slashed through. The destroyer *Patterson* had been bypassed, being cuffed about by secondary batteries and suffering nineteen casualties. She had gamely fired sixty rounds of 5-inchers in her own defense, but hit nothing.

There was pandemonium abroad in the roadstead as Mikawa's eight vessels bore down on the *Chicago*. Captain Bode, still half asleep, had staggered to the bridge and tried to untangle a score of conflicting reports at once. Somebody pointed out three moving silhouettes against the blazing *Canberra*. ''Train the forward 5-incher on the one leaving,'' Ping Bode ordered. ''And get up a star shell so we can see what the hell it is we're shooting at.''

Too late.

''Wake to starboard,'' called the bridge lookout. Captain Bode whirled around.

''Two torpedo wakes to port,'' came the voice of the main battery commander.

''Full left rudder,'' the captain shouted. The *Chicago* was bracketed, and the battle was less than four minutes along. The first dreaded Long Lance passed seventy yards in front of the bow, hissing off into the channel. A second torpedo streaked even closer past the snaking ship. There were gritted teeth aplenty among those on deck who witnessed the near misses.

And then, with a grinding, crashing roar the ship seemed to come to a complete stop, shuddering for what seemed like forever before a mountain of spray appeared off the port bow. The bow disappeared in a shower of plates, chains, sea anchors. A gaping hole of tangled steel was all that was left. The *Chicago* yawed violently.

"My God," was all that Comdr. Cecil Adell could think to say. A moment later an 8-inch salvo crashed into the foremast, near the forward funnel. Adell felt his throat constrict. A small piece of shrapnel had passed between his jugular vein and his windpipe. He crawled over bodies to the aid station amidships where the ship's dentist, Lt. Comdr. Ben Oesterling, sewed him up—without an anesthetic.

There was nothing that could be done for the *Chicago*. She was left wallowing, barely afloat, out of the fight. As with the *Canberra*, her main batteries had not fired a single round. The so-called "southern force" had been wiped out.

It had been a kaleidoscopic five minutes for Admiral Mikawa. The tail of his column was only then swinging into the channel in the end run around Savo. He now ordered a change of course to the northeast where he knew the remainder of the American cruiser force to be deployed. Would they be ready for him? Or, having inflicted this much damage without suffering casualties, should he cut and run?

He conferred briefly by wireless with Rear Adm. Aritomo Goto, his second in command, who was aboard the *Kako* directly behind the *Chokai*. Radio silence, by then, was academic.

"Goto from Mikawa . . . Changing fleet course NNE. Please give opinion. Should we seek further action?"

"Mikawa from Goto . . . Advise continued action."

Mikawa's men, from battery pointers to black gang, were naked to the waist, sweat welling from every pore as they feverishly went about their task of destroying the emperor's enemies. The *Banzais* heard on deck were echoed in the firerooms. Torpedo tubes were frantically reloaded. Turrets of the mighty 8-inch guns swung like cobra heads in the night, searching for new targets. And the eyes of the fleet, trained for this moment, scanned the dark waters to aid that search.

There had been a revolution in naval architecture during the past two decades, United States planners and designers having opted for the "big gun" concept for cruisers. The Japanese, favoring close action, had designed their cruiser fleet for torpedoes, heavy cruisers packing eight tubes, light cruisers six. In Mikawa's fleet there were fifty-six torpedo tubes loaded with the deadly Long Lance. There were none in the three enemy vessels they were now stalking from the rear.

Brashly, Mikawa divided his forces, sending the *Chokai, Aoba,* and *Kinugasa* to the right of the American column; the *Furutaka, Tenryu*, and *Yubari* swung to the left, or east. At twenty-six knots, Mikawa was overtaking the three U.S. cruisers at a steady rate of sixteen knots.

Lookouts on the *Chokai*'s bows relayed a warning to the bridge. Mikawa's hand described yet another arc downward, and seconds later three aerial flares hung in the sky, sending down their eerie greenish-white luminescence to bathe the sea below and the ships upon it in a black and white montage of death.

A finger of light pierced the overcast as the *Chokai*'s powerful searchlight was turned on, picking up first the *Vincennes*, then the *Quincy*, and finally the *Astoria*, dead ahead off the *Chokai*'s port beam.

On the *Vincennes*, Captain Riefkohl turned to Lt. Comdr. Cleveland Miller, his officer of the deck and cracked out a query: "Whose spotlight is that, Miller?"

"I don't know, sir." Miller had been trying to fill in his skipper, just returned to the bridge, as best he knew. "Must be ours."

"Turn off the spot," blinked *Vincenne*'s semaphore. "We're friendly."

Mikawa considerately obliged. He would run in a little closer. Orders flashed through the *Chokai*; turrets rumbled as range-finders cranked out corrections. Two more spotlights flicked on and off to the east, pinpointing the targets.

"Who in the hell is running this goddamned show?" Riefkohl blurted out.

"Radar reports sighting at eight thousand yards, sir."

Riefkohl waited no longer. "Ring the engine room, fifteen knots." Whoever was running the show, Fearless Freddie wanted more speed.

On the *Astoria*, meanwhile, the OOD thought he heard an underwater explosion off the stern. "Maybe it's a destroyer dropping a depth charge," he told Lt. (jg.) N. A. Burkey, Jr. "Whatever it is, get Captain Greenman."

Flares lit up the sky. To Burkey's utter astonishment he heard his own main battery go off.

"Who gave the general alarm?" Greenman snapped. "Who gave the order to fire?"

The answer was not slow in coming. Lt. Comdr. Bill Truesdell had been working on a faulty fire-control radar system. Having patched it up with CPO John Datko, Jr. and Ens. Ray Herzberger, he had just come up on deck. He was witness to the first Japanese salvo plopping into the water, yards ahead of the *Astoria*. Hooked up by phone, he had commanded, "Commence firing, commence firing. Cruiser Nachi Class to port."

From the bridge: "What are you firing at?" And then: "Cease fire, cease fire."

Truesdell: "Jap cruiser, bridge. Request permission to continue fire."

Greenman had had a substantiating report from the bow lookout about the salvo dead ahead. He hesitated no more. "Commence fire!" he ordered. And then, to the engine room, "Full speed ahead."

The turbines had barely started throbbing to the full-speed order when all doubt was removed. The first salvo from the *Chokai*'s 8-inchers fell five hundred yards short, in full view from the starboard wing of the bridge. Then a second salvo, two hundred yards short; and a third, less than one hundred yards, its splashdown drenching the bridge. Mikawa was using creeping fire. He could not afford the luxury of bracketing fire lest one of the "overs" crash into his second column, steaming up on the other side of *Astoria*.

The fourth salvo came in like an express train

through an open switch. It staggered the *Astoria* in perhaps her most vulnerable spot—just amidships, where the planes, catapults, oil, and gas were stored. In a matter of seconds the ship was a blazing torch.

Ahead, Greenman saw the lead ships of his column also take fire, the *Quincy* first, and then the *Vincennes*. At full speed, *Astoria* was already overtaking *Quincy*. Now he himself was taking salvos from both sides; his turrets II and III reported their controls gone, shot out. But they continued the fight, the ship rolling with her counterbattery fire.

Between 0201 and 0206 hours, the *Astoria* absorbed 109 hits from 8-inch and 5-inch shells. She was a shambles, and at 0207 Captain Greenman ordered the helmsman: "Hard astarboard." She responded to the helm, barely avoiding a collision with the *Quincy*, which was ablaze from stern to stern, almost dead in the water.

Aboard the *Quincy*, a direct hit had turned the bridge into a charnel house. Comdr. Bill Gray, the exec, was dead, as were Lt. Comdr. Ed Metcalf, the navigator, and Ray Tuttle, the damage control officer. Lt. (jg.) J. H. Mee looked in from the companionway aft. He thought all were gone, that no one could have survived in the awful wreckage. But then something stirred to the right of the shattered helm. It was Captain Moore. He raised his head, and in a calm voice ordered the kneeling Mee to "transfer control to Battery Two."

In the corner of the bridge stood a completely dazed quartermaster. "The captain told me to beach the ship." His voice was charged with frustration. "But I can't steer." Mee held him up. "The captain is dead," the quartermaster said.

Into the wrecked bridge stumbled another figure, half his face shot away. It was Lieutenant Commander Billings, the bridge phone-talker. "I'm all right, keep calm, keep calm." The words came slowly from the bloody mask. "Everything will be okay. The ship will go down fighting."

He was right. A lone 5-incher cranked off a solitary round as if to emphasize Billings's words. The *Quincy* sank in five hundred fathoms at 0235 hours. It had taken sixty-three direct hits and three torpedoes to send her to the bottom.

Up ahead, the *Vincennes* lasted only fifteen minutes longer, going down at 0250 with a new set of colors flying. Her skipper, knowing his vessel was mortally wounded, had ordered a second set reefed to the mast to replace the flag Mikawa had shot down. Riefkohl had waited and waited for orders from his superiors. They never arrived. He had thought at the beginning of the action that the southern squadron must be up against a sub pack, or perhaps a destroyer screen slipping through for a torpedo attack. That had been his surmise. As he told his exec: "We're in a good position to cut them off if they try to sail out."

But a second searchlight caught the Vinnie Maru in her glare.

"Get 'em off my vessel," he ordered. It was duly cranked out on the semaphore. This time a full, armor-piercing salvo was his answer. That was the convincer.

"Hard aport. Full speed," was the next bridge order.

Too late, again. Moments later a full 8-inch salvo caught the *Vincennes* right behind the stack.

Torpedoes streaked toward her; one got home, slamming into her side between the Number 1 and Number 4 firerooms. Another salvo knocked out her main battery control.

"Captain, we have absolutely no more guns. Everything is out," reported gunnery officer Robert Lee Adams.

"Okay, Bob, you tell the men to get down below from exposed positions and see if they can take cover."

Up to then, the Vinnie Maru tried. She was the lead duck in a shooting gallery, and she kept fighting under a barrage from both sides. It took eighty or more direct hits to silence her guns, and two torpedoes to send her beneath the waves. She had answered with fifty-three rounds from her batteries.

When water closed in over her bridge, only the *Astoria* was left afloat, though not for long. She was abandoned at 0445, destroyers picking up her survivors.

Iron Bottom Bay had been christened. The toll was awesome. Six cruisers had been on station protecting the approaches. Now five were sunk, and one had been so badly crippled she was given little chance of ever fighting again. Of the 4,417 officers and men aboard, 1,042 were killed, 709 were wounded: a fearful price. An enormous down payment for the contracted beginning of America's first assault landing.

Americans would be shocked.

And yet, it could have been worse: Mikawa's fleet might have descended upon the huddled transports anchored off Kukum and Tulagi, to score even more heavily. The twenty-three transports, still unloading in the night, had been saved.

A lucky shot from the Vinnie Maru had slammed into the *Chokai*, wrecking the communications network and killing thirty-four Japanese sailors. Only one other of Mikawa's men was lost.

It was a tremendous Japanese victory—and, proportionately, America's most severe naval defeat. At Kure Naval Base, Fleet Admiral Yamamoto was properly grateful. Scurrying up the Slot, and worrying about the carrier retaliation that never came, Mikawa received this message from his chief: "Appreciate the courageous and hard fighting of every man in your organization." And then, in the concluding sentence, Yamamoto set the pattern for the reconquest of Guadalcanal. "I will expect you to expand your activities."

Before dawn, the last U.S. transport had scuttled south. The carriers were long gone. The battleship, the remaining cruisers, the planes, the whole weaponry of invasion had withdrawn. The marines were on the beach; and the navy which had brought them to this place, far from "expanding its activities," had restricted them.

Yamamoto wasted no time announcing the U.S. naval debacle. The Japanese radio did not report the loss of any imperial vessels in the dispatch. There was, however, one. Next morning, 10 August, John R. (Dinty) Moore, commander of the elderly United States submarine S-44, put the cross hairs of his telescope on the prow of the cruiser *Kako*, returning from the raid. Dinty Moore didn't have the Long Lance. But what he had proved sufficient. The S-44 fired a spread of torpedoes, and they streaked home. Within five minutes the 7,100-ton cruiser was beneath the waves. Most of her crew of 50 officers and

589 men were picked up.

Thanks to Dinty, the Yanks had exacted a price for their humiliation. It was a very small one.

7

"WE HAVE GAINED A TOE HOLD"

Dawn broke on August 9. The driving rain poured through the palm fronds that marked divisional headquarters like birdshot through a tin horn. The battle of Savo Island was over. The booming of the big guns, the yellow flashes of torpedoes crashing home, and the pyrotechnic display of giant searchlights on the bay and aerial flares over it had ceased several hours ago.

A sputtering fire, tended gently by many hands, somehow managed to stay live. It licked up the blackened sides of a five-gallon tin. Dirty hands reached down, now and then, to scoop up a canteen cup of bubbling Navy-issue coffee, as thick as a corporal's head and twice as strong. But it was hot.

General Vandegrift, still soaking wet, presided over the pot. He sipped appreciatively at the hot aluminum rim of the cup, which any marine will tell you always remains ten degrees hotter than its contents, and nodded his approval. "Not bad joe," he said, gesturing to those around him that the conference had convened. He was the ranking honcho in the Solomons now that Admiral Turner was headed south in the

Wacky Mac, taking with him the transport fleet and "a hell of a lot of stuff we sure could use."

The Guadalcanal brass had jeeped or splashed afoot to the division command post, located near Alligator Creek; Higgins boats had ferried the Tulagi contingent for the meeting. Now, as they conferred, the mists lifted slightly over Sealark Channel and the tropical sun came filtering through. Offshore, the truncated shape of a prowless gray cruiser took form, slowly making its tortured way eastward in the company of two destroyers.

"For God's sake, look at that," came the awed voice of one of the staff. The company was hushed.

"It's the *Chicago*," the whisper ran around. "They've shot the bow off her."

It was time, Vandegrift felt, to accentuate the positive. He went at it hard and heavy. The navy had taken its lumps, he pointed out, "but they did get us here, goddammit, and it's up to us to hold the ground. They did their job, now we've got to do ours."

The tasks of each unit were spelled out and assigned. Vandegrift listed the priorities. The notebooks and pencils were busy. Then the maps came out. "You'll get all this confirmed in writing when James gets his mimeograph working." That brought forth a chuckle.

The general wound up by kicking over the empty coffee tin. His summation told the group that the offensive was over, for the time being. "What's wrong with the defensive, it's part of our job, too, huh?" He closed with a reminder to pass the word along to every last man. "Just tell 'em to forget about the navy. We're marines!"

A small grey rodent scurried when the can was

kicked, disappearing between the legs of the departing officers and into the bush.

"Just a minute, doctor!" The division surgeon paused. "Let's get those atabrine tablets going." He was referring to the malaria suppressant that was being used in the place of quinine. "And, Doc, I'd like a report on rat-control measures being taken by all units, by 1900 hours." He turned to his chief of staff. "Let's get to work, James, we can't make any money here."

The marines would dig in and wait.

In the ten days that followed that first conference the marines battled the elements a lot more than they did the Japanese. Tulagi had been cleaned up and made secure. The last of the Japanese holed up in caves on Tanambogo and Gavutu had been smoked out by satchel charges and grenades placed on the end of bamboo poles. It was simple and effective.

But it was hard for the marines to understand the Oriental mind. "Why don't those little yellow monkeys just give up?" they asked. Since no answer was forthcoming, the marines adjusted to a new philosophy of warfare even as they did to the equally implacable jungle and its deadly menaces.

"Keep those socks up or keep those leggins on," was a daily reminder from squad and platoon leaders to their troops. The medics had not been idle; the "socks up" edict had been a preventive measure against exposure to the typhus-infected mites that infested every jungle rat. And there were a lot of rats.

The other major health worry, malaria, was already taking its toll, and atabrine quickly turned every man on the 'canal as yellow as a gourd.

"I can't send you out on patrol," one gunny-sarge told his nineteen-year-old point man. "You're yellower than a Jap." It had been the scuttlebutt that the drug made a man impotent. There were a lot of twenty-year-old marines who feared this more than they feared a Japanese bullet: "A dead marine, maybe, but an impotent marine, never!" Accordingly, strict measures of atabrine discipline had to be maintained, including the threat of court-martial.

Coursing down into Sealark Channel from the rain forests above, two rivers figured in the marine master plan for the defense of the airstrip. The Tenaru (or Alligator Creek, as it was first mistakenly called) was on the right flank; the Lunga River, about three miles to the west as the crow flies, formed the left flank. Inland between the two rivers, and running a mile and a half to two miles deep, a rough arc encircled the airstrip. This was the perimeter.

It was far from completed when Vandegrift called in his division D-2 to chart it out on the headquarters map. The need for exact information regarding the enemy forces of the original garrison was the major topic of discussion.

Lt. Col. Frank Goettge, the intelligence officer for the division, bent over the map and its overlays. His finger traced westward to a third river, farther up the coast toward Cape Esperance. "We think they moved along this line," he said, pointing to the Matanikau River.

The terrain of Guadalcanal looked simple on a map, but between the inland extremities of each flank lay a chaotic jumble of ridges, ravines, and flat jungle country. It appeared, from the very beginning, to be impossible to establish a continuous line across such terrain, even had there been sufficient marines available for the task. Vandegrift and his D-2 realized that any attack from inland could result in a penetration of the perimeter, which was blocked out neatly on the map but which existed only on paper.

The alternative to a continuous-line defense was to dispose various units in compact areas, or strong points, along the general defensive line, and to maintain contact and security by a system of outposts. The results of penetration could then be canalized, and the disruptive effects minimized. The patrols were to be moved inland from each strong point regularly to a depth of fifteen hundred yards.

The two men straightened up from their study.

"It's really a mother, General."

Vandegrift agreed with his D-2's estimate of the situation with a sigh. "Now, Frank, find out what those Nips are doing up along the Matanikau."

Goettge called together the leaders of two previous patrols to the west. On August 9 and again on August 10, a patrol from the 5th Marines operating just outside the Kukum sector had met heavily armed enemy patrols, and casualties had been suffered on both sides. Another patrol of the 5th Marines had moved down the coastal track to the actual mouth of the Matanikau and had been met by automatic-weapons fire from entrenched positions on the left bank.

Goettge, a gung-ho marine with tremendous energy and drive, jeeped up to the Kukum area for a conference with Capt. Wilfred H. Ringer, intelligence officer of the 5th Marines. They quickly got their heads together in the battered shed, its corrugation pierced by fragments from H-E shells and seemingly held together only by the maps and overlays hung on the walls.

"Our first patrols went down here." Ringer pointed down four miles of coastal track that linked the Lunga River and the Matanikau.

"How did the Nips react?"

"They were pretty aggressive, our guys thought. Some of them stood right out in the open. But here," Ringer pinpointed the left bank of the Matanikau, "is a real boar's nest."

"Automatic weapons?"

"Yeah, and dug in deep. We took quite a few casualties, probing 'em."

"How about artillery or mortars?"

"Negative. They do have some of those knee mortars, we know. They pooped out a few rounds as we moved in."

"What's this I hear about a white flag?"

Ringer paused, going to one of the overlays. "Right here is where the guys thought—I repeat, *thought*—they saw something white waving. It might not have been. I can't confirm it. It just might have been one of their battle flags."

The senior intelligence officer rubbed his closely shaven chin. He had "shaved cold in his helmet" earlier and the skin was still tender. "Reason I bring it up is that we've got a Jap naval rating in the division stockade right now." Goettge waved with deprecation at the term used in describing the prisoner lockup. It was just a G.I. pyramidal tent with a few strands of barbed wire around it. "He's not exactly 'one of the emperor's finest.' Fact is, he's a construction worker we picked up wandering around. He told us after considerable questioning that there might be a chance of surrender by the guys who hightailed it down there. What do you think?''

''Could be. You know the flag was reported seen after our guys unlimbered that pom-pom we liberated. We must have thrown a thousand rounds down their way.''

Goettge grinned. ''Heard about that.'' The report had reached the division D-2 that marines had made use of a captured four-barrel anti-aircraft gun mounted on Kukum dock. He continued, ''The little Nip appears sincere. I just sort of put two and two together.''

Goettge then outlined a plan he had for an amphibious end run by a patrol to be landed west of the Matanikau, near Tetere. He was convinced that there ''were a lot of Japs wandering around in that area who would opt for capture rather than death by starvation or worse.''

The original plan called for an early start on August 12 so that the landing could be made by daylight and there would be ample time for reconnaissance before the patrol went into bivouac. Additional details, most of them developing from Goettge's humane attitude toward ''the little Nips,'' caused delays and changes in the planning and composition of the patrol.

Frank Goettge was not cast in the mold of the military man who believes that most human suffering is a matter meriting instant sympathy but requiring indefinite postponement thereof. Nor did he feel that death to an enemy, like vintage wine, mellows with the years until it reaches the stage where its memory might be savored. In the patrol he included a doctor, Lt. Comdr. Malcolm Pratt—the 5th Marine regimental surgeon—in case there were wounds to be bound, and a Japanese-speaking linguist, Lt. Ralph Cory, in case of language barriers that might impede surrender. Almost the entire intelligence section of the 5th Marines worked their way into the act, and as a result the combat effectiveness of the patrol was further reduced. The inclusion of these "office pinkies," as they were derisively called by the front-line marines, left only twenty-five of the latter on the roster of forty-three.

It was an invitation to disaster.

The first humanitarian-combat patrol of the war was finally formed at 1800 hours as the sun bent to the west, some ten hours later than originally scheduled. The Higgins craft would take them north and west from the perimeter and land them, four hours later, on Point Cruz, far to the west of the mouth of the Matanikau.

"Stay away from that beach, Colonel," was the collective advice of those members of the patrol who, three days earlier, had carried away their casualties. "Them Japs ain't the surrendering kind. Flag or no flag, them bastards are dug-in and mean." At headquarters, Col. William J. Whaling, executive officer of the Fifth Marines, added a like warning.

Two hours before midnight, the landing craft approached the beach, its motors muffled and running dead slow. Silent, stealthy figures splashed ashore, arm signals alone indicating the assembly area along a narrow outcropping of logs and sand at the high-tide mark. Orders were whispered; the patrol was organized, a point set, flank guards designated. The landing craft backed off and slowly headed out. When the throb of its diesels was lost in the distance, Goettge waved his arm, the signal to advance.

Almost immediately the patrol was taken under intense rifle and machine-gun fire. It came, said Sgt. Charles Arndt, from all sides. The marines had walked into a deadly trap. Colonel Goettge was among the first to fall. As the unequal battle continued, three messengers were dispatched to the rear at intervals, beginning at 1130 hours with Sergeant Arndt, who managed to run back to the beach. The sound of the firefight behind him increased as the marine survivors opened up. But at midnight, firing sputtered to a halt, leaving only the firecracker sound of the small-bore Japanese .25-calibers cranking out a few last rounds.

Arndt, the first messenger, worked his way down the coastline and entered the marine perimeter at 0220. It had taken him three hours to cover the four miles. He reported that the patrol had been pinned down, and that all firing had ceased around midnight. He could only conclude that all his buddies had perished in the ambush. Further confirmation came at 0725 when Cpl. Joe Spaulding staggered past the perimeter guards, to be followed a half hour later by the third messenger, Platoon Sgt. Frank L. Few.

Spaulding and Few had crawled back to the landing beach and had concealed themselves in the outcropping of logs and sand. After the firing ceased inland, the Japanese sent a patrol down the path on which they had retreated, searching for survivors. They were noisy, Few said; they chattered excitedly, "like monkeys," and they had finally left.

When all was quiet, the two men had come out of hiding and left on their own.

"God damn them to hell," sobbed Spaulding. "They got every last fuckin' one of 'em. They must have."

A relief party from Company A, 5th Marines, was sent out immediately. Reinforced by two platoons of Company L, 5th Marines, and a section of light machine guns, they landed at Point Cruz, where the Goettge patrol was supposed to have disembarked, and retraced the coastal road to the mouth of the Matanikau. They were looking for a fight, but they didn't get one. The Japanese ambush party had vanished into the bush.

Neither did they find any trace whatever of the Goettge patrol. The jungle rapidly hides its dead, and the marines had learned a bitter lesson. It was quickly passed around the perimeter.

The 1st Engineer Battalion, under Maj. James G. Frazer, had been hard at it since August 8, when they had moved up from Beach Red to the captured airfield. Like a doughty wagonmaster of the Old West, Jim Frazer had his outfit going round-the-clock. The bad news, he would tell you, was that only fifteen percent of his heavy equipment had been put ashore from the supply ship *Fomalhaut*, which had followed the fleet over the southern horizon. Despite that crucial shortage, however, the Engineers had extended the existing runway by 1,178 feet in just seven days. It was now 160 feet wide, 3,778 feet long, and as yet unnamed. The unfinished Japanese control tower was alive with Engineer carpenters banging away hammer and tongs. "She was designed with a pagoda-prow roofline, and that's how she stays," said Major Frazer. "She's good enough for the fly-boys the way she is."

The perimeter had been completed almost as efficiently. Its arc from Alligator Creek to the Lunga had been developed in depth. But it was from the sea that most marines believed that counterinvasion would come; and for the first ten days the signs of its coming were manifest.

There was "Louie the Louse," whose daily advents became ever bolder and more detestable. He would come by daylight or by night, singly or in squadrons of two, four, or a dozen. In any number or formation he was still Louie, buzzing in arrogantly, dropping his bomb load on the field or on the perimeter with equal impartiality, then banking lazily for Rabaul. His insolence was maddening.

Whenever Condition Red was sounded to announce the arrival of Louie the Louse, Engineer Corporal Cates would drop whatever job he was on and head his R-4 bulldozer for the airstrip, ready to patch up the runway as soon as Louie and his pals had left. The earth-mover was the only machine unloaded for the 1st Pioneer Battalion before the fleet sailed away. Cates allowed no one to touch her as he guided her almost around the clock, filling craters, lengthening the runway, 'dozing supply roads to Kukum dock, even burying Japanese dead.

Even more insolent than Louie—because they were slower and stayed around longer—were the surface ships, and even submarines, that would stand off the beach and casually pump salvo after salvo of high explosives into troop positions and onto the landing strip.

110

The situation called for any countermeasure of defiance that might be improvised, and the marines dug deeply into their bag of tricks. They would haul pack-75s to the beach and pump round after round in mostly vain counterbattery-fire against the might and weight of Japanese naval eight-inchers or 4.7s. They mounted an 81-mm mortar in a Higgins boat one day and nearly blew out the bottom of the craft trying for a high-angle lucky hit. However futile, it was better, the marines would tell you, than just crawling into a sandbagged hole and waiting it out until their tormentors chose to leave.

The Japanese didn't know it, but the marines were being psyched into a murderous mood. After the Goettge ambuscade, what had been casual patrols became aggressive. Ack-ack battery crews were getting mad. The Engineers, who saw their runways pitted with bomb holes and eight-incher craters, were thoroughly enraged. Frustration supplied what amounted to a vital antitoxin, curing the few cases of combat phobia: they were spoiling for a fight.

But the one thing that all on the perimeter fretted about with equal perplexity was, when was all this "sit and wait horseshit" going to end? "For Christ's sake, when do we get our 'muscle'?"

On August 20, thirteen long days after the landings, some of it finally arrived. From a point two hundred miles south of the island, a flight of nineteen F4Fs, led by Maj. John L. Smith took off from the flight deck of the converted carrier *Long Island* at 1330 hours. They were closely followed by twelve SBD3s under the command of Col. Richard C. Mangrum.

General Vandegrift was on the line to shake Major

Smith's hand when the man who was to become the leading marine ace clambered down from his stubby fighter plane. The day before, in anticipation of the event, Vandegrift had christened the airstrip in honor of Loftus Henderson, the marine hero of Midway. A captured bottle of sake, broken at the Pagoda, highlighted the ceremony.

Beauty, as the saying goes, is in the eyes of the beholder. And Smith's ugly little plane was a thing of considerable beauty to the harassed ground commander trying to put the pieces of his defense together to meet the counterinvasion he knew was imminent.

"Welcome aboard, Major." He gestured around at the half-finished pagoda tower and the smiling staff who crowded in.

"Glad to be aboard, sir," came the familiar response. Goggles and headset removed, the major grinned, revealing a handsome Buzz Sawyerish countenance with beetle brows dominating a pair of wide-set eyes. He saluted smartly, and the two men walked towards the operations shack.

There was little time to clue him in.

Tomorrow would mark the second full week of Operation Watchtower. Only the primary mission, seizure of the nearly completed Japanese airfield, had been obtained. American forces held just a tiny corner of the ninety-mile island, and their hold on that was, at best, tenuous. The enemy commanded the sea routes from Rabaul, only six hundred miles away. Between the two points, stretching southeast like a necklace, was a veritable inland sea, dotted by the hundreds of large and small islands that make up the Solomons chain. This was "the Slot," and the Japanese

112

owned it lock, stock, and barrel.

Louie the Louse considered the Slot his private domain, Smith was told. Taking off from one of five airfields in and around Simpson Bay, Louie could head southeast by south over the southern tip of New Ireland, then over Buka, Bougainville, Buin, Choiseul, Santa Isabel, Florida, and Savo. By then he was home free and in position to drop his calling card.

Small landing craft, often escorted by destroyers, could ply their way south through this same sheltered chain, taking refuge at night, if they wished, among the many coves and bays along the way. The Tokyo Express, likewise, had been provided almost total immunity from U.S. surface retaliation to date. This collection of battlewagons, cruisers, destroyers, and subs could freely make use of the fine harbors of Rekata Bay, Bougainville, and Kavieng for refueling, victualing, and repair.

The Japanese forces, in short, were operating on interior lines of communication. Such was the picture Smith and Mangrum were given in their briefing by the general and his staff. A wireless report to division headquarters that very morning had been particularly ominous. Admiral Turner, far to the south, had forwarded intelligence received from Pearl Harbor that a strong counterinvasion force was being gathered to the east of the perimeter, some sixteen to twenty miles away. Somebody had intercepted a Japanese battle order and Washington had broken its code.

In the days leading up to the arrival of the two air squadrons, marine patrols had been bringing back reports of increased land activity to the east as well as to the west of the perimeter. Turner's relayed message of

113

the Japanese battle order provided confirmation.

Lt. Col. Edmund J. Buckley, who had replaced Goettge as D-2 for the division, had daily summarized his intelligence data to the general and his staff. "They're landing troops in strength up here." He indicated a spot several miles east of the Tenaru River. "Also down here, to the west."

"We'll be getting it from both sides, huh?"

"Looks like it, sir."

The Tokyo Express in recent days, indicated Buckley, was bringing in more than just large-caliber shells to lob onto airfield and beach positions. Fast Japanese destroyers, freely ranging up and down the Slot, were acting as troop carriers, landing arms, artillery, and personnel on both sides of the perimeter.

Three days earlier, native scouts of the Solomon Islands Constabulary, under the direction of "Bonzo Boy" Martin Clemens, had brought back word through the perimeter that a battalion-strength unit designated as the Yokosuka Special Landing Force had been put ashore during the night at Tassafaronga Point, off the Bonegi River, some twelve miles west of the marine positions. This was eight miles farther down the coastal track from where the Goettge patrol had been annihilated.

Vandegrift studied the map more closely when the pointer was moved back to the Matanikau. "On his way down," the memory of Goettge still sharp and poignant, "did Captain Clemens find any sign of the patrol?"

"Negative, sir. Lots of empty casings, ours too." Buckley shook his head. "But not a single body."

"Well, keep looking."

"Yes, sir, we will."

"Now about the other side." Vandegrift pointed to the overlay east of the Tenaru. "What do you make of this report by Captain Brush?"

"Kinda shakes me up, general."

"You're durned tootin' it does." The soft-spoken man from Lynchburg, West Virginia was not, except on highly special occasions, given to harsher expletives. "If these people down there," he gestured towards the area east of the Tenaru, "have got this kind of line on us, we're in for a whole peck of trouble."

His intelligence officer nodded assent.

Capt. Charles A. Brush had led a patrol drawn from Company A, 1st Marines, on a reconnaissance mission toward a dot on the map called Tetere, east of the marine lines. With the mission of confirming the presence of any buildup in enemy forces along their line of march, the patrol had left the perimeter at 0700 August 19.

The planned route lay along the narrow coastal road that led from the Lunga River to the Koli Point-Tetere area. By noon the formation had sneaked silently down the coast for about five or six miles. Oppressed by the heat, the men dropped in their tracks on command, to break out the K-rations. Pfc. Tony Jones and Sergeant Jachym, who had been this far with a previous patrol, informed Brush that there was a grove of fruit trees a short distance ahead.

"Okay, so we move out and get some fruit. But make it quiet," he warned. The patrol resumed its stealthy progress, scouts out well in advance. It passed through a deserted village and had just regained the road when the scouts hit the deck, bringing up their

115

rifles from the prone position on their backs, up and down, up and down, the signal announcing "enemy in sight."

Brush waved down the patrol and crept forward. He caught his breath. In and around a jungle clearing there were Japanese, a lot of them. They were not in combat formation; they were laying wire, it seemed, and intent only on that. Few even carried weapons. Some of their .25-caliber rifles were stacked near the clearing. There was a lot of chattering going on. The captain judged that there were between twenty-five and thirty Japanese. No supporting or covering force was in evidence. He snapped his binoculars back into their case and slipped back to the rear.

Down the road, the attack was organized. Jachym struck out in a wide arc to his right, through the jungle, with part of the patrol. Their mission was simple: get to the left flank and rear of the unsuspecting Japanese communications team. "Open up when you get into position," the captain whispered. They moved out.

The balance of the patrol extended itself into a skirmish line and sighted-in its automatic weapons. Fingers tightened on the triggers, safeties were snapped off, bolts silently worked a round from the belts into the machine-gun chambers. They waited. The chattering from the clearing continued.

At long last, Captain Brush heard the first shot fired. Then came the *bump-bump-bump* of a three-round burst by a BAR. "Open fire!" Two Japanese carrying a roll of wire were the first to go down. Then others, running for their rifle stacks, were hit. The envelopment had been complete. The firefight continued briskly, but in a few minutes it was all over. Four Japanese managed to dodge to the rear through the murderous hail. Four enemy officers and thirty-one men perished. Brush signalled "Cease fire," and the marines moved forward to collect the documentary material they had been sent to find. Brush counted his own casualties: three killed and three wounded.

"Let's go home. In fact, let's get the hell out of here."

The captured documents and maps were now before the general, appended to a brief action-report from Captain Brush. "It seemed to me," Brush wrote, "that the enemy detachment we surprised was the advance party of a much larger force. The maps the Japanese had of our positions were good enough to startle me. They showed our weak spots all too clearly."

The general cleared his throat.

"What do you make of it, Buck?" he asked.

"I'd guess they were coming at us tonight," opined his D-2.

"I'd have to say you could be right," The men looked at their watches. It was 2300 hours.

Earlier that same evening, a member of the Solomon Islands Constabulary had staggered through the lines of the 2d Battalion, 1st Marines, badly wounded. He was identified as Sergeant Major Vouza, one of Martin Clemens's men. He had been caught by the Japanese the day before, near his village east of the perimeter. Intelligence conjectured that his captors might have been the same group that Brush's patrol had destroyed. When he refused to give the Japanese the information they believed he had, he had been tortured and left for dead.

117

The Vouza incident and the report of the Brush Patrol had a sobering effect on those within the perimeter. Tension crackled over the command network and out to the defense positions.

"I got a feeling they're comin'," said the gunner of a sandbagged heavy machine-gun, "you can kind of smell 'em."

The work of "wiring in" the strong points for all-around defense proceeded with renewed attention to detail. Machine-gun "final protective lines" had been tested earlier, and the gaps, which the flat-trajectory fire of the .30-caliber Browning water-cooled weapons could not cover, had been registered for mortar fire. Aiming stakes had been plotted to deliver the fire by night.

Back at headquarters, work continued behind darkened, sandbagged revetments; only the tiny wink of lantern light remained visible from the outside through a chink in the blackout curtains.

And while the presence of enemy forces to both the east and the west had been established, the attack from the west across the Tenaru was, by midnight, considered inevitable.

The Lunga River defenses had already assumed the basic form plotted for them by the divisional D-3 section, Col. Gerald C. Thomas in command.

"But it's down here," Thomas pointed to where the Tenaru bends left toward the sea, "that Buck and I agree they'll hit us tonight." He looked at his wristwatch. "Correction, make that this morning."

General Vandegrift noted the correction with a grin. "Get it right, you two. What is your estimated time?"

Thomas looked over toward Colonel Buckley, the intelligence officer. "We think at dawn." Buckley nodded agreement. "A couple of Clemens's scouts checked in an hour ago. The head of the Jap column, they said, was about four miles down the trail. And not very quiet, either."

"OK, we'll just sit here and sweat it out."

"We'll be ready for 'em, sir."

Vandegrift went back to the map. He had lengthened his flank to about three thousand yards along the left bank of the Tenaru. What worried him most was that no permanent fortifications had as yet been built. Time had not permitted it, nor had the engineering facilities been available.

He had five rifle battalions at his disposal. The entire 1st Marine Regiment, all three battalions, were on hand. The 5th Marine Regiment still lacked its 2d Battalion, which had been detached prior to D-Day for service on Tulagi. Four of the five battalions were committed to perimeter defense. His only reserve was the 1st Battalion, 1st Regiment.

Two options had been presented to the general by his planners. The first called for the deployment of the reserve in the late afternoon, sending it down the coast to meet the Japanese advance head-on. He had immediately rejected this. The second proposed holding the reserve battalion near the airstrip, ready for a counterthrust to be supported by light tanks. This was adopted.

And now it was past midnight. All his troops were in position. Their morale, he believed, was good. That afternoon before the sun went down, Vandegrift had watched two marines wade out from their machine-gun position into Sealark Channel and wade back with a giant sea clam suspended from a knotted rope.

Morale? It could be equated with clam chowder, he mused.

Chowder was not on the White House menu on Thursday, August 20. But the President, half a world away, must have sensed some of that morale. In a cable, written that day to Marshal Josef Stalin in Moscow, he reflected upon it. "We have gained, I believe," he wrote, "a toehold in the Southwest Pacific." Secretary of the Navy Frank Knox, parrying a question at his news conference, proved less sanguine. "I don't want to make any predictions," Knox said, "but I believe that every man on Guadalcanal will give a good account of himself."

As for toeholds, the President might well have been a little premature in his judgment. The marines would rest their case on Frank Knox's evaluation in just a few hours.

8

THE BATTLE OF THE TENARU

One mile west of the Tenaru River a swamp stream with the imposing name of Block Four River moves with turgid reluctance to empty into Sealark Channel. A small man of evident authority waded to its left bank and barked a single command. There was a scurry all around him. Then a single flashlight illuminated the utter darkness, revealing a lean, sallow face with a jutting jaw over which a tiny pencil mustache presided.

Col. Kiyono Ichiki studied the map that was quickly produced. His staff huddled about him, watching as the colonel's finger moved and stopped. "Here!" he snapped. The light clicked off. He had indicated the mouth of the Tenaru. He had also issued the attack order, remarkable in its brevity.

Brevity and simplicity. Both are admirable military traits. But they can be overworked, and they had become so ingrained in the colonel's professional character that each had taken on the color of an idiosyncracy. In the tradition of the Japanese samurai, of which Colonel Ichiki might be considered a distinct prototype, the qualities of leadership most admired were arrogance and contempt. The colonel affected both.

The Japanese, Ichiki was fond of pointing out to awed junior officers, had not suffered defeat in three thousand years. They had humbled the mighty Russian navy in a single afternoon at Tsushima Strait. The fact that another Roosevelt, President Teddy, had acted as a mediator in settling the truce of that Russo-Japanese conflict of 1905, was treated by Ichiki with like contempt. "The Yankees," he told his men, "are mediators, not warriors."

He had been thwarted earlier in his role of avenger by the course of events at the battle of Midway. Designated commander of the unit that was to have taken the island, he was on his way home to Japan with his outfit, for rest and rehabilitation, when the marines landed.

That had been two weeks ago. Intercepted en route, the reinforced battalion of the 28th Infantry Regiment, 7th Division, was at this moment struggling up the coastal track toward Block Four River where at 0100 the colonel had given his one-word battle order and snapped out his flashlight. Nearly a thousand men stumbled down the inky black trail behind him. Route-march discipline was less than strict. Flashlights made yellow pinpricks in the night. There were groans as men stumbled over jungle creepers and fallen coconut trees. Now and then there was chatter as officers struggled to close up the column. The rear detachment had already passed the clearing where the marines had trapped the Japanese communication group.

No matter. Ichiki would spend the final hour before combat on rest and meditation. He ordered his staff to set up command headquarters. As the bustle about him intensified, Ichiki readjusted the pistol at his hip and touched the comforting folds of the personal battle flag he'd wound around his waist. He would review the orders from his commander, Lt. Gen. Harukichi Hyakutake, commanding officer of the newly formed Nineteenth Imperial Army, with headquarters at Rabaul.

These orders, also, had been short and simple. The Nineteenth would be run in that manner, Ichiki had been told. Fresh from the tea-houses of Japan, the general had only during the past week set up his headquarters. There would eventually be fifty thousand troops assigned to his command, including crack units now underway from China, the Philippines, and Borneo.

Hyakutake had confided in the colonel that it might not be necessary to send Ichiki many troops. "The character of the American is lacking in tenacity and battle leadership," the general had mentioned over a glass of rice wine, and Ichiki had nodded solemn agreement. "Further," his superior officer had continued, "when they suffer a setback, they have a tendency to abandon one plan for another. Perhaps you may inflict that first setback and exploit their confusion."

"I am honored, sir, by the opportunity."

"Your orders, Colonel." Hyakutake shuffled papers. "Six destroyers will take you to this point, about sixteen miles from the American lines. You will organize your approach-march and attack. It is a great moment for you. I wish," he sighed, "that I myself could be there. But. . . ." He had spread his hands.

The destroyers had carried a heavy manifest of arrogance. Colonel Ichiki was sitting on a bundle of it, amid the boxes of ammo and materiel in his head-quarters on Block Four, at 0300 on August 21.

Across the Tenaru, a marine sentinel posted at the mouth of the river sang out a challenge. The Constabulary scouts had drifted back earlier, one at a time. There was no response; only a stirring in the brush that lined the far bank of the river.

"Hey sarge!" the sentry called back to his squad leader in a hole nearby. "They's something moving over there."

"Give 'em a burst."

The sentry's trigger-finger tightened; the Thompson rattled and hemstitched the far bank. "Another!" Again no response.

But at 0310 all hell broke loose along the Tenaru.

With a howl somehow akin to the old rebel yell, some 250 Japanese, the spearhead of the Ichiki Detachment, flung themselves in a violent and headlong attack across the sandbar at the mouth of the river, firing as they ran.

"Banzai!"

The battle cry tugged at the gut. It bristled the hair at the nape of the neck. It had spread fear on a dozen fronts, from Borneo to Indochina. It had sown panic in a hundred engagements from Manchuria to Malaya. It was supposedly infallible.

But against the dug-in marines along the Tenaru, the code of *seishan* was to prove less effective.

The marines had new weapons in their hands, though some were not so new. The ancient .30-caliber water-cooled machine gun, the Browning A-1, had been emplaced on the left bank, its tripod legs heavily sandbagged. It was the workhorse of American ground-defense, eight to a battalion; and it was a carry-over, with minor modifications, from the trench warfare of World War I. With proper head-space adjustment and a good corporal at the trigger assembly, it could attain a cyclic rate of five hundred rounds per minute. That was two belts of copper-nosed bullets with a tracer every fifth round. At six rounds per burst, it could fire all day and half the night.

Interlocked on the final protective line was the A-1's little sister, the .30-caliber light machine gun, an air-cooled weapon assigned to rifle companies. It was new to combat and a little more temperamental because of this. It could get out one belt per minute in bursts of three. Because it was air-cooled, it was hard on barrels. "Another belt, another barrel," was the derisive tag hung on it by the water-cooled crowd.

Two brand-new high-angle mortars were receiving their baptism of fire. They had replaced the old Stokes mortar of the last war, and because the shells were finned they had far better accuracy. The 81mm mortar, designed as battalion support, could lob high-explosive shells into the dead zones not covered by machine guns. When targeted, a good 81 crew could put nine rounds into the air at the same time while firing for effect.

The little 60mm was the company commander's artillery. On the final protective line it filled in the gaps.

Also brand-new to combat were the regiment's 37mm guns. These were primarily designed as antitank weaponry, but along the Tenaru they had been emplaced to fire canister shells.

In the hands of the rifle squads were the M-1's,

replacing the old bolt-action Springfields of World War I. The M-1's 2,700-foot-per-second muzzle velocity would tear through a coconut log and kill at three hundred yards.

Such was the arsenal of the defense as the enemy came pouring across the sandbar. The marines did not run. They sat and they stood and they worked their pieces. The sand pit and the beach disappeared under a suddenly descending curtain of bright yellow flashes. The eruption was producing an almost impenetrable wall of water, coral, sand, and flying lead and fragments.

Yet Ichiki's men came on.

Lieutenant Colonel Pollock's 2d Battalion, 1st Marines found itself in the fight of its life. The colonel had just hit the sack when the attack was made. He was up, fully clothed, in a second, and on the line to division. At the other end was Ed Buckley, soon to be the busiest man within the perimeter.

"Buck? Pollock. They've hit us down here . . . Yeah, I guess you can hear . . . Yes, I've got Company G in reserve. I'll move 'em in to the beach if they're needed."

There was another pause. Then, "No, for Christ's sake don't send anybody down by jeep, they're liable to get their ass shot off." Major Bill Chalfant, his exec, was talking to one of the front-line positions. "What you got, Bill?"

"Art Larsen tells me some of the Japs got through. They're chewing hell through our rear."

"Any idea how many?"

"Just small groups, says Art. We got most of that first wave stacked up." The fire outside battalion CP had noticeably slackened.

"Better get G Company to move up," Pollock ordered.

The clock in division headquarters pointed straight up: 0400 hours. The sound of firing from the Tenaru was reduced to an occasional crackle of small arms. Pollock had just reported that G Company was mopping up on the survivors of the initial attack. The battle was only fifty minutes old, and the pieces were being put together on the situation map hung up on the wall and presided over by Gerry Thomas, the D-3. Vandegrift moved to the map and studied the changes. "Looks like they've got a considerable number of uncommitted forces located right in this area, Colonel." He thumped the map to the south of the sand bar.

Japanese mortar fire and pack artillery had started cranking out rounds against the 2d Battalion positions. Their *thump, thump, thump* could now be heard clearly at headquarters. Vandegrift had already ordered counterbattery fire from the 75mm batteries of the 11th Marines, and at just that moment these opened up. They settled into a dull cannonade as their barrage descended on the Japanese positions.

The cannon fire awakened the press corps on Guadalcanal. The correspondents noted red and white flares going up. At 0515 the artillery barrage, which had slackened, was renewed with intense fury. It continued, intermittently, until dawn began to lighten the skies to the east.

"Those guys out there are getting a pasting, that's for sure," said Maj. Bill Phipps, the regimental operations officer who had just talked to Gerry Thomas at division. Phipps beckoned his commanding officer, Colonel Hunt, to follow him outside the earshot of the correspondents. "Gerry says the flank of the Jap force has been determined."

"Are we going to be called in?"

"Not yet, Colonel. The general is sending in Cresswell." Lt. Col. Leonard Cresswell commanded the 1st Battalion, 1st Marines.

"Did Gerry give you the scoop?"

"Yes sir. Cresswell will go upstream, cross the river, and attack to the northwest along the right bank."

Colonel Hunt checked the route on his map. "That'll put 1st Battalion to the rear and on the Jap left flank."

"Affirmative. The general thinks now that the Japs are concentrated pretty much in this small area." Phipps drew a circle that looked like a smoked ham, with the shank end toward the Tenaru and the butt near Block Four River.

"Okay, we just sit tight."

It was past six o'clock, and from the airstrip could be heard the sound of engines warming up.

"Looks like the fly-boys want some of the action," observed the regimental commander.

"Yeah, keep 'em warm. We may be able to use 'em."

Col. Gerald C. Thomas was everywhere that morning of August 21. After a quick breakfast of boiled captured rice, he hopped into his jeep and headed for the CP of the 1st Marines and a confab with its C.O., Col. Clifton B. Cates. Together with Cresswell, they quickly plotted the envelopment strategy Vandegrift

128

had outlined.

"Can you get tanks through that area?" Thomas inquired uneasily.

Cresswell had a slow Louisiana drawl. His shirt was sweat-soaked even at this early hour. He had evidently been out in the bush. "Sure can, Gerry." He rolled out a map of the area. "Right here, upstream, they's real good dry footing."

That was good enough for the fast-moving Thomas. "Cresswell gets a platoon of light tanks."

Cates nodded approval. The division D-3 continued in his brisk manner. "Al is going to contain them from this end." He pointed out Pollock's position at the mouth of the river. "When he pushes this way, you roll up their flank. And maybe you can get the tanks into their rear."

They went over details, but the main battle plan was set: "It's just you n' Al, and the general figgers between you . . . well, you can get the job done."

Thomas was on his way to round up the tanks.

The execution of the movement was a picturebook success. The battalion crossed the dry upper streambed of the creek, debouching from the jungle onto a grassy plain some three thousand yards inland. Cresswell formed up for the attack, Company A on the left, Company C on the right, with Company B in reserve. Heavy weapons from Company D were split up, a platoon of heavy machine-guns assigned to each of the attack groups. The 81mm mortars of D Company followed with the reserve.

At 1115 Cresswell radioed back that he was advancing. Cates received the message. So did the man on the move, Gerry Thomas. "Good luck," was their joint message.

Word of the advance reached Pollock on the sand spit that had just been christened "Hell Point." It was over Hell Point that Ichiki had launched his abortive attack. Almost two hundred Japanese corpses still lay draped along the beach and over the wire around Pollock's position. A Japanese survivor, badly wounded, waved a white flag from the far shore. "For Christ's sake, there's one that wants to surrender. I can't believe it," a machine-gun section sergeant from Company G observed. The man came wading, feebly waving his banner. There was a sharp crack from behind the bushes across the river. One of his former mates was trying to cancel the surrender. A light machine gun burst covered the man's approach as he stumbled up the bank to join the marines.

"Poor slob. Hey, come on over here, we'll fix you up."

Pollock's G Company, the men who had "tended the store" and mended the river line last night, moved across Hell Point and disappeared into the jungle. From the southeast the presence of 1st Battalion was clearly marked by distant machine gun and mortar fire, increasing now in intensity as the sides of the Japanese pocket were being compressed. During the early afternoon the tanks rumbled into position. One hit a Japanese mine and was lost; the others inflicted only moderate casualties on the enemy. But Guadalcanal was not tank country. Here the mortar and the machine gun were kings of the hill. By 1500 hours encirclement was complete.

By 1700 it was all over.

In the sixteen hours of continuous fighting, more

than nine hundred Japanese had been killed. Only a handful managed to escape, including their arrogant commander, who had led brave troops to suicidal death. Only fifteen permitted themselves "the dishonor of life" by surrendering.

Next day a patrol found the remains of Col. Kiyono Ichiki far down the jungle track of his disgrace. He had dispatched himself with his own pistol in a final, ceremonial act of *hari-kari*. Before he put the pistol to his head, the colonel had burned his personal battle flag.

The battle of the Tenaru had cost the marines 109 casualties, 34 of whom, by no means "lacking in tenacity," had paid the ultimate price for the destruction of a Japanese myth.

9

CACTUS AIR FORCE

The thirty-one newly arrived pilots had not slept well during their first night on Guadalcanal.

Lt. Col. Charles Hayes, who had flown in from Espiritu Santo two days after the initial landing, had worked with Corporal Cates and the lone bulldozer on the monumental task of making the airfield operational. There were a lot of rough spots left. But what could be expected from one 'dozer, one corporal, one light colonel, and 140 green, young sailors from an obscure naval unit with the strangely appropriate designation of CUB-1?

By 1730 hours on August 20, however, the last SBD and the final F4F had been parked in their designated locations. The revetments were not yet fully completed. And the Cub unit, under the direction of an enthusiastic young ensign, George Polk, was forced to tug and haul each plane into place, so rough were the taxi areas.

That wasn't the only thing they had to move by muscle-power. There were also no bomb-handling trucks. These, too, were still deep in the hold of a ship far to the south. The five-hundred-pounders were not so bad, beaming Ensign Polk confided, but those thousand-pounders that had to be swung up into the bellies of the SBDs, somehow. . . .

There was the matter of refueling. No pumping gear on Guadalcanal. No sir. It was the handpump all the way, from fifty-five-gallon drums into the wing tanks. None of the Cubs had more than four months' service, but they all turned to with "vigah."

By 1800 the last airman had been jeeped to his BOQ, a veritable Jungle Hilton consisting of pyramidal tents, canvas cots, mosquito nettings, and spray bombs. Four cots to the tent, natural dirt floors, and a big Lister bag in lieu of running water: it was luxury living at its best. Mangrum and Smith, the two squadron leaders, were being given a briefing by Fog Hayes, who was understood to be C.O. of something called VMO-251, chief honcho and operational boss of the lash-up. Things were so flaky and off-the-cuff that one wonders whether the name "Cactus Air Force" came from that first operational meeting or whether it derived from the code name, "Cactus" for Guadalcanal and was itself a coded designation.

For Cactus Air Force it was to become.

That first meeting set up routine morning and evening search missions for the heavier SBDs, who were under orders not to attack anything smaller than a cruiser. Combat patrols were slated for the F4Fs, and the Bonzo network was discussed in detail as the best early warning system available.

What the group of officers and correspondents gathered along the Tenaru had heard warming up in the predawn hour of August 21 was the first search mission, getting out of the revetments and being muscled down the rough taxi-lane by the men of CUB-1. The two squadron leaders had flaked out early the evening before. So had most of their pilots. At 0310 had come the first interruption, guns along the Tenaru. Then an hour later the roar of the 75s made further sleep impossible. There was to be little shut-eye after that, that night or almost any given night.

The routine flights got off the deck and flew their missions. Other pilots, not assigned, went aloft for "observation flights" ostensibly, but turned them into strafing missions on the trapped Japanese, much to the glee of the circling marines, who cautiously held up fire when the fly-boys zapped in.

The forenoon was all but gone when Major Smith, in company with enlisted pilot Sgt. Johnny Lindley and two wingmen, got into the first scramble. They were at fourteen thousand feet just south of Savo Island when one of the wingmen spotted a dot in the sky, some five hundred feet above and half a mile away.

"Bandit at two o'clock."

Fortunately it was noontime; there was no sun side to sneak up on. Smith immediately recognized the silhouette as a Zero. Suddenly there were six of them flashing by, one exposing his belly as he banked and pulled up. Smith got in a good burst, but his attention was immediately taken by two more Zeros on his tail. He shook them, heading back towards Savo.

When the division formed up again, Lindley was missing. So was one Zero. It had crashed off Savo. Lindley, his oil tank shattered and his wheels up, made the first dead-stick landing at Henderson . . . and walked away from it. Smith followed him in.

"They were just as scared of us as we were of them,"

Smith reported with becoming modesty as he was being congratulated on the ground a few minutes later.

"How'd she handle?" The pilots were gathered around their captain, throwing questions at him. "Was it a Zeke?" "How's their top speed compared to ours?" "How much did you lead him?" On and on. Smith and his fellow fliers in the action clued them in. None of the four had flown in combat before. Neither had most of the others; some of the men of Fighting 223 had had less than sixteen days' total training. In their new profession they badly wanted to become proficient fast because that meant staying alive.

The euphoria produced by the Tenaru victory and by Captain Smith's first kill of the dreaded Zeke was contagious. But it did not last long. Two days later, on August 23, the SBDs and the Bonzo network spotted a new Japanese invasion force coming down the Slot. There were eleven vessels in the convoy, Vandegrift was told. But heavy rains and squalls, thundering down from the north, concealed the progress of the invasion fleet.

It also drenched the perimeter and turned the Jungle Hilton into a soggy, canvas-topped swamp. The field looked like a lake, its incomplete revetments standing out like islands.

At 1630 hours that afternoon a worried General Vandegrift stood by the Henderson Field airstrip and watched Colonel Mangrum's flight of nine SBDs take off on a search-and-destroy mission, accompanied by twelve F4F fighters commanded by Major Smith. Walking back to "the Pagoda," as the Operations building had been tagged, the general was as gloomy as the weather. "I feel as if I have just committed my last reserve," he confided to Gerry Thomas.

"You had no option, sir," Thomas tried to comfort his chief. He estimated that the new Japanese fleet was bringing in the balance of the enemy's 28th Infantry, around two thousand men.

Unknown to the general, a lot of things had been happening that day. Far to the south at Graciosa Bay, at Ndeni, and from Espiritu Santo, Adm. John McCain's long-range PBYs were probing north of Guadalcanal. They, too, located the new counter-invasion fleet and reported its composition with fair accuracy.

Also getting into the act was Admiral Fletcher's Task Force 61 which, since it had sailed away on August 9, had been "passively patrolling" to the south of the Solomons with a force that now included three carriers, one battleship, seven cruisers, and eighteen destroyers. What was more important, Fletcher's aircraft on the flattops had been reinforced to number 256. Now they were some seventy miles east of Malaita, less than 150 miles from Henderson Field, and well within supporting range.

Rear Admiral Tanaka, commanding the attack forces, was well-apprised of Fletcher's presence in the area. Vandegrift was not. It was but another chapter in the strange history of wartime intelligence. When Tanaka got his reading of Fletcher's position from two Japanese submarines operating on the surface that morning, he changed his course. That and the storm served nicely to confuse the hunters.

Within an hour after takeoff, the marine flights from Guadalcanal ran into a vicious line-squall and were turned back. They had found nothing. As the pilots trooped soggily into the Pagoda for debriefing, they found a grim-visaged ground commander who tried hard not to show his disappointment. "Don't worry about it, fellows, you've done all you could." By the light of a single, dangling 50-watt bulb it was actually rather difficult to determine just who was the more upset, the general or his airmen.

Out of the debriefing came at least this much of an intelligence summary: the Japanese landing force might possibly reach Guadalcanal as early as sometime around midnight. Gerry Thomas and Ed Buckley, the D-3 and D-2 of the division, to whom this raw information was most vital, shook their collective heads: it would not do. Still, there had been one event of some encouragement to the shoestring Cactus Air Force: Admiral McCain's own personal PBY had landed during their absence, bringing in a supply of the oxygen bottles so badly needed by the pilots.

And then, about 1830, after CUB-1 had begun the handpump refueling process that was to last well into the night, crackling through the tower came a sudden torrent of messages from aircraft overhead.

"For Christ's sake, they want landing instructions! . . . Sure I'm sure they're ours. The guy knows Ted Williams's batting average!"

The man over Henderson requesting landing instructions was a short, tough, and, for those days, experienced pilot. He was the air-group commander of the *Saratoga*, and he was bringing in thirty-one SBDs and six TBFs. They had taken off from the deck of the gallant Old Lady four hours earlier to search out the Japanese attack force. Frank Jack Fletcher, too, had heard from McCain's morning search by PBY from

Ndeni, and he had decided to do something about it.

But Comdr. Donald Felt, who had led the dive-bombers from the *Lexington* at Coral Sea, had been baffled and buffeted by the same line-squall that had frustrated Mangrum and Smith, and he had followed his optional orders to put down on Guadalcanal rather than risk the longer flight back to the carrier and land after dark.

The most astonished and delighted of them all was General Vandegrift. The navy had somehow come back. To hell with the details.

The night dragged on endlessly for Don Felt's fliers. Accustomed to clean quarters, showers, comfortable beds with sheets, and all the conveniences of a carrier, they found the blacked-out tents, the cots, the mosquitoes, the rattle of gun fire, and the weird jungle noises little to their liking. And in the small hours they were treated to a furious 8-inch barrage by the *Kagero*, a Japanese cruiser that had crept unnoticed down the Slot.

Thanks to the hard work of George Polk's men, their planes were refueled and armed by dawn. After Mangrum's SBDs had shoved off for their morning patrol, Felt's fliers took off for the Sara, not without a pungent assortment of comments and expressions of relief. They left behind them twenty-seven thousand-pound bombs, badly needed by the marines. They were the only ones in Mangrum's arsenal, and he would make good use of them before the day was over.

Morning on August 24 passed by with little new intelligence coming in until the Bonzo network reported the presence of a Japanese carrier within the Slot, keeping Mangrum's and Smith's men on edge. At

1300 hours, confirmation arrived from a coastwatcher on Malaita.

"I say, old boy, we've got something stirring over here. Looks like you've got twenty-eight meatballs coming to tea."

Fighting 223 scrambled at 1420, its three-bladed props surging the Grummans off the strip. They were poised over the east coast of the island when the Japanese came in at the suicidally low altitude of nine thousand feet. The fourteen F4Fs went to work with dispatch. They caught a mixed bag: the Japanese even had Kate torpedo-planes carrying bombs. Ten of them were shot down; six fought their way through to the airfield and dropped their loads.

There were twelve Zekes flying cover; six of these were splashed. Capt. Marion Carl was in the thick of it; he shot down two torpedo planes and a Zeke. It was an impressive start for the man who was to become one of America's top aces. But victory exacted its price: three young lieutenants of the equally young Cactus Air Force failed to return.

Word got around fast. And this time Jack Fletcher, annoyed by the previous day's negative reports, ordered his carriers into action. The Japanese flattop had by now been identified as the light carrier *Ryujo*. Her planes had been picked up by the *Saratoga*'s radar scope.

So at 1415 hours, Don Felt's weary warriors took off again, this time with an established target. Divisions of SBDs and TBFs roared off the Sara's bow, now turned into the wind. It was a beautiful sight for all save those on board the *Ryujo*, which was by now that most useless of naval vessels, a carrier without her brood.

She took hit after hit by the *Saratoga*'s planes before going under, ablaze from stem to stern. Her companion, the seaplane carrier *Chitose*, was badly damaged and limped out of action toward Rabaul.

Meanwhile, the transport division of the counter-invasion fleet continued to steam south by another route, still undetected. It did indeed carry the rest of the 28th Infantry Regiment as well as the 5th Yokosuka Special Landing Force. It was Vandegrift's main concern. It consisted of four old destroyers, the auxiliary cruiser *Kinryu Maru*, and the light cruiser *Jintsu*.

Late in the day word came in to the Pagoda that this force had been sighted, slinking between the islands of the Slot. A flight of twelve SBDs rose from Henderson and headed north. It was dusk when they returned, and the word they brought back was heartening. The *Jintsu* was last seen heading back the way she came, smoke pouring from multiple hits. The *Kinryu Maru* was afire and was being abandoned. The surviving transport-destroyers had scattered for their lives and were now on a course for Rabaul, not the 'Canal.

Their withdrawal was later confirmed by a long-range army B-17 Flying Fortress, up from Espiritu Santo to see what was going on. In the setting sun the crew spotted, from twenty thousand feet, a pillar of smoke and two slow-moving objects on the calm sea. It was the doomed cruiser *Kinryu Maru*, with the destroyer *Mutsuki* standing by. The Flying Fort closed in. The bombardier, his eyes glued to a new invention called the Norden Bombsight, directed the flight of the plane by voice intercom to the pilot.

"Talk about your rainbarrel, skipper . . . a little left . . . a little more . . . There you go. Bombs away!" He pressed the button, and a two-thousand-pounder glided down in its prescribed arc.

"Let's head for home, men." The pilot made a slow bank to his left. He looked back. "Good shot," he said. Black smoke still billowed, but the cruiser was going down by the head. She was the only thing in sight. The *Mutsuki* had already disappeared on her way to the bottom.

There had been more activity at Henderson than ever before, these past twenty-four hours. At 1845 Vandegrift once more returned to the Pagoda. That was where the action was, and it wasn't over yet by any means.

The jury-rigged landing lights had just been turned on. They didn't make much of a show along the runaway, but they looked pretty bright in the growing dusk to the stack of planes circling the field.

In the rickety control tower there was a two-way radio communication going on.

"Request landing instruction for Flight 300, over."

"Uh . . . Flight 300, roger. Do you read?"

"Tower, this is Flight 300. I read you five by five, over."

"Uh . . . take Runway One, 300. Repeat, Runway One."

It was the local joke. There was, of course, no Two. Corporal Cates and his 'dozer hadn't quite made it that far.

However, one runway proved adequate to handle Lt. Col. Turner Caldwell and his sixteen planes from the carrier *Enterprise*. The Big E had suffered a hit, most probably from one of the aircraft of the doomed *Ryujo*. Caldwell and his flight had been aloft at the time. Now

141

they were instructed to touch down at Henderson, the *Enterprise* having been pulled out of the line and headed south again.

Thus ended what has been termed the battle of the Eastern Solomons. The Americans had sunk a small carrier at the price of damage to one of their three big ones. A Mexican standoff, strategically speaking.

Tactically it was a different story, particularly for the marines. They had beaten off and partially destroyed one counterinvasion force. Others were on the way.

Vandegrift welcomed his new guests. He was glad to have them, even if the reinforcement they brought him was only temporary.

Late that night, the general gathered his staff around him for an evaluation of the day's work. There was every reason to believe, he told them, that Japanese envelopment forces around the perimeter now numbered more than four thousand. The Bonzos were reporting that more and more small landing-craft, holding from forty to fifty men each, were snaking down the island chain by night, holing up in jungle coves by day. They carried with them pack artillery, mortars, communications gear, and the like. Each boat meant a platoon-sized reinforcement, fully contained.

Still, it had been a good day, the general observed wearily. "The best thing about it, I guess, is that our navy seems to be back with us."

"Can we relax now, general?" somebody wise-cracked in the shadows.

Vandegrift allowed himself the luxury of a smile. "Not just yet, I'm afraid," he went along, good naturedly.

10

KAWAGUCHI: NEW MENACE

As the invasion month of August rolled to a close, one thing was becoming clearly apparent: you could throw the book right out the window. All the texts for future operations were being written by a special new breed of military men.

They had taken their lumps, but they had stuck it out. The press had reported their exploits; the folks back home had read about them and applauded. The marines on Guadalcanal had become a national symbol, a powerful antitoxin against the malaise of defeat. Wake, Guam, Pearl Harbor, even Bataan, were now a part of yesterday. The 'Canal was today. The marines had carved out a little piece of the jungle and, as Secretary of the Navy Frank Knox had predicted, were giving "a good account of themselves."

With Vandegrift's men, as August came to a close, two things stood out: innovation and flexibility. The Cactus Air Force was Exhibit A. In the ten days since Major Smith had led the first flight of fighters to Henderson Field, an almost perfect model of interservice cooperation had been achieved. That was something often bandied about in the high echelons of command but rarely brought into reality. But Cactus was doing it.

Its men came in all sizes and shapes. They flew an odd assortment of planes. They cannibalized some to get others aloft. They wired and taped and patched them together. They manhandled the planes in and out of revetments and hand-loaded the bomb racks. But the planes flew, and that was the important thing to the harassed marine general who saw, more clearly than anyone, the gathering clouds of a major counter-invasion effort.

On August 30, the Cactus Air Force mustered sixty-four planes, the newest arrivals being the army's 67th Fighter Squadron under Capt. Dale Brannon. Brannon had island-hopped his way up from Noumea in a bird originally destined for the European theater. It was a P-400, a hopped-up version of the old P-40, and as the 67th touched down at Henderson, ground crews took note that its snout had been painted like those on Chennault's Flying Tigers.

The P-400 couldn't be used for fighting Zeros. High-pressure oxygen bottles, needed to make it operational as an interceptor, were not available in the theater. But it could do low-level reconnaissance work, and that too was badly needed.

The old Bells, as the P-400s were called, were on the line at 0930 on August 30 when coastwatcher Paul Mason called down to report an unusual flight of single-engine Japanese planes heading down the Slot.

"Right-o, now these aren't twin-engine Bettys, you know. I rather think they're carrier-based Zeros. Yes, eighteen of them."

Cactus Operations checked Mason's description on

their charts. Stub-winged, huh? They were probably Hamps, the clipped-wing carrier versions of the Zero.

At 1100 hours John Smith's seven Grummans snarled down the runway for the intercept. After them came Dale Brannon's Bells. Another squadron of four P-400s had taken off earlier and was circling cover over a grounded supply ship, the *William Ward Burroughs*. There were nineteen flyable fighters available for duty at Henderson that morning. All nineteen were in the air.

The Grummans climbed to only fifteen thousand feet, in deference to the army pilots' lack of proper oxygen equipment. Smith led the first division, Rivers Morrell the second. Over Savo Island, Smith executed a wide, slow bank toward Cape Esperance, the P-400s riding on the outside, unable to maneuver like the stubby Grummans. Smith kept the formation for forty minutes, checking his watch and the solid front of clouds moving northwest up Sealark Channel, its thunderheads reaching to forty thousand feet.

"They could come at us from that cover," he thought aloud, the voice going out over the unusually quiet intercom system. And then, "What in the hell . . . ?"

Out of the corner of his eye he saw a flash of olive drab going down. Then six more flashed by. Dale Brannon had spotted enemy ships swarming around the *William Ward Burroughs* and the four Bells protecting her. He had moved to the attack.

Smith leveled off to get the sun behind his back and, with the flight in position, headed down. The blue-and-gray Grummans whined in. "Pick one bogey and stay with him," he ordered.

It worked. The Japanese, preoccupied with their task, were caught with their pants down. Eight Hamps were blown out of formation by the first pass.

The F4Fs pulled up for another run. Smith saw a Hamp on the tail of his wingman, Willis Lees. He gave the Japanese a burst and shot him off as Lees ducked into a cloud bank. He was just about to follow suit when he met head-on with another enemy plane. Smith gave one long burst with all six guns, right into the Hamp's engine. Strike another. This time he did duck for cover. The melee was over in three very long minutes. And then came the short glide back to Henderson and the nose count.

The debriefing that followed was a scene of restrained excitement. It was a remarkable victory, the tote board showed. Eight Hamps had been shot down in the initial melee. Two more stubbed-wing Zeros were badly damaged and never returned to Buka. Ten out of eighteen. Not bad. The eight F4Fs all made it home, although three were hemstitched pretty badly and would be off the line for a few days.

The army boys had not fared quite as well. Four of Brannon's game-but-outclassed Bells had failed to return, although two of the pilots managed to bail out and were later picked up.

It was a good victory, but could the Cactus Air Force stand the attrition rate? This morning they had had nineteen operational fighters on the strip. This afternoon there were twelve. Make that five; they had seven in the shop for minor repairs.

A little after 1500 hours the acute shortage was highlighted. The old four-stack destroyer *Calhoun*, a veteran of World War I, had been assigned as a ferry to lug spare parts, supplies, and troops between Tulagi and Guadalcanal. She was halfway across Sealark Channel when eighteen Bettys, swooped down on her.

The five flyable Grummans couldn't do a thing about it. Ensign Polk and his hand-crankers just hadn't been able to pump fast enough to top their tanks. The Bettys pounced and splashed a beautiful pattern around the old four-piper, and down she went. Then, unmolested, they headed back up the Slot.

It was a matter of timing, the luck of the draw, the fortunes of war. A couple of hours would have made a real difference, for as August 30 waned, three flights of reinforcements flew up from the south: nineteen more F4Fs, twelve SBDs. They were led by Col. Bill Wallace, group commander and veteran marine flyer, Maj. Robert Galer, and Maj. Leo Smith. At the Pagoda they were met and welcomed by a distinguished delegation: Archer Vandegrift and, by his side, Rear Adm. John Sidney McCain.

As Commander Air, South Pacific, McCain was responsible for the whole ball of wax. A tough little Mississippian with a vocabulary of expletives to match, he was essentially a "quarterdeck flyer"; he had gone into naval aviation late in his career, graduating as a pilot from Pensacola in his fifties. He was a no-nonsense guy, with no fear of "laying it on the line" to his superiors if he felt this to be necessary. And after one day on the 'Canal he felt he had the situation pegged. The pitiful showing of the P-400s triggered his resentment. The sinking of the old four-piper was the last straw.

Closeted with Vandegrift on the next morning, he laid out his summation before the general. "This will blister Ghormley's butt, I know, but it's got to go out." It was a dispatch addressed to Admiral Chester Nimitz in Pearl Harbor. Direct. Not through channels. McCain watched closely as the general read. Vandegrift shook his head slowly, his lips curving in a big it's-about-time smile, ear to ear.

"Your ass is gonna be in a big sling, John."

"Hell, it's been there before."

The two went on to discuss Ghormley's "black pessimism" and how it had affected the higher echelons of the entire theater. "Thank God it hasn't infected the kids out there." McCain waved to include the entire marine perimeter. He slapped the paper on the table between them. "Hot or cold, as they say at an Irish wake, it goes out this morning."

The message was blunt indeed. It read as follows:

Reinforcement 19 F4F-4, 12 SBD arrived just in time afternoon August 30. Pilots on Cactus very tired. Of 19 F4F-4 put in August 20, 5 flyable, an attrition rate of 14 in 10 days. Cactus designed by enemy as major base, for which admirably located, and is making major effort to recapture, of which daily bombings are a part. Against enemy power thus far shown 40 flyable fighters necessary to protect. P-400s no good at altitude and disheartening to the brave men who fly them. F4F more successful, due in part to belly tanks on Zeros, in part to cool maneuvering and expert gunnery. P-38s believed better, but 2 full squadrons of P-38s or F4Fs in addition to present strength should be put into Cactus at once, with replacements in training to south. One of these types should be replacement and reinforcement planes for those P-400 and P-39 pilots in South Pacific who are highly trained. The situation admits no delay whatever. No help can or should be expected of carrier fighters unless based ashore. With substantially the reinforcement requested, Cactus can be a sinkhole for enemy air power and can be consolidated, expanded, and exploited to enemy's mortal hurt. The reverse is true if we lose Cactus. If the reinforcement requested is not made available, Cactus cannot be supplied and hence cannot be held.

McCain

Far to the south, meanwhile, near the tip of San Cristobal Island, the Japanese submarine I-26 up-periscoped during a mission to the Coral Sea and put her cross hairs on the gallant *Saratoga*, zig-zagging leisurely at thirteen knots. A spread of six Long Lances sped out silently, and one of them got home. The Sara staggered. She'd been hit amidships, near the island. The wound was not mortal. Old Sara was tough, she had been torpedoed once before, off the California coast, and had returned to fight again. She limped away, but she would not be available for more than a month.

Injured aboard was Frank Jack Fletcher. He, too, would be beached for a spell. The *Saratoga*'s skipper, Duke Ramsey, flew off all his bombers, fighters, and torpedo squadrons to Espiritu Santo and Efate with a "well done" message and a hope that they would carry on as in the past.

Many of them would do so from an unsinkable

carrier named Guadalcanal. McCain's message had borne fruit. In a telegram to King in Washington, Nimitz relayed his decision to employ ''all aircraft that can be spared from the *Enterprise* and *Saratoga*'' in the Cactus Air Force, emphasizing that no suitable army planes were then available.

As the month ended, Vandegrift himself put the postscript to that message. Writing somewhat more boldly now to his theater commander, Vandegrift told Ghormley that the P-400 ''will not be employed further except in extreme emergencies.''

Despite it all, the Henderson Field box score, posted on the Pagoda, was becoming impressive indeed. Fifty-six tiny Japanese flags had been posted as September came in. Cactus had lost eleven.

Guadalcanal was becoming a three-service flattop.

Air, by itself, has its limitations. If you can't see 'em, you can't sink 'em. During the first week in September, swift Japanese destroyers, operating under the cover of night, continued to land reinforcements to both the east and west of the encircled marines. Probing action now grew stronger from within the perimeter. A second reconnaissance was organized by 1st Battalion, 5th Marines, to see what the Japanese were up to along the Matanikau. Col. William E. (Bill) Maxwell reported back that he had found a force of between 2,500 and 3,000 Japanese well dug-in along the left bank.

To the east, however, was the greatest threat, Vandegrift felt. There, down the line along which Ichiki's troops had advanced, was a dot on the map representing the native village of Tasimboko. It was twelve miles away as the crow flies.

Native constabulary, sneaking in and out, had brought back strange tales of Japanese atrocities. Two priests, Father Arthur C. Duhamel and Father Henry Oude-Engberink, who had refused to leave their flock, had been tortured and killed, as had Sister Sylvia, a French nun, and Sister Odilia, of Italy. These murders, the constables reported, had been witnessed by a third nun, Sister Edmée, also French.

The priests and nuns had been taken captive by survivors of the Ichiki Detachment, said the scouts. They had been ordered by a Japanese spy named Ishimoto to enter the American lines and spread the word that a large Japanese army had been landed. The Catholic delegation, it was said, would act in the humanitarian role of mediators for the marine surrender. When they refused on the grounds that they took no part in anything but religious matters, they were subjected to a week of torture and starvation. Pale, weak, but still stubborn, they were bayoneted to death.

Tales of the atrocity spread over the jungle telegraph. The marines were steamed. ''Those little piss ants, those dirty little sonsabitches—'' these were among the milder of the epithets aimed at the enemy now building up on their eastern flank.

They had come in by dribs and drabs: sampans, small landing-craft, and swift destroyer-transports. But by September 6, Maj. Gen. Kiyotake Kawaguchi could count four thousand troops present and available for duty, including the handful of survivors of the Ichiki Detachment. This was the advance element of the Japanese 35th Infantry Brigade.

Like his predecessor, Kawaguchi was an impatient man. Before leaving Japan for his new assignment, he had made a solemn pledge to his emperor. The marines on Guadalcanal would die. He would himself raise the banner of the rising sun over Henderson Field.

When he had arrived at Rabaul to confer with his superior, Lieutenant General Hyakutake, even the timetable of conquest had been set, and the exact spot designated along the Lunga River where the American surrender was to take place.

Hyakutake and Kawaguchi went over the master plan. The senior officer had the peculiar Japanese faculty of calling events, not as they were, but as they would appear to others such as Tojo and the emperor. The Ichiki debacle, as one example, was to be written off as "a glorious withdrawal of unshaken discipline." Such is the lexicon of face-saving.

Hyakutake had further elaborated his report on the defeat with this bit of philosophical flimflam: "The attack of the detachment was not entirely unsuccessful." Still, he had one warning for the 35th Brigade commander: avoid the Ichikis. The survivors of the Tenaru battle must now be considered pariahs. They were to be isolated from the brigade. In defeat they had become dishonored. In survival they had lost much face. "They must not be allowed," Hyakutake emphasized, "to infect others with their pessimism."

The two stuck pins in the big map, pondered them, nodded in agreement, and adjourned, solemnly bowing to each other. They had decided that there would be no need to await further buildup of their forces in the field. The attack would be made on September 12.

A command car whisked Kawaguchi and his baggage to a darkened dock in Simpson Harbor. The general was off to war. Inside the baggage, neatly packed and crisply starched, was a set of formal dress whites, complete with epaulettes and medal-ribbons meticulously in place. He fully intended to wear that uniform at the ceremony of surrender.

Despite his impeccable dress and fierce handlebar mustache, Kawaguchi was a man of tremendous drive, the kind of officer who might have been expected to tackle the building of a bridge over the River Kwai without turning a hair. As it was, he would have to build a road, twelve miles in length, through the jungle. This, he noted with an unbecoming lack of modesty, was to be called the "Kawaguchi Trail." Over this jungle road would be carried—hand-carried for the most part—the artillery, the ammo, the supplies.

Awaiting his trailblazing was a collection of rather elementary equipment: a few trucks, a load of axes and shovels, and very little else. The general wasted little time. Upon his arrival, he called in his unit leaders, brought out the map, and pointed them in the right direction. The 35th Brigade laid down its weapons to shoulder the axes and the shovels.

For six days the jungle reverberated with their sound. By then, amazingly, the two-lane trail reached out for seven miles from base camp. Five tortuous miles to go, to reach the eastern flank of the marine perimeter. . . .

The general himself made a habit of visiting the working parties, leaving behind a substantial force to cover his headquarters at Tasimboko. And so it came about that on the night of September 7 the general bivouacked with his troops on the Kawaguchi Trail.

Col. Merrit "Red Mike" Edson had been inactive of late, a situation not at all appreciated by the man who had stormed the Japanese caves on Tulagi just one month before, and who had kept his hand in by smoking out the final Japanese resistance on nearby Florida Island in the weeks that followed. Now the job across Sealark Channel was finished, the island secure. And Red Mike was looking for action. So were the Raiders.

As pressure built up against the perimeter, Vandegrift ordered the Raiders back to Guadalcanal. He plugged them into the defenses around Kukum; and when he looked around for somebody to find out what the Japanese were up to in the Tasimboko area, his eye fell on Red Mike.

Edson was not hard to get, his Raiders would tell you. "Glory Hound," they tagged him affectionately. "If there's a tough, miserable, shitty job lying around, ol' Red Mike will find it for us." News of the recent atrocities, the torture and bayoneting of Catholic priests and nuns, added fresh fuel to marine resolve.

That news and other matters came up for discussion at division headquarters on the morning of September 7, as Edson was being briefed on his assignment. Red Mike's exec, Lt. Col. Sam Griffith, was there; so were Maj. Bob Brown, the battalion's S-3, or operations chief, and Martin Clemens, chief of the native scouts.

Gerry Thomas, pointer in hand, led it off. "Gentlemen, Captain Clemens here says that the Nips have at least three companies, and maybe more, dug-in right about here." Clemens nodded as the pointer indicated a spot just west of the village of Tasimboko. "As far as we can determine, this force is lightly armed, although it may have a few bits and pieces of artillery. Now your job will be to land here, and here. And you'll envelop around here." The arrows grew in number. Purpose of the operation: the destruction of the Kawaguchi base camp.

"You will load at 1800 hours. You've got the YP boats *Manley* and *McKean*," Thomas smiled broadly. "And a Portuguese skipper named Joaquin Theodore. You'll go ashore in landing craft just before dawn. That's about it, gentlemen. . . . And don't forget to call for air support. It's yours if you need it."

The newcomer at Vandegrift's side confirmed this with a nod that shook the wattles below the strong jaw which dominated his jovial, avuncular countenance. He had come aboard four days earlier as the newly appointed boss of Cactus Air Force. He was Maj. Gen. Roy S. Geiger, veteran marine aviation commander, whose 1st Marine Air Wing headquarters would henceforth direct the mixed, all-service operations.

At dusk the converted tuna clippers *Manley* and *McKean* took on their consignment of Raiders. Edson and his staff were last on board. The two little ships were packed, above decks and below. Captain Theodore shoved off into rain and a rough sea. The little tuna boats rolled heavily; the night proved to be long. The noisy labor of the straining diesels bothered even those on deck who had preferred a damp ride in the open to the steaming hold. Somehow the galley managed sandwiches and coffee before unloading was commenced at 0500 hours.

As the first Higgins boat chugged slowly toward

shore a small convoy passed close, escorted by destroyers. "Who the hell are they?" someone demanded.

Red Mike had the answer. "They're ours, heading for Kukum." It was a fortuitous coincidence. If there were enemy observers within range they would be likely to believe the Raiders' vessels to be part of a much larger force.

The ship-to-shore movement continued without incident as the first wave of landing craft hit the beach and returned for the remainder of the troops still lining the rail and peering at the jungle. "Jesus, it's quiet," said a light machine-gunner, shouldering his piece and slipping over the rail into the bobbing landing-craft. "Yeah, pal, but not for long," came the rejoinder.

The operation was proceeding just as it had been laid out on the division headquarters map. Company B was on the beach and holding. Company A came ashore on its left and kept contact by a line of file-closers. Charlie Company, assigned to the envelopment, moved inland on its extended route march. Suddenly, just at the break of dawn, the whipcrack of a single shot came from the jungle.

"Christalmighty!" Eight hundred and fifty men sharply took in their breath. Then, as the seconds passed, the movement forward was resumed, with riflemen at high port and machine-gunners ready to drop and mount at an instant, ammo-carriers lugging their backbreaking loads. "Some shithead forgot to lock his piece."

Soon, Charlie Company came across evidence of enemy confusion or unreadiness, or both. There, on a side trail, sat a Nip 37mm gun, its trail split, ammo stacked, but unattended. Packs, shovels, even shoes, were strewn around the site. No signs of trap or ambush, and no rhyme or reason. The marines continued on their way. More field fortifications were unmasked, including two more 37s. These, too were unmanned.

"Just what the hell are we getting into?" Red Mike asked himself. He checked his watch. Unbelievably, its hands showed 0630. They had been ashore for a solid hour. Edson, at the head of the column, was now in sight of the village. There was a distant drone of engines to the south and east. It rapidly grew louder. He waved his radio section forward, and they came stumbling, toting the battalion two-way wireless.

General Geiger was about to launch his first strike in support. At 0635 the formation roared in, targeting on the thatched roofs and the corrugated iron sheds of the Japanese base camp. Bomb loads from the leading SBDs rocked the jungle and sent debris flying through the village. Four P-400s streaked by on the low-level strafing mission for which they were admirably suited. They banked in, banked out, their guns stitching the workshops and the warehouses. At the same instant, both the *Manley* and the *McKean* got on target, lobbing three-inch shells from their deck guns, adding to the smoke and fire.

By 0855 Edson and his Raiders had closed in, surrounding Tasimboko. There had been some return fire by then. Red Mike called in to headquarters at Henderson.

"We're doing nicely, thanks." The flat crack of a Japanese .25 rifle came in over the air. Then a machine-gun burst. "Yep, they're getting together for

157

a counterattack, I do believe.''

So it went, back and forth. The situation was becoming slightly murky. Edson believed he was faced with some one thousand enemy troops. He suggested that bombers be kept in the air for continuous support, on call.

Two more hours went by. The fire had increased. The Raider commander got on the horn again. ''Is it possible to send more troops around to the west of Tasimboko?'' he inquired.

Division was getting worried. ''Negative, Mike. Suggest you re-embark and return to the perimeter.''

''Is that an order?''

''Negative again. You call the shots.''

The Raiders continued to infiltrate the Japanese defenses. They captured several field pieces that had been firing point-blank into the marine encirclement. Back at headquarters their progress was noted; also noted were the reports that contact between the three companies, lost for about an hour, had been re-established.

Edson breathed a sigh of relief and resumed the attack. He called for the P-400s again, and four responded on a strafing mission that silenced more of the gathering Japanese 47mm guns. By early afternoon Tasimboko was entered; not, however, before most of its defenders had fled up the Kawaguchi Trail and into the bush.

The entire base was reduced to rubble. Mission completed. The cost had been incredibly small: two American personnel had been killed, six wounded.

The Japanese covering force had suffered total surprise, and it had not fought well. That was the opinion of an irate Kawaguchi upon his receipt of the news, far up the trail. He had left a thousand men behind him, and considered their defeat a disgrace to the 35th Brigade. It could be wiped out only by the surrender ceremony he had planned in such detail.

One small detail would be missing, however. There would be no white starched uniform for the general to wear. As the rear detachment of the Raiders was completing its wrecking chores, removing and destroying artillery breech-blocks and fuses, setting fire to what buildings still stood, one of Red Mike's men came across a battered trunk. He opened it.

"Well, will you lookee here!" He'd found a still-sparkling white tunic. Then he pulled out Kawaguchi's breeches. "Hey, let's give 'em to Red Mike!" He and his buddies trotted back towards the shore and to the waiting Higgins boats, waving their prize. Their colonel might have a use for it, in case he ever met up with the Japanese general.

11

THE BATTLE OF EDSON'S RIDGE

Snaking south and east of the perimeter, patrols of the 2d Battalion, 1st Marines encountered opposition with increasing frequency. The Kawaguchi Trail was being pushed forward with renewed vigor. The head of the road was less than four miles out. Mountain guns, singly and in batteries, were spotted at various points within range of the airfield. They had been hand-carried forward, camouflaged, and were awaiting only crews and ammunition.

Native scouts added to the information buildup. Kawaguchi's trailblazers were in deep-forest country, far to the south of the field. All signs now indicated that it was from this direction that the attack would be mounted.

Vandegrift moved his headquarters on September 9 to meet this danger. Now it was located on the inland side of the airfield, at the base of a small, jungle-covered hill.

The 1st Amphibian Tractor Battalion, under the command of Lt. Col. Walt Barr, was given the assignment of preparing defensive positions on a ridge that commanded the enemy approach. The Engineer

Battalion tied in with the left flank of the 1st Marines, who in turn extended themselves to reach the lines of the Parachute Battalion. And so it went. Patch up those holes and stretch those lines. Try to make two marines cover the space that should be handled by a full platoon. Assign a company to do the defensive work of a battalion.

There just weren't enough men to go around.

Still, there was always the reserve—and Red Mike Edson. On the morning of September 12, Vandegrift called him in.

"Colonel, we've got a problem." He put a bony finger on the map. "This ridge is it."

"Sir, I'm your man."

They talked it out. South of the airfield, the terrain began to fold into the jumbled foothills that led up into the rain forest. Here and there, a patch of *kunai* grass appeared. One of these ridges was a thousand yards long, pointing like a dagger at the airfield just a mile away. It was the subject of their full attention. It stood out like a drawbridge crossing a moat.

"Let's go out there and take a look."

On the ground it looked worse. The ridge fell off on one side toward the Lunga, on the other towards the Tenaru. Deep ravines, heavily wooded, formed four distinct spurs that slanted down into impenetrable jungle growth.

What Red Mike saw he didn't like. He sent back his exec to collect the Raiders. "Bring plenty of wire." Lieutenant Colonel Griffith nodded. Red Mike and a single runner continued the reconnaissance. On a slight eminence, called Hill 2 on his map, Edson dropped his musette bag. "This is headquarters, Sam. Start digging."

161

As the Raiders toiled up the ridge later they groused, "Where's old Glory Hound taking us now?" But they went right to work, the dirt flying, aprons of barbed wire being thrown out in all directions from machine-gun emplacements and rifle pits. All during the day, as the marines dug in, they could hear enemy troops moving across their front, from left to right toward the Lunga River. The final segment of the Kawaguchi Trail from Tasimboko to the Lunga had been completed. Scouts slipping back had reported that a general's battle flag now flew on the Lunga River. Kawaguchi had arrived.

A worried Vandegrift joined Edson on Hill 2. The marine-aviator-turned-ground-soldier tried to cheer up his general.

"They're making quite a racket out there, sir."

"They are indeed, Mike. Can you make out what they're chanting?" It sounded for all the world like a high-school football crowd yelling, "Shove 'em back, shove 'em back! All the way, all the way!"

The division interpreter translated. "They're saying, sir," he said, "U.S. Marines be dead tomorrow, U.S. Marines be dead tomorrow."

The marines were unimpressed. All along the ridge they mimicked the Japanese chant, with appropriate epithets thrown in.

To Archer Vandegrift the earthy language of the line was almost like a tonic. He was actually stimulated by it when the multifarious, sometimes near-insoluble problems of command threatened him with depression. On September 12 a good supply of these problems was very much at hand. Before he had rejoined Red Mike, the daily conference at division headquarters had brought him more than its customary quota of bad news. The Cactus Air Force reported that the Slot was teeming with Japanese ships. The SBD search team had identified a cruiser and three destroyers forty miles down from Rendova. Others had brought back intelligence of two more destroyers off the northern tip of Santa Isabel. It was now fairly obvious that this was the advance guard of the fleet that would support the Kawaguchi attack.

Meanwhile, from Espiritu Santo in a Command R4D, Admiral Turner had arrived, clean-shaven and in a freshly pressed uniform. Greetings over, the man who had sailed away thirty-four days ago, leaving Vandegrift "bare-assed," was ready to drop another bombshell. McCain was with him. The three sat down in the new headquarters of the division, at the bottom of the hill.

"Just take a look at this," Turner requested, handing over a six-page message form.

The general looked, his strong Dutch face blanching. It was from Ghormley. Its cynical defeatism was awesome, overwhelming. It really had to be heard to be believed. Gerry Thomas, taking the paper from his obviously shaken commander, read it aloud in tones of growing disbelief.

The Japanese were massing a big fleet at Truk. The air strength at Rabaul and Kavieng was increasing much beyond previous estimates. Important troop concentrations had been reported at Rabaul. A major Japanese effort to retake Guadalcanal must be expected within ten days.

The liturgy of defeatism continued with an appraisal of the weakness of the Guadalcanal garrison;

163

employment and tactics of the division were discussed and criticized in considerable detail. At this point Gerry Thomas had thrown up his hands. Ignoring Turner, he had asked Vandegrift: "For Christ's sake, sir, are we that bad?"

The general had merely waved him on again, and the D-3, his voice shaking with anger, had proceeded with the staff conclusions: Ghormley as COMSOPAC could no longer support the marine position. It was as simple as that. He'd been advised, and he intended to throw in the sponge.

Kelly Turner, he of the Wacky Mac, was sympathetic. He pulled out a bottle of Scotch from his briefcase and poured a hooker all around. "Okay, you say you can hang in, right? What if I get Ghormley to release the 7th Marines and send 'em in?" Vandegrift's third regiment had been held back in New Caledonia. "Would that help?"

"Is the Pope Catholic?" the irrepressible Thomas broke in. Admiral Turner smiled. "Okay, we'll say we had a meeting and that this is our considered opinion," he suggested. "We want the 7th."

It would be a joint message, it was agreed, signed by Turner, Vandegrift, and McCain. The meeting broke up and Vandegrift hustled up the hill.

The two admirals spent a sleepless night within the perimeter, but so did everybody else. By mid-afternoon it had become obvious that action was imminent. The chanting Kawaguchis were still closing in on what was now being referred to as "Edson's Ridge." A flight of Bettys, sneaking by the weary Cactus defense, dropped a dozen sticks of bombs along the ridge line, emphasizing even further that this was indeed the spot selected for the breakthrough. Reports of new enemy surface vessels continued to come in from the coast-watchers. Clearly the warnings Admiral Turner had brought of a major attack were being proved valid. Tension mounted.

In the early evening, Archer Vandegrift paid a visit to his friend and comrade of thirty-three years, General Roy Geiger. "How are your fellows making it?" Vandegrift asked the white-haired Cactus boss.

"We'll make it, Arch, don't worry. The boys are tired but they're okay." The two men left the Pagoda for a short stroll, Geiger talking animatedly as if to pump new confidence into the quiet Virginia gentleman at his side.

Fighting 223 had accounted for seven Japanese planes that day, and its commander, Major Smith, had shot down two more. "How many has he got now? Gee, I dunno. Trowbridge and Frazier got two Bettys each, and Lees splashed a Zeke."

The new squadrons, VMF 224 and VF5, had been credited with six, but they'd lost two of their own. They were still learning. Vandegrift halted Geiger's recital in mid-sentence and gestured at the fliers' BOQ area. He knew they were doing a great job, he said. He was grateful for their tireless work; he was aware of their sacrifices. But he had to lay it on the line. There was a chance, a good chance, that the Japs might break through. Edson's battalion, like all the marine battalions, was down to damn near half-strength. Malaria, jungle rot, typhus, the wounded, the KIAs: they all added up. He paused, looking squarely into the kindly face of his old friend.

"Roy, if they do break through, I don't want any

fliers turned into infantry, you understand? I want you to get those planes out. And that's an order."

Geiger's blue eyes shone as he blinked back his tears. He would comply. "We'll fly 'em out, Arch. But whatever happens, I'm staying right here with you."

They headed back to the Pagoda.

It was dark by then. On Edson's Ridge, Red Mike was with his company commanders. In a final disposition, he'd sent Charlie Company into the unbroken jungle of the two spurs to the right, where they sloped down toward the Lunga. The map they were looking at showed the river to be only five hundred yards away.

Company B had been ordered to dig in as a connecting force. They had already done so; they were locked up tight, with double aprons of barbed wire strung out.

The light machine-guns, and the attached heavies, had been sited to provide interlocking fire. At least the map overlay showed that to be so. But on the ground, as always, it was quite another matter. How could you secure interlocking fire with a flat-trajectory weapon when the ridge itself, its little hills and hummocks and ravines, got in the way? "What we need," Red Mike kidded his C.C.s, "is a .30-caliber bullet that will follow the contours of the terrain." Still, most of the dead spots had been marked on the overlay.

Back on the ridge, where A and D companies had dug in as a reserve around the battalion command post, the mortars were emplaced to cover them: the big-tubed 81s and the short, stubby 60s, ammo stacked neatly in yellow-finned rows by the gun pits.

Edson clued-in the company commanders on their

primary mission: they were to stay put. The artillery behind them would deliver fire-support when called upon. Communication wire was in and checked. To the left were the Engineers, who in turn locked in with two understrength companies of the Parachutists.

Such was the main line of resistance. It had a lot of holes in it, but if they needed help, Red Mike had his reserve close at hand. He reminded his company commanders that he wouldn't hesitate to bring in the artillery fire right on top of their positions if it looked like they'd been overrun.

"So keep your heads down. And for Christ's sake, don't let some chowderhead wander around during the night. That's about it, gentlemen, let's check our watches."

It was 2100 hours—9:00 P.M. straight-up. The eight company commanders and their runners left Red Mike's CP, and watchful sentries challenged their return. It was pitch-black and quiet. Except for an intermittent burst of automatic weapons fire, and an occasional Jap chanting "Marine, you die," it had been quiet since the Bettys had deposited their string of bombs along the thousand-yard axis of the ridge. There had been no casualties. A little wire had been chewed up, a few craters had been dug.

When would it come?

Suddenly the ridge was illuminated by one parachute flare, then another. As they slowly floated down, the defenders' faces staring up at them took on a greenish pallor. "Hey, you look like Boris Karloff, Sarge," whispered one of his squad. "Damned if he doesn't," said another. Somehow the laughter was choked off in their throats.

167

Half an hour later a series of flashes winked far out in Sealark Channel. Naval salvos. The winking continued faster, looking for all the world like sparklers on the Fourth of July. Up on Edson's Ridge, the call was passed from post to post along the line: "Here they come. Duck!" The first eight-inchers came in like freight trains crashing through a siding. Moments later the five-inch salvo arrived. It struck some twenty yards below the 5th Battalion CP. The ridge lit up like the proverbial Christmas tree.

Edson's phone bell jangled between salvos. "Yeah, we're getting plastered pretty good. There's creeping fire all the way down the lines."

"It's that Jap fleet we lost this afternoon up the Slot. Looks like you're catching it all, Red. Four destroyers and a heavy cruiser. They seem to be concentrating on you."

"Thanks a lot for nothing."

"Hang in there."

The naval barrage lasted twenty minutes. It chewed up some of the communications wire linking the companies with the battalion CP. It worried Edson, although not as much as the red flare that dangled low over his right. He whirled the hand-crank on his line into division. "The Nips have fired a red flare over Baker Company, close to the Lunga River. Here they come."

The distant chanting of the Kawaguchis could be heard, punctuated now by strings of firecrackers, hundreds of them, popping all across the front. The Japanese had completely discarded any attempts at stealth; they were relying on Bushido. On they came, screeching through the night, firing as they advanced.

Two strong thrusts were initially made along the east bank of a lagoon that constituted the dividing line between B and C Companies. Communications to the battalion CP had gone out. The right platoon of B was driven from its positions. A second *banzai* charge ripped the left flank of C Company and isolated its command. For two hours the jungle raged with rifle and machine-gun fire. The action on Edson's imperiled right turned into a free-for-all, with friend and foe inextricably entangled.

Division came back on the line. "What is your situation, Mike?"

"I've lost contact with both Baker and Charlie. Nothing's happened on my left."

"What do you plan to do?"

"I'm going to have to commit my reserve. If I can't patch that hole the Nips'll have a straight shot at the airfield."

A and D Company stood ready. But at midnight all the firing sputtered to a stop. The Raider boss looked up at Colonel Griffith. "What do you think, Sam?"

The exec cupped his ear. "Sounds like axes and shovels, entrenching. Maybe they've called it a night, huh?"

"Maybe." The phone at Edson's side rang again. It was the line from Charlie Company. "Colonel?" The voice spoke perfect English, accent-free, but Edson did not recognize it. The reason was immediately clear: it had to be a Japanese officer. "Everything down here, Colonel, is going fine. Goodnight, sir."

"Well, I'll be Goddamned." Red Mike hung up. His defense had been bent like a horseshoe around the ridge. Only one narrow access-road to the battlefield below was left. The Raiders had been stunned.

At midnight exactly, for a full forty-five minutes, the Japanese naval shelling resumed. This time the airfield, Vandegrift's headquarters, and Red Mike's as-yet-untouched left flank receipted for the bombardment.

Sam Griffith had guessed right. The Japanese had dug in for the night.

At his command post on the Lunga, Major General Kiyotake Kawaguchi still had work to do. First, there would be a word of thanks by radio to Admiral Mikawa for his splendid support in providing not just one, as he had requested, but two naval bombardments. Then, more important, a report on the night's action to Lieutenant General Hyakutake in Rabaul.

The Kawaguchi Trail and its planning had been brought to successful fruition near the headwaters of the Lunga, Kawaguchi advised. "We have cracked the marine perimeter, and we shall exploit the breach. You will be perfectly safe, my dear General, in announcing that Henderson Field, as the American marines have called it, has been recaptured. I shall raise our flag over it tomorrow."

His one regret he thought it best not to announce to his superior. It was that he would not be properly attired. The Raiders were responsible for that, and he would make them suffer punishment accordingly.

At Noumea, on September 12, Admiral Ghormley's forward headquarters was literally burning the midnight oil. The gloom hung pretty thick. News of the day had flashed up along the chain of command,

and there were many on the staff just about ready to admit the worst. The fall of Henderson Field, they judged, was now almost inevitable, and would constitute a worse disaster than Bataan.

The message signed jointly by Turner, McCain, and Vandegrift, requesting the 7th Marines, was received with a curious sense of relief. "Well, if they're asking for the 7th, maybe things aren't really so bad. And after all, they're on the ground. Let's kick this thing around and take it in to the Old Man."

The F4Fs from the *Saratoga* had been sent to Henderson. That should help Cactus. It sure ought to. Now, let's see, what else did we provide . . . Talk brightened quite a bit. New estimates were cranked out, checked, evaluated. Seventh Marines had been destined for MacArthur, but they *could* be spared. "Of course we'll have to clear it with Pearl." "Oh sure, we'll need Nimitz's approval. But that shouldn't present much of a problem, should it? After all, *we're* on the ground, aren't we?"

Back at Pearl, the message from Noumea greatly puzzled Nimitz. "What the hell is going on down there?" But the request for reassignment of the 7th Marines was bounced back, approved.

On the 'Canal there had been no such yo-yoing as dawn broke on September 13. In the predawn hours even the dank, steaming jungle could turn chilling to the bone. Down the perimeter, men yawned and stretched, scratched themselves, and wondered anxiously what the day would bring. Up on the ridge, Mike Edson crawled out from under his poncho. "Where's the commo officer? Check out those phones! We've got to get new lines."

Red Mike was early on the job. Runners from B and C were coming in. "Yes, sir, we got the hell shot out of us, but we're still in there." The two companies on Edson's right had been cut off and isolated. But they were dug-in. The enemy had filtered through. There were a lot of Japanese between them and the airstrip.

Though it was a Sunday morning, there was no church call. But in the rear areas, and even up front where intermittent firing was still going on, battalion and regimental chaplains were busy conducting brief services for small groups. Even among the less devout, there was a lot of praying going on.

Vandegrift ducked into his tent and went over the action reports that were now reaching headquarters in flood stage. Their consensus was pretty grim. A hole had been punched through the right flank of the defenses. They'd be back tonight, that was for damned sure. Edson could never handle it alone; this time he would need help. The D-1, the SX, the D-2 and D-3 laid their problems on the line: supply, ammo, men present for duty, casualties, medical reports, information of the enemy—the works: all that was needed to arrive at a command decision.

Staff had done its duty. Now it was up to Archer Vandegrift. The fortress-keeper sighed, his head bowed as if in brief prayer, thought one staffer.

"Get me Whaling!"

The perimeter's final reserve would be committed. Gerry Thomas had picked up the phone and turned its crank three times. "Get me 2d Battalion, 5th Marines." Then, after a short pause: "Hello, Bill? This is Gerry. Better come on up . . . Yeah, that's right. We've got a job for you."

The decision, a fateful one, had been made.

Down at the Pagoda, the battered clock on the wall read 0645 as Cactus Operations cleared the sleek R4D revving up at the end of the runway, and she gunned forward, gathering takeoff speed. She banked left, toward Espiritu Santo. Aboard were two very tired admirals, McCain and Turner. They hadn't slept very well either. McCain, however, had spent his last few moments on Guadalcanal talking to pilots. In his rumpled pocket was a copy of a further dispatch he'd sent COMSOPAC: "When I left today, materiel situation OK except for gas shortage and no Marston mat. Personnel very tired—no rest at night due to bombardment, or by day because of air alerts." McCain had stated his case. Now he rolled himself up in a ball on the floor of the plane and went to sleep.

Within the hour, eighteen F4Fs from the *Hornet* settled down on Henderson. Their pilots would exchange clean sheets and juicy steaks for stretchers, soggy ponchos, and the doubtful gourmet menu of the "Book-Cadillac." As they were jeeped into the sagging tent-area they would call home, there was a spate of good-natured grousing. Standing ankle-deep in mud, one of the Hornet fliers offered an opinion. "If the world needed an enema," he cracked, "this would be the right place to put in the hose."

"Welcome to Guadalcanal," came back the jeering reply.

Just then a Red Alert was sounded. "Cripes, they don't even give you time to find the head. Where'n hell's the head?"

On that Sunday morning the Japanese, no doubt wondering if they would be able to land on Henderson

Field as promised, sent twenty Zekes down the Slot from Rabaul. The Cactus Air Force promptly relieved them of any misapprehension. The Red Alert sent seventeen F4Fs scrambling off the pad to meet them. The press corps, searching for a grandstand seat, whirled off in jeeps for Kukum, a place they knew would afford them the best seat in the house.

In the melee that followed, three Zekes were shot down. Fighting Five lost two of its own. Ens. Don Innis, who parachuted into the channel and was picked up later, had been badly shot-up.

Ground activity during the morning and afternoon hours consisted of attempts by the marines to re-establish their positions along the ridge; and on the part of the Japanese, to consolidate and organize the ground they had gained. It soon became evident, after the Raiders had failed to eliminate the salient west of the ridge, that B Company's present position was untenable.

The phone line to B had been reinstated. Edson got on it. "Sweeney, get out of there. Pull back to the ridge." Captain Sweeney fought his way out, his men bringing out their weapons and wounded. They dug in anew, on lines adjacent to B Company, 1st Engineer Battalion. The ridge defenses were indeed bending back like a horseshoe.

Meanwhile, Col. William Whaling summoned his company commanders. "You might be committed piecemeal. A unit here, a platoon there. I dunno. I do know I want you guys to study and learn the terrain like the back of your hand," Whaling told them.

And so it went with the marines that Sunday afternoon. "Move that heavy over here. That's better.

174

Put an extra sandbag on that gun pit. One more strand of barbed wire down there, and clear away that tree, you'll have a better field of fire. We're as well sited as we'll ever be. Let 'em come.''

And in the gathering twilight they came.

Howling threats and obscenities, the Kawaguchis charged the Raiders, driving between A and B Companies. Marines along the line worked their weapons until their shoulders and their trigger fingers became numb. Enemy corpses stacked up on the wire. But still the soldiers of the Rising Sun came on, wave after wave. The Raiders' right shook, and once more threatened to crack. Marines stood up and battled hand-to-hand as their positions were overrun.

The carnage was horrendous.

And yet, at the very moment when it seemed as if Edson's right flank must collapse under the ferocity of the attack, the pressure miraculously eased up. A gap of some two hundred yards existed between the flank companies. One more charge through this undefended hole and the road to the airstrip would inevitably have opened. But that charge failed to materialize.

It was by then 2030 hours; the attack on the right had been sustained for two hours. The ridge was dark and almost quiet. Firing had dwindled to a halt. Here and there, men shouted at each other, some of them jeering at the enemy, some calling out for ammo bearers or for medics to assist the wounded. From behind the Japanese lines came the vague sounds of movement that could only mean one thing. They were regrouping there, and being resupplied.

A strange gray mist crept up the ridge and drifted into the ravines. It was reported to division. ''What is it, gas?'' demanded Gerry Thomas.

"Negative. The Japs have kicked out a few smoke shells.''

The division D-3 looked at his watch: 2130. The sound of a sudden fusillade came in clearly over the still-open phone.

"They're at us again, Gerry. Hold your hat.''

The Kawaguchis had launched their second assault of the night. All down the ridgeline they came, yelling, screaming, cursing. They hit the wire, and the dying and dead served them as a carpet.

The marine artillery, which had been delivering interdiction fire on the assembly areas and possible approach routes, now lowered its sights to almost point-blank range. One battery of the 11th Marines had manhandled its four 105mm howitzers up the ridge during the afternoon. Now, with forward observers in the foxholes, their telephone lines passing through the Raider Battalion switchboard, permission was asked to reduce the range even more.

Red Mike granted it readily. "Drop it two hundred yards!'' he bellowed. The next salvo from the four guns clipped the jungle brush and *kunai* grass above his command post. It slammed in close behind the advancing Japanese. They wavered. "Down one hundred!'' The muzzles dropped another notch and belched again. "You're on!'' reported the observers. "Fire for effect!'' As fast as each piece could be loaded, it was fired, the cannonade continuing until the barrels of the 105s were blistering hot.

The cannon stopped the Japanese charge cold. "Bring up the other batteries of the 11th,'' the request came from the ridge.

The 105mm howitzer is a lot of gun. Normally, it takes a big prime-mover to tow the piece and wheel it into battery. But prime movers were in very short supply on the 'Canal. This night it was up to the ubiquitous jeep and a few amphibian tractors, plus all the manhandling available.

And time was short. There was another pause in the action, but there was also every sign that a third wave was about to be launched.

The Raider defenses, after the initial assault, were tenuous, at best. Baker Company, on the inside of the horseshoe, had been decimated. Its flanks dangled. The Parachute Battalion on its left had been hard-hit. One more attack like the last, and the entire position could fall apart. Communications were thoroughly muddled.

Edson sent a corporal crawling forward. "Tell Captain Sweeney it's okay to withdraw," he ordered. A few minutes earlier he had sent out another messenger with a box of grenades, and the messenger had walked straight through Baker Company's position without realizing it, so attenuated were its lines. Captain Sweeney took advantage of the lull to pull his men back up the ridge. He brought out only sixty marines. (A rifle company's normal strength is 225.)

At 2200 hours the marine artillery opened up again, pouring a devastating barrage into the Japanese assembly-areas. Edson's plan of action was relayed to Division. It was as simple as it was necessary. He would shorten the defense line around his command post—located on a high knob dominating the northern half of the ridge—and hope that the Japanese would attempt to dislodge him there. The 105s were sighted down along that ridge. These were almost Civil War tactics, the cannons right up front as they had been with Lee on Marye's Ridge before Fredericksburg.

For four hours, attack after attack was received, the barrages of the 105s performing like a wall of steel against each new wave. Those few enemy who somehow penetrated it came under intense fire from rifles and automatic weapons at short range. And still the situation to the rear became further confused as Japanese snipers, individually and in small units, managed to infiltrate behind division headquarters.

By 0300 hours on September 14 the ammunition supply on the ridge had become critical. "Hang in there, Mike, it's on its way up," Gerry Thomas relayed. It did arrive: boxes of machine-gun belts, clips of rifle ammo, and grenades. Thomas was a busy man on the phone. He even managed to relay observer information to the 105 batteries. "I'm dropping it five-zero and walking it back and forth across the ridge," Thomas said. The artillery banged out the request.

Word got back to him. "Colonel Edson says the range is perfect. You're knocking the shit out of them."

A bullet whizzed through the operations tent. "Goddamned snipers, General. They've filtered through."

"Let 'em. We'll take care of them in the morning." The general was very calm. His watch said 0400. The attack, incredibly, had lasted close to seven hours.

And while the main assault had been on Edson's Ridge, several other parts of the perimeter had been heavily engaged as well. The 3d Battalion, 1st Marines, were emplaced with their left flank on the Tenaru. It was against this strong defensive position that the 1st Battalion, 124th Japanese Infantry, had attacked at midnight. The marines had held his diversionary attack in check all through the night.

On the opposite edge of the perimeter, another thrust had been made against the lines of the 3d Battalion, 5th Marines, along the Matanikau River.

"I'm committing my last reserves, General," announced Mike Edson on the phone. "Have you got anything left to replace it?"

Vandegrift looked at the Operations map. "I'm afraid it's negative, Mike. They've got us tied down on the Matanikau and at Alligator."

"Well, I'm sending in the 2d Battalion." There was a pause. "Is that okay with you, sir?"

"Go ahead, Mike. Sorry I can do no more for you. Daylight'll be here soon."

"Sir, I've been wondering if it ever would."

The final reserve, Bill Whaling's 2d Battalion, 5th Marines, crawled forward to its prearranged positions, a company here, a platoon there, wherever the line threatened to crack. And so, in the end, there was no reserve left at all. Everything, literally, was on the line—a thin, curved line.

At 0430 the Japanese attacked again. This time they wilted quickly when the marine artillery opened up. The stacks of empty shell-cases had to be kicked away from the trails of the 105s by the gun crews, so tired were the ammo bearers. They had expended more than two thousand rounds. The 75mm pack howitzers had cranked out almost another thousand. Never before had such a barrage been fired with modern artillery at point-blank ranges.

Up on the ridge knob, the Raiders held. They yelled their defiance as the artillery zeroed-in its curtain of protective fire to within fifty yards of their positions. "Shorts" inevitably dropped on their own people. One of the shorts prompted a grizzled noncom to quote the legendary battle cry of Sgt. Dan Daly, a veteran of Belleau Woods: "Quit bitching, you guys. You wanna live forever?"

At dawn it was all over, and Red Mike clambered down to division headquarters to shake hands with his commanding general. There were still snipers around; one in a nearby tree snapped off a round in the direction of the press corps tent as the correspondents scrambled for cover.

"What have you got there, boy?" The general poked a finger in a bullet hole in Edson's jacket.

"That one was pretty close at that," Red Mike admitted wryly. "I hadn't noticed it before." They were joined by Maj. Kenneth Bailey, who was being kidded about his helmet. A Japanese .25 had ventilated it, front and rear. He had been hurt but was still going strong.

"Better draw another from supply, Ken," joked the general. He would write up both men for the Medal of Honor for their work on Edson's Ridge.

As for the Japanese, they had begun a painful retreat back down the Kawaguchi Trail. Along Edson's Ridge, an estimated 1,000 lay dead. They had counted on Bushido, and it had failed them. It had also failed some 250 Japanese at the Tenaru and another 100 who had charged the lines of the 5th Marines on Alligator Creek. Along the trail, the survivors slipped, slithered, and fell in the mud, hundreds of walking wounded

180

bringing up the rear.

Far out in Sealark Channel, the darkened ships of Admiral Mikawa waited in vain for the victory signal from shore. As dawn broke they, too, joined the retreat.

12

DIG IN AND HOLD

Sixty days on the line had left their mark on those who held it. The marine cemetery near Lunga Point was growing. The Graves Registration Service had forwarded white wooden crosses along with the regular division supplies. Thirty-two fresh markers went up, the day Edson's Raiders buried their dead. Red Mike's men had suffered twenty percent casualties, and 103 of them lay on stretchers in the evacuation hospital, awaiting shipment out.

On September 18, five days after the action on the ridge, the 7th Marine Regiment landed. The newcomers looked like creatures from another world. Their uniforms were new; their web equipment sparkled. Only their shiny, well-oiled rifles and machine-guns could be matched by the men they passed on their way up from Kukum dock. Veterans on the 'Canal had learned the price of a fouled piece the hard way. But the big difference that struck one and all was around the eyes: the veterans had an older look. Sgt. John Basilone, who earlier had noted the look, summed it up best: "There ain't no apple-cheeked kids left."

There was considerable and universal relief, heartfelt

but carefully concealed, at the arrival of the 7th Marines. Few on the perimeter experienced it more strongly than General Vandegrift, even though these four thousand fresh marines hardly made up for the attrition suffered from killed, wounded, and sick.

The overriding strategy was still defense—there was an airfield to be held. That meant more of the same mission: dig in and wait. The initiative still rested with the forces of the Rising Sun.

The Bonzo network had not taken time out since Edson's Ridge. Neither had the Cactus Air Force. And the snap, crackle, and pop of their transmitters had brought one sobering fact sharply into focus: Japanese destroyers, slipping through with increasing boldness, were putting ashore an estimated nine hundred troops every night at Kamimbo Bay, twenty-five miles from the perimeter, on the western tip of the island.

This time the Japanese were building-up to the west. At Tasimboko, to the east, the remnants of the Kawaguchi Brigade and the surviving members of the Ichiki Detachment had dug in, and were being supplied by small landing craft. No major troop movements had been reported by the scouts in that sector. In view of the buildup to the west, it now became critical, staff felt, to probe past the Matanikau, beyond the Bonegi River, clear up to Cape Esperance. With the 7th at hand perhaps this would be possible.

Meanwhile, General Geiger's Cactus Air Force was operating with an efficiency that puzzled the experts flying desks at Noumea, Pearl, and Washington. Geiger had certainly found the best use for the variety of planes on hand. On the morning when the Kawaguchi Brigade had called it quits on Edson's

Ridge, he had sent his P-400s to strafe and harass the Japanese withdrawal, turning it into a scene of bloody disaster. They had buzzed the trail with awesome effectiveness, and this was noted with grim satisfaction by Colonel Edson when, on the next day, he led a patrol some few miles toward Tasimboko. Members of the press corps had been given the okay to tag along. They had been somber witnesses to the mass destruction of men and materiel.

Geiger, who was fast becoming a legend in his own time, managed the joint Navy-Army-Marine lash-up with bewildering informality. But it was working. So although his methods caused rear-echelon brass to shake their collective heads, Geiger was left free from administrative meddling. That was the important factor. He spent half of his time "casing the front lines" and the other half keeping his few dozen operational planes busy.

Little flags had begun appearing along Cactus cockpits, and now, as October came, there were 171 "meatballs" pasted on the fuselages, each representing a kill. Major Smith, who had knocked down the first plane on the very day of his arrival, now had nineteen of these insignia. They had earned him a Medal of Honor. Capt. Marion Carl had sixteen and Maj. Bob Galer thirteen. Galer had been shot down three times in aerial combat, surviving each bail-out. On his third time back, Geiger had written him up for the Medal of Honor.

But there had been setbacks, too.

Probing toward the endangered west during the last days of September, marine ground-forces had been given a bloody nose along the Matanikau River, four miles outside the perimeter. Three battalions were involved in what turned out to be a bitter and confused firefight. The marines had carried back two hundred battle casualties. There was little to show for this prodigious sacrifice save the positive intelligence that the enemy buildup was indeed real and that any probing toward Esperance would be met by increasingly deadly counterblows.

The action of September 24–26 had been planned initially as two separate, though closely related, operations. The mission was simple: search out and disrupt any enemy buildup in the coastal area lying between the Kokumbona and Matanikau rivers.

Cactus fliers and coastwatchers had provided the major intelligence data to headquarters. For three days the ominous notes of the latest Japanese movements were dutifully compiled by Lt. Col. Edmund J. Buckley, the division D-2. At evening mess on the night of September 21, Buckley expressed his deep concern to his commanding general.

"They're getting bold as hell, General."

Vandegrift chewed slowly, scanning the pile of notes at his elbow. He pushed his plate away. "Let's get Geiger and his people over here tonight to see what we can do about it."

Geiger, as usual, provided a positive approach to the problem that evening. "We've built up quite a stock of aerial flares. Let's hit the sonsabitches as they come in." He glanced around the tent. "We'll operate a dusk-till-dawn striking force for three nights in the Kokumbona-Matanikau landing sectors. How does that grab you?"

The idea was adopted and expanded: Cactus would

punish the Japanese destroyer-transport fleet as it hit the beaches; two marine battalions, operating independently, would harry the survivors. By midnight of September 21 the joint operation was underway as occasional flares lit up the skies west of the perimeter and Cactus night squadrons took off at intervals.

Positive reports were forthcoming over the next three critical days. Three old nemeses, the destroyer-transports *Kagero*, *Kawakaze*, and *Umikaze*, were hit and set ablaze as they headed for the landing beaches. A fourth unidentified destroyer was also badly mauled. Perhaps as many as eight others, however, snaked through the cordon and landed their troops unharmed. The Japanese had paid a price. But they were prepared for that sacrifice.

How many got through? That was the dilemma facing Vandegrift as the 1st Battalion of the newly arrived 7th Regiment moved out of its assembly area on the morning of September 23, with Lt. Col. Lewis B. (Chesty) Puller in command.

Puller's orders were to "conduct a reconnaissance-in-force" of the hilly country between the Mambulo and Kokumbona rivers, and his operational (D-3) journal noted that the first day passed without incident. The journal, compiled under the direction of Capt. Charles Beasley, recorded that the battalion set up all-around defenses as it went into bivouac that night, and moved out shortly after dawn. The morning hours of September 24 were uneventful, the journal continued, "but early in the afternoon the battalion met and engaged an enemy force of undetermined strength, whom we surprised in bivouac." In the resulting firefight, which ended at nightfall, the Japanese withdrew. "We inflicted casualties," the journal continued, "but how many is unknown."

Later that evening, a summary of the day's action was radioed back to headquarters. One vital statistic had a sobering effect: the battalion had suffered thirty-two casualties in the skirmish, including seven killed and eighteen stretcher cases.

There were a lot of long faces.

"Just how in hell is Chesty going to get his wounded out of there without impairing his combat strength?" Vandegrift asked his staff.

The question was directed mainly at Col. Gerald Thomas, who had that day replaced Col. Capers James as divisional chief of staff. At the moment he was still doubling in the role of D-3, or operations officer.

Thomas deferred, momentarily, to Lt. Col. Merrill B. Twining, his successor, with a nod of the head. At a sign from Twining he moved ahead to answer the general's question.

"It's a bitchy problem, sir," he admitted. "It'll take maybe a hundred men to get 'em out. Right, Merrill?" The new D-3 nodded.

It was hard for Thomas to change hats. He continued: "From my view, I say we air-drop the stretchers. If possible we'll give ol' Chesty some air support and let him make his own decision about whether to come out or not." He looked around. "Agreed?"

It was agreed. Lewis Puller was one of the storied veterans of the Marine Corps. He had served in the Nicaraguan campaigns. He had helped write the book on jungle warfare.

Around midnight, the word got back to Chesty

Puller. His earlier requests for morning air support and stretchers had been approved, and he would receive reinforcements.

Next morning Chesty was up early. The reconnaissance-in-force resumed. Stretcher parties moved out to the rear. So did the guides posted to direct the reinforcements—Lt. Col. Walker Reaves's 2d Battalion, 5th Marines. By mid-morning, advance scouts working up ahead of the main party signalled a halt. The battalion, wary and alert, halted in place while the scouts scrambled back down the line with news for the commander.

"Seems the scouts have spotted a Jap party up ahead taking a late breakfast over rice fires," Puller told his officers. A few staccato-like orders followed. There was a brief pause, then: "Let's go get 'em!"

The column moved into high gear, silently stealing up the western slopes of Mount Austen. The automatic weapons were moved forward; the riflemen extended their lines around the cul-de-sac where the Japanese unit lingered over ceremonial tea. A chattering automatic rifle on the right opened up a deadly fire on those below. It was joined by rifle and machine-gun fire from a semicircle drawn about the ambuscade. A few 60mm mortars joined in late, dropping their rounds into the center of the impact area. And suddenly it was all over. The Japanese party had been obliterated.

But within the hour a larger Japanese unit was observed making its way up the slopes where Puller had his battalion dug-in. A heavy firefight developed and continued through the afternoon, sputtering out as darkness covered the field. The Japanese withdrew, this time leaving their dead behind.

Once more it was a night bivouac, with Chesty's men sleeping on their arms and closing gaps in the perimeter defense. In the early morning, sounds back along the trail heralded the approach march of the 2d Battalion, 5th Marines; by 0845 the two forces had linked up. Puller acknowledged the reinforcement and sent the following message to Vandegrift: "Am sending A and B Companies, 7th Regiment, back to perimeter with remainder of casualties. Will continue reconnaissance with your approval."

Now the decks were cleared for Puller's movement. From the eminence of his observation post, the panorama was breathtaking. Four miles away, past grass-covered *kunai* ridges that dropped into the dense jungle of the ravines beyond, was Sealark Channel. The early-morning sun had sown a million diamonds on its surface. Yet the sun's brilliance did not disclose the presence in the jungle of a single enemy soldier.

Puller drew the curtain on the command tableau. "Any questions?" He looked around the circle of staff and company commanders and glanced at his wristwatch. "It's 9:38." Arms flexed all around as the unit leaders checked their own timepieces. "Okay, let's move out."

The advance march proceeded for three hours without incident. It was slow going as the two battalions cut and thrust at the jungle creepers and dense growth blocking their progress down Mount Austen. Then, around 1400 hours, with the head of the column approaching the deserted native village of Matanikau on the coastal road, enemy automatic weapons opened up, pinning down the point. A skirmish line was hastily thrown out and it, too, was halted in its tracks. The crash of heavy mortars was heard all across the marine front.

Patrols were dispatched from the main body to ascertain the enemy intention. After taking moderate losses, they scurried back with the information. It wasn't good. The ridges west of the Matanikau River were held by the enemy in considerable strength. Further probing determined quickly that the Japanese had the advantage of previously prepared positions in dominating terrain. To continue the attack head-on would be to play the other guy's game. And old jungle-fighter Puller was too cagey for that.

Sitting tight, on the other hand, soon became a noisy and expensive alternative. The hammering of the mortar fire was stepped up. The automatic-weapons fire, sporadic a few minutes before, grew in intensity. Walking casualties began stumbling back past the command post to the aid station just to the rear. A well-timed counterattack by the Japanese at this point could cause no end of hell, Chesty Puller told Reaves. "Christ, we're strung out all along the trail." Runners came stumbling into the command post from units as yet not engaged. The orders poured out: "Close up, dig in, form an all-around defense line. We may get hit from the rear. Get the mortars in."

By mid-afternoon the marine fire died down. Inexplicably, so did the Japanese fire. By then, Division was back on the radio with revised plans. Vandegrift had changed signals. Like a quarterback who finds himself confronted by a "stacked defense," he had called an "audible" on the line of scrimmage. The 1st Raider Battalion, under the command of Lt.

Col. Sam Griffith, had been ordered to force a river-crossing at the mouth of the Matanikau and link up with Puller's force.

This operation was to ease Puller's position. It seemed to be feasible, and on the map it looked easy. Griffith was already underway; the attack on the river mouth could begin within the hour. "You're close enough to hear 'em open up," Puller was told.

An hour later Chesty did hear them. The only snag was that the answering Japanese fire appeared to be heavier.

Puller got back on the radio to Gerald Thomas, the new chief of staff. "What's wrong?" asked Thomas.

"Just too many goddamned Japs at the river mouth. Griffith's pinned down."

"Did he make it across?"

"Negative. They hit him with everything but the kitchen sink, front and flank. Lots of casualties, I'm afraid. They cranked a round into Griffith's CP; it wounded Sam and killed Ken Bailey."

"Jesus!"

"Yeah, she's rough as a cob." Maj. Ken Bailey, one of the heroes of the Bloody Ridge battle, had been the Raiders' executive officer. Now, before the relief column was even launched, its top two men were out of action. The Raiders, far from getting across the river, had been forced to set up a perimeter defense and were fighting for survival.

Here we are, Vandegrift mused, three of my battalions out there, cut off, maybe surrounded. He nervously fingered the latest field message from the Cactus people down at the Pagoda. One of the SBD planes, flying over the Matanikau river mouth, had seen the word HELP spelled out in white letters within the Raider perimeter.

"When was this message checked in?" he asked the D-2 staff sergeant.

"Just five minutes ago, sir."

"Well, gentlemen," he turned to his staff, seated about him. "I dunno about you, but I've had enough." The staff, for whom nothing had gone right this day, fidgeted nervously. "Let's get 'em the hell out of there!"

Gone were the indecision, the frustration, and the doubt of the past forty-eight hours. The situation remained grave; but a snafu was about to be disentangled before it became worse. A serious error in tactical judgment had been acknowledged. The losses were to be cut. There was an audible sigh of relief from the men.

At almost that exact moment a jeep rattled up the hill. Out of the front seat jumped a rumpled figure. The guards were tossed the briefest highball as he scurried by.

"For Christ's sake, Chesty, we were just talking about you. How'd you get here?"

"I bummed a ride from one of the landing craft that was poking around west of Matanikau Village, General."

Vandegrift looked sharply at his D-2, Ed Buckley. "Did you know about that, Ed?"

"Yessir! We sent two LCVPs down there this afternoon to snoop around for a possible evac beach. Just in case."

Vandegrift grinned at Puller and slapped him on the shoulder. "Glad we've got a couple of guys on the ball," he said. "Let's get to work on how we get you out of there, Colonel Puller."

Within the hour the boat people down at Kukum dock were alerted and the logistics of support defined. The artillery command was briefed. Cactus was brought into the picture and its required assistance outlined.

"This sure as hell beats yakking over the damned radio," Puller said in an aside to Gerald Thomas, Vandegrift's chief of staff, as he left the command tent.

"Sure does, Chesty." Thomas whacked him on the seat of the pants as the grizzled jungle-fighter clambered into his jeep. The two men shook hands. "Bring 'em back, sir."

"I'll do my damndest." The jeep roared away toward the docks.

The withdrawal order specified that Puller's two battalions would disengage immediately and withdraw to a specified beach west of the Matanikau. Artillery and air-strikes would cover the movement. While the Japanese were thus engaged, the Raiders would time their breakout through the encirclement on the east bank of the river. Darkness was approaching; that would help. But timing was of the very essence. And soon the 105s and the 155s began their covering barrage, the roar of the guns deepening as the shades of evening fell. Silver streaks from Cactus moved in off the channel, their wings picking up the last rays of the setting sun, their bombs hurtling down into the growing gloom.

At the water's edge on the specified evacuation beach, Sgt. Bob Raysbrook pulled out his semaphores and began signalling to the destroyer *Ballard*. The

Ballard's skipper saw him and began shepherding the landing craft ashore. He saw tracers streaking toward the sergeant on the beach and marvelled to himself at how the skipping and dancing sergeant stayed alive. The *Ballard*'s batteries opened up in support of the lone figure.

By then, other dim figures were taking cover near the beach, by half-squads, squads, and then platoons. Chesty's men had reached their tropical Dunkirk and were being embarked. Lt. Dale Leslie of the Cactus Air Force observed the action from his VMSB-23, one of the planes flying cover for the withdrawal. A weary marine, watching Leslie strafe the bushes from treetop level, was half hauled into the bottom of a Higgins boat. "Ain't he wonderful. Ain't he jist wonderful." Leslie and his mates kept up their flying passes until the last boat was landed. Then there was much wing-wagging as the flotilla headed for home.

On the other side of the river, Platoon Sgt. Tony Malinowski, Jr., A Company, 1st Raider Battalion, received word of withdrawal calmly and set his men in motion when the heavy artillery stepped up its barrage. The last of the platoon file-closers, moving out on his way to the rear, noted that Malinowski was still straddled out flat, the bipod of his Browning automatic rifle set and BAR clips all around him.

"Hey, Sarge, you coming?" A burst from a Nambu light machine-gun hemstitched across their front. The file-closer hit the deck. Malinowski gave him a pat.

"You okay?"

"Yeah."

"Move out then. I'll be along soon."

As the file-closer scurried through the brush he could

hear the *bump-bump-bump* as Malinowski got off a burst of three. Then another, and yet another. The sergeant was covering his platoon's retreat. He never made it back.

Aside from toting up the casualties, the operation was over. As well as it had gone, the withdrawal was not without its price. Vandegrift had committed nearly one-third of his combat infantry strength. The Japanese had nearly succeeded in destroying one battalion, and they had successfully cut off and isolated two others. It was estimated that more than two thousand Japanese had taken part in the action.

"They're tough, they're well led, and they know how to use their weapons," said Chesty Puller in his evaluation of the operation. "We're just damned lucky we didn't get the royal shit kicked out of us."

There was a collective sigh of relief as the final boat docked at Kukum and the last straggler from the Raider Battalion limped into the perimeter. Tomorrow, twenty-four new crosses would be added to the Lunga cemetery. It could have been worse. There was, however, little cause to cheer.

There had been much cheering a few days earlier at Hinomiya Stadium in Tokyo. A high-ranking government official, the loudspeakers said, would make an important announcement in behalf of Premier Tojo.

There was a hush over the stadium as the jam-packed thousands listened intently. This must be something big, surely, something which could touch each one personally in the common communion of war.

The speakers crackled and then the voice, tense with

195

emotion, read Tojo's words; slowly, even haltingly, as though to savor every syllable of every word. "His Imperial Majesty's Government is pleased to announce," there was a pause, "that Guadalcanal airfield has been captured!"

The remainder of the announcement was drowned by a wall of sound, pierced through by hysterical *banzais*.

Later, as the tumult subsided, the crowd was told of "other glorious Japanese victories," these more factual. The mighty United States carrier *Wasp*, it was announced, had been sunk! More thunderous applause. The greatest U.S. battleship, *North Carolina*, is also believed to have been sunk.

In the thunder that rocked the Tokyo stadium that evening, truth and fiction received equal billing. Waxing eloquent, Tojo's spokesman concluded with this announcement: "This night," he said, pausing for dramatic effect, "this night, ten thousand U.S. marines, the victims of Franklin D. Roosevelt's criminal ambitions, are now stranded on Guadalcanal and all but wiped out."

As W. C. Fields would have said, "There wasn't a dry eye in the place." And for one performance, at least, Tojo had topped Herr Goebbels as the world's most nimble propagandist.

The Tokyo press and radio next morning carried details of the critical naval battle that had taken place in the waters between Guadalcanal and Espiritu Santo. Truth mixed with propaganda, but the real statistics were pretty grim.

The *North Carolina* had taken a torpedo and had limped off in company with the carrier *Hornet*, seven heavy cruisers, and fifteen destroyers. The fleet once more had headed south. But the gallant *Wasp* was gone. She had taken three fish. And only Japanese eyes were on her as she sank beneath the waves, burning from stem to stern. Her crew, her planes had been evacuated from her decks. She died alone. It was a sad fate for the ship that had helped launch Operation Watchtower and put the Marines ashore on Guadalcanal back on August 7.

There were, however, high Japanese officers who rightfully assessed the value of truth as against propaganda. Among these was General Hyakutake, who at that moment was assembling twenty thousand fresh troops at Rabaul for the purpose of liquidating "the victims of FDR's criminal ambitions."

To avoid that very thing, Vandegrift next day put out Operations Order No. 11. Now that he had the 7th Marine Regiment at hand and had been promised the 164th Infantry Regiment of the U.S. Army "in the very near future," Vandegrift's staff divided the perimeter into ten defense sectors; each sector commander was to know every molehill like the back of his hand, Vandegrift told his men.

It was still pretty much the same old ballpark, four miles long between the Tenaru and Matanikau rivers, two miles or so in depth from Sealark Channel to the old Kawaguchi Trail. The marines had by now fought over nearly every inch of it. Even, Vandegrift thought wryly, outside it. Henderson Field was like the pitcher's mound, right in the middle of the diamond.

"Figure it out," Vandegrift told his ten sector commanders when it was all lined out and assigned. "We've got twelve miles of front and less than a division to hold it. Gentlemen, it's your ballpark."

Thereafter, axes rang in the jungle. Wire entanglements crept out from the water's edge, making it tough on the clam-hunters but equally tough, it was hoped, on any Japanese trying to get across it. The positions along the rivers were deepened and strengthened. Many of the coconut trees were chopped down to provide abutments and beams for bombproof shelters. Sandbags by the thousands were filled and piled on new gun-pits.

Supply ships filtered in, usually at daybreak. And the latest cargos included some badly needed items of combat clothing. Two months of being shot up, washed up, and beaten up by the Japanese and the elements had produced some odd-looking scarecrows. As the bundles were broken out and distributed to companies, the effect was, in many cases, one of high comedy.

"Hey, look at me," the squad comedian invited, spinning around for examination. "It's the Easter Parade, men."

Bulldozers by the dozen had been put over the sides of transports at Kukum docks. They were hustled up to the airfield to replace Corporal Cates's old Caterpillar, which had, inevitably, collapsed in a heap.

Up north, at Rabaul, a new man had been solemnly appointed to arrange the American surrender. He was Lt. Gen. Masoa Maruyama, commander of the crack Sendai Division. The Sendais were a proud and distinguished outfit boasting a long tradition of military victories in the emperor's service. Their assignment this time, Maruyama felt, should be much less exacting than previous ones, all things considered.

They were to move a mere twenty miles to reach the marine perimeter along the Matanikau. Their primary and elementary objective: Seize the right bank of the river, crack into the airfield, and raise the imperial flag. They would be assisted in the breakthrough by a sweep around the marines' right flank, using a new trail to bring forward heavy artillery and supporting fire.

With such an elite force at hand, Hyakutake would not have to rely on Bushido alone. With the Sendais he had Bushido plus muscle.

This time there would be no gamble. He would use all of the twenty thousand troops available to him in one massive strike from a new direction. What was more, he had been pledged the full cooperation of Nippon's mighty fleet. Now her soldiers, her sailors, and her indomitable airmen would drive the hated Yankees into the sea.

Maruyama, of course, would precede him. But Hyakutake himself would arrive in mid-October to preside over the once-postponed surrender formalities.

13

THIRD MATANIKAU

Back at Pearl Harbor his gray eminence, Adm. Chester Nimitz, stood looking out his window toward ''Battleship Row'' on Ford Island. The beauty of the early-morning scene below was not lost on him. The sun, just up, sparkled on the bay, and the first cat's-paw of the Hawaiian trades gently stirred the sea beyond. The scent of ginger blossoms filled the room; the admiral took in its full fragrance with a deep sigh.

By tradition, the early-morning hour belonged to him alone. It was a time for reflection, meditation, and inner prayer. For some weeks, Nimitz had been deeply troubled during these quiet hours. What he had read from Southwest Pacific headquarters bothered him. There was something between the lines of the routine reports that was disturbing. It was an intangible, true, but woven in the fabric of recent American successes appeared the constant thread of pessimism. This morning he had reached a painful conclusion. Someone's dauber was down, a situation calling for immediate correction.

There was a gentle knock on the door. An aide entered and coughed discreetly. Nimitz looked up.

"Please wire ahead," he said. "I'm going to see Ghormley."

On the long plane-ride down to Noumea, Nimitz took stock. He, himself, had appointed Robert Lee Ghormley to the position of theater boss. Now he anguished over the question of whether he'd given this man the support needed to do the job. It had been a shoestring operation, admittedly. But Admiral King had specified that condition when Watchtower had first been conceived. "Make the best of what you've got," had been King's orders.

The conference between CINCPAC and COMSOPAC took place in Ghormley's plush and shining headquarters on October 3. Spit and polish abounded. This somehow irritated Chester Nimitz, but he ascribed the irritation to the long flight, which had left him dead tired.

Nevertheless, as he sat across the desk from Ghormley, the fatigue did not show, for above all, Chester Nimitz was one hell of a poker player. He had traveled thousands of miles to listen, and listen he did: hard, long, and with few interruptions.

Ghormley rose and paced back and forth before the big wall map, occasionally slapping at it with the back of his hand. "If I strip these areas, the Japs could break through here . . . or here. If I shore up the forces on Guadalcanal, what happens to my back door?" There were a great many other problems about communications, shipping, landing craft, spare parts, nuts and bolts. But through it all, eventually, came the one unmistakable sound that Nimitz did not want to hear—the thin, shrill overtone of failure.

At almost the same moment, Lieutenant General Maruyama, commander of the prestigious Sendai Division, was bowing a formal farewell to his chief, General Hyakutake, and closing a conference of similar importance. In this one, however, optimism had been the keynote. This was to be the third and largest counterinvasion. It would also be the last, of course. Both generals laughed politely at this. A staff car whisked them off for the dockside area of Simpson Bay where a cruiser, aptly named *Sendai*, was awaiting Maruyama's embarkation. Aboard the cruiser and its six accompanying destroyers, in spotless tropical attire, were the men of the peerless 29th Infantry Regiment. The 4th Regiment of the Sendai Division had been landed safely four days before at Kamimbo Bay.

Everything was progressing splendidly. There was only one small problem remaining, and Hyakutake had reserved this for a last-minute admonition at dockside. It was something of a personal matter—the army's honor, so to speak. "These fine warriors," he waved toward the men lining the rails, "must not be infected with the germ of defeat. *Seishan* must be of the highest priority."

Maruyama bowed in agreement.

It was an awkward matter, his superior continued, since it concerned the remnants of the Ichiki Detachment and the Kawaguchi Brigade. "They, of course, will come under your command. I fear there are those among them who lack or who have lost the true spirit of Bushido. It is sad but it is so." The issue here, Hyakutake went on, was a grave one involving morale. The Sendais would have to be quarantined. They must, at all costs, be kept apart from those who fought on the Tenaru and along the Kawaguchi Trail. It was not for their eyes to see or their ears to hear of the piles of glistening bones still unburied at Block Four River or along the jungle paths to Tasimboko.

There would be a new roadway built to attack the marine perimeter. "We shall call it the Maruyama Trail, if you have no objection, my dear general. And along it will move artillery of the heaviest caliber. There will be tanks. There will be additional aircraft, more ships, more supplies. Above all, there must be Bushido of the highest quality, unaffected and untouched by defeat." The generals bowed yet once more. They had settled a sticky matter in an honorable fashion. Maruyama was piped aboard with due formality and the heavy cruiser weighed anchor.

Vandegrift had been driving his staff hard, and on October 3, Plan 2-42 came off the planning boards. Its strategic thrust was defense, pure and simple. Keep the attackers off-balance; jab where they least expect it; organize in depth with mutually supporting fires. The strategy called for the employment of five of the division's nine infantry battalions: the 2d and 3d battalions of the 5th Regiment; the 1st and 2d battalions of the newly arrived 7th; and the 3d Battalion of the 2d Regiment. The date scheduled for the movement outside the perimeter was October 7; the date for the joint attack, October 8.

With luck it just might work.

Two battalions of the 5th would track through the jungle to a point one mile upstream on the Lunga River. That was the thrust on the left. Chesty Puller would be on the right. The main effort would be made at the mouth of the Matanikau by two battalions of the 7th and the 3d Battalion of the 2d Marines, plus a detachment of scout-snipers. This force had been dubbed the ''Whaling Group'' after Col. Bill Whaling, its commander. They were to effect a crossing, move down the coastal road, and once more secure the abandoned village of Matanikau.

The Matanikau River was not one of Vandegrift's favorite rivers these days. Just mentioning its name evoked somber reflections. The memory of the Goettge Patrol ambuscade in August still rankled and hurt. The sobering fact that three of his nine infantry battalions had been trapped on the far bank kept haunting him. It would, he vowed, never happen again.

It was 0100 on October 6 when General Maruyama stepped off his darkened ship and into an awaiting lighter at Kamimbo Bay. The six destroyers and the heavy cruiser that had brought the Sendai Division to Guadalcanal had entered the two-hundred-mile-radius area at sunset and had cleared Cape Esperance in less than seven hours.

That was the pattern.

The Japanese had the formula for night approaches down to a fine science. Baggage quickly followed the general overside, and in less than thirty minutes he was ashore, seated on his steamer trunk, and composing General Order No. 1.

Headquarters
2nd Division, Imperial Army
Guadalcanal, 6 Oct. 1942

* * *

From now on, occupying of Guadalcanal is under the observation of the whole world. Do not expect to return, not even one man, if occupation is not successful. Everyone must remember the honor of the Emperor, fear no enemy, yield in no material matters, show the strong points as of steel or of rocks, and advance valiantly and ferociously. Hit the enemy opponents so hard they will not be able to get up again.

Maruyama
Lt. Gen. Commanding

The General Order applied equally to the Ichiki Detachment and Kawaguchi Brigade survivors who, stripped of dignity by defeat, huddled outside the Sendai bivouac, hopeful of a meager issue of rice.

Up ahead of division headquarters, somewhere on the coastal road to the Matanikau, was Colonel Nakaguma, commander of the 4th Infantry. Nakaguma had advance detachments forward of his command post, the farthest detachment already occupying the right bank of the river.

By messenger, Maruyama sent Nakaguma a copy of General Order No. 1, along with a note that he had arrived safely with the 124th Infantry. The Colonel got the message before dawn.

As an added thought, the general had appended a postscript. The Japanese attack across the Matanikau to strengthen an already existing bridgehead was to be made on 7 October.

The tail end of the column moved past a small group

of drenched men standing beside the trail. The rain, which had been pelting down steadily all night, slanted even more heavily now in the half-light of dawn. It was October 7. Plan 2-42 was operative, and General Vandegrift had slogged his way to the line of departure. At a strong-point overlooking the main line of resistance, he stepped out of the line of march to watch the last battalion leave the perimeter.

Five had left; five remained.

In his biggest gamble of the campaign, he had sent forward six thousand marines to secure both banks of the river against an attack he now felt was inevitable. Now the toughest job of all, the agony of command, was his alone. He had to wait.

By mid-morning, reports drifted back that contact with the enemy had been made by the 3d Battalion, 5th Marines. Maj. Bob Bowen, its commanding officer, had radioed back that Japanese pickets were falling back slowly. "They have to be dug out, one by one. They're tough bastards."

Upstream the marines were likewise finding the going tough. Their assigned mission for the first day was to attack northward from a point identified as "Nippon Bridge" and continue toward the high ground on the far side of the river: on the maps this high ground led down to and dominated Matanikau Village. Midstream, a third marine column hacked and cut its way through solid rain forest. But by nightfall the five battalions had reached their assigned positions. The attack was set for the following morning.

Radios crackled, and often failed. The jungle and the constant downpour made wireless an uncertain medium for the transmission of orders and information. Runners splashed back to fill the gaps. It was exhausting work. So was the hand-carrying of machine-gun tripods, mortar base-plates, tubes, mortar ammo, and belts of ammunition.

As the brief jungle twilight merged with the blackness of night, six thousand men dug in, dead tired. The deluge continued. It was going to be a long, wet night.

Earlier Bill Whaling had been on the line to Division.

"What's up, Bill?"

"We've surrounded a pocket of Japs holed up on the right bank."

"How big, do you estimate?"

"Oh, maybe seventy-five to a hundred. They're well dug-in. I don't consider it advisable to try to smoke 'em out at night. What do you think?"

"I think you're right. Is it raining out there?"

"Coming down in buckets."

"If it keeps up we might have to scrub. We'll keep you posted."

"Roger."

Around midnight, Whaling was back on the horn. The surrounded Japanese had staged a *banzai*, attempting to cut their way out. "A few made it. We had the 81s and 60s on them pretty good. Dumped a lot of rounds in there."

"Yeah, we heard the racket."

"There was some hand-to-hand stuff reported by the platoon nearest the river, but it's all quiet now. I don't think we took many casualties. I'm checking on it."

By the first light of morning the Whaling Group scouts moved down into the battle area. The body count was fifty-nine Japanese. The marines had won the first hand. It was raining cats and dogs, and the Matanikau was raging from bank to bank. Huge trees, uprooted upstream, were barreling down to the sea. The sandbar at the river's mouth had vanished. Vandegrift was worried. Does the attack go on, his five battalion commanders wanted to know?

Staff presented the options. Go now and you've got the raging Matanikau to ford. If it gets worse, how do we get back? On the other hand, wait and we lose the element of surprise.

It was still coming down in sheets at mid-morning when the daily intelligence came over the wireless. A vast new concentration of ships was reported at Rabaul. Plan 2-42, off to a wet start and a small unit victory, would have to be altered.

It had, ambitiously it seemed now, projected a quick clearout of enemy forces on the other side of the river and a push westward up the coast to secure the village of Kokumbona, five miles east. Upon securing Kokumbona, a permanent outpost garrison was to have been established there by the 5th Marine Regiment. From that defensive outpost, perhaps, the pressure might be relieved on the perimeter itself. Now the monsoon had changed all that.

The orders went out. Attack reset for October 9. Dig in and sit tight. Cancel Kokumbona. Mission with more limited objectives to be announced later, rains permitting.

As so often happens in the tropics, the morning of October 9 opened clear and fair: not a cloud in the sky. And for those latitudes, where the humidity and the sea-water temperature usually match each other on their respective graphs at around an even 100, the air was strangely invigorating. It could have been a beautiful fall day anywhere.

Lt. Col. Chesty Puller and the men of the 1st Battalion, 7th Marines, were up at the crack of dawn and on the phone to Col. Amor Sims, Puller's regimental commander.

"Looks like the weather's cooperating, Colonel. We're moving out in ten minutes."

"Right. Keep in touch. And Chesty?" There was a slight pause.

"Yes sir?"

"You know the revised orders. Reconnoiter the coastal road toward Kokumbona, but don't get involved in a large action."

"Wilco, out."

The Whaling Group was on the move, too. The Raider battalion attached to it had lost heavily in the night engagement, with twelve killed and twenty-two wounded. At mid-morning they were attacking toward the sea, with their right flank on the left bank of the Matanikau. The 2d Battalion, 7th Marines, reported meeting strong resistance after crossing the river. Lt. Col. Herman Hanneken huddled with his executive officer, Maj. Odell Conoley, and Capt. Art Sherwood, the battalion 3.

"What's it look like, Art?"

"The point is up near the village, sir, but we're moving."

Amor Sims rang back Colonel Whaling.

"Looks like we can take Matanikau Village without too much trouble. Can we advance beyond?" He looked at his map. "Say to Point Cruz?"

"Go to it." Point Cruz jutted out into Sealark Channel like a fighter's jaw. It would be a good place to anchor the right. The mouth of the river was secure. Point Cruz, up ahead, would offer good defensive positions.

Upstream, Puller's men crossed the river and debouched from the dense rain forest along the bottom. In advance-guard formation, his scouts were operating along the grassy ridges that dominated a series of overgrown ravines. The *kunai* grass was waist high. Farther back along the column, on the heels of the file-closers, came the automatic weapons of the battalion, the mortars, and the communications platoon. Everything was all hand-carried, and the men of the 1st Battalion sweated at their toil.

One last ridge remained between them and the coastal road; the road could be seen now by the advance guard. From the river bottom to the ridgeline the battalion had been under light sniper-fire which, like a swarm of gnats, had been batted aside. Puller's men remained in route column. The opposition had not caused them to deploy.

They had been two hours on the march when Puller's lead scout scrambled back down the trail to mid-column, where the battalion CP was traveling en route. The scout was goggle-eyed with excitement. The flank guard, operating some distance to the left of the column march, had stumbled onto a Japanese assembly area, unobserved. The Japanese appeared to be bivouacked in a deep ravine, almost hidden by the heavy tangle of jungle growth.

"How many Japs in there?"

"The captain says a whole ravine-full, sir."

The staff looked at Chesty. He stood up, slipping on his combat pack over a soaked fatigue jacket. "Come on," he said to Capt. Charles Beasley, his operations officer. "We're going up to have a look." Chesty crooked a finger at his commo officer. "Bring your stuff." He meant the field radio. "We might have a message for somebody."

They moved up the column, which was now sprawled alongside the trail. "Keep 'em down until I contact you," was his parting shot to his exec, Maj. John Weber.

It took some time for them to get to the head of the motionless battalion. But within minutes of their arrival, Chesty had seen quite enough. "I'll be goddamned. Get me Division on the radio."

Runners began slipping back to their units with messages for deployment. The move forward to surround the tangled bivouac area was silent. The heavy weapon were sited. Mortar crews stumbled forward slowly to set their tubes in defilade. Ammo carriers dropped their loads at their assigned places. Rifle squads peeked over the rim.

Back at Division, orders rang out to the artillery units. Maps were unrolled; the ravine was pinpointed on the firing grids. The "on-target" signal flashed back from batteries to 105s and 75s to Division.

"We're ready when you are, Colonel."

"Have you figgered out what unit's down there?" Chesty wanted his foe identified, if possible. Queries were in a hushed tone. There was a stillness along the ridge.

"We think it's the 4th Regiment of the Sendais."

"The hell you say!"

"They must have moved up sometime yesterday. They're part of the 2d Division, that's for sure."

Chesty Puller looked around him. He nodded briskly. "Well, gentlemen, let's have at 'em."

By now the sun was past the zenith. From far to the rear came the unmistakable crack of the sharp-barking 75s. It was followed a milli-second later by the deep *crump* of the bigger howitzers. But even before that sound reached the ridge, there was the whistling scream of descending shells into the valley below.

"By God, that's good shooting." The artillery forward-observers corrected fire: "Down two hundred, left ten." And behind the ridge, the high-angle fire of the 81s and 60s began joining in. In half a minute the valley below rocked with the violence of tree bursts, cascading plumes of debris and dirt and, over all, a red and orange winking and blinking, here, there, everywhere.

Death became wholesale in the valley below.

Out of the maelstrom of the artillery barrage came the Japanese, singly and in small groups. They were like ants whose hill had suddenly and unexpectedly been stomped. The surprise, it was apparent, had been complete.

What followed was a process of extermination, carried out with terrible exactness. The heavy and light machine-guns on the ridge took a horrendous toll as "targets of opportunity" raced out of the jungle. It was plunging fire with free traverse, and its victims dropped in windrows; only a few escaped the cul-de-sac, most of them because ammunition on the ridge soon began to run short and spare barrels for the machine-guns were being used up.

"Cease fire!" The message was relayed back from the ridge to the artillery batteries. A deadly quiet, disturbed here and there by the cries of the wounded below, crept up to the ridge. The marines moved cautiously forward. Chesty Puller came down the hill with them. The gruesome work of body count, identification, and intelligence began.

It was, unmistakably, part of the 4th Infantry of the elite Sendai Division. Documents found on the body of one of its officers substantiated both this and the amazing fact that only the monsoon had prevented a planned attack by the force on the very day the marines had scheduled their operation. A meeting engagement, an action dreaded by every commander, had been avoided.

Important new intelligence was also discovered, including a copy of Maruyama's General Order No. 1. There would be, division intelligence deduced as the captured documents were translated, adequate replacements for those who had fallen in the slaughter pen. Matanikau had been a Yank victory, but the Japanese would be back, in even greater strength. Their timetable had been posted and noted.

And so, that afternoon as the sun went down, the marines retired once more within their perimeter, carrying a tender burden of one hundred and five wounded comrades to the field hospital at Kukum. They also carried sixty-five dead marines whose dog tags would be affixed to the small white crosses now growing in number in the cemetery beyond.

In all, more than a thousand Sendais, who had been told "not to expect to return, not even one man," lay mostly unburied along the Matanikau.

14

THE BATTLE OF CAPE ESPERANCE

News of the American victory along the Matanikau was received at home on October 10 with undisguised relief and joy. There had been hints of disaster, rumors of defeat. But now, for the first time in weeks, the official communiqués from the war zone contained a new note of optimism and hope.

The marines, the nation's press and radio seemed to indicate, "had the situation well in hand." Newspaper sidebars and magazine features carried, among other things, the "box scores" of leading Cactus aces. The names of Joe Foss, John Smith, Marion Carl, Bob Galer, Bill Maronate, Ken Frazier, and Gene Trowbridge were fast becoming household words. Gregory (Pappy) Boyington and his Baa Baa Black Sheep squadron, perhaps the most colorful air warriors of the Solomons campaign, were still offstage, waiting for history's cue.

The wire services, Associated Press and United Press, had done their best to enlighten the American public. Some of the original Guadalcanal press corps, including Richard Tregaskis, had been rotated home. But their replacements continued in the best tradition. They shared the hardships and dangers, and they wrote about the men: Sgt. Mitchell Paige, Sgt. John Basilone, Maj. Kenneth Bailey, squadron commander Harold Bauer. These men were among the Medal of Honor winners.

And there were those who shared heroism with the men they led: Vandegrift, Geiger, Puller, Edson, Cates, Maj. Lewis Walt. The names were becoming legion, and valor the expected.

There were certain statistics to which the press was privy but which, for reasons of military security, were not being reported. The 1st Raider Battalion, for instance, was down from its assigned Table of Organization strength of one thousand men to less than two hundred. It was carried on the division rolls as a battalion, but its real fighting worth amounted to little more than that of a company. Under Lt. Col. Bill Barba, the Raiders had suffered heavily in the fighting of October 7. Four companies averaged around forty men each; battalion headquarters counted thirty. D Company existed only on paper.

Attrition due to combat action, sickness, and disease was alarming. Even more disturbing to Col. Robert C. Kilmartin, the division D-1 or personnel officer, was that after two long, agonizing months, theater headquarters still had set no definite policy regarding replacements.

The division supply officer, Col. Randolph Pate, added his voice in the staff conference following the Matanikau foray: medical supplies, ammunition, even food were on the critical list of shortages.

There were serious difficulties to be solved in the resupply of the Guadalcanal garrison. The men on the perimeter were well aware of them. By night, the Japanese owned the Slot. But thanks to the Cactus squadrons and their "unsinkable flattop," Henderson Field, the Americans were able to exert a measure of control of the waters surrounding the 'Canal by day.

Why don't we use the daylight hours more efficiently? was a frequently asked question at Division that had been echoed in early September in the office of Secretary of the Navy Frank Knox in Washington.

Among all the top brass of the navy, none was more disturbed by the apparently dilatory effect of resupply than Knox's undersecretary, James V. Forrestal. Ordered by his chief to make a personal evaluation of the situation, Forrestal had flown out to the Pacific in the first week of October, quietly and without fanfare. As he left Washington, Knox told his deputy: "Jim, I want you to get at the very bottom of this matter. I want a no-nonsense, no-horseshit answer to one question: Can we hold Guadalcanal or can't we?"

The undersecretary began his probe at the top. On arrival in Noumea on October 6 he met privately with the theater commander. Unlike his conference with Chester Nimitz three days earlier, this conversation confronted Ghormley with a lot of sharply worded questions.

Using the answers as a point of reference, Forrestal next went down the shiny corridors of COMSOPAC, posing more pointed questions to the command staff. "What's this unit doing here? What's its mission? How about the replacements for Cactus? How much artillery ammo do you have in reserve? What about this food shortage on Guadalcanal? I hear they're still on two-a-day rations, including Jap rice? What plans do you have in the works for navy task forces? When do you propose to gain a measure of initiative at night in the waters around Guadalcanal?

On and on it went, deeper and deeper. The gobbledygook of official communiqués was slashed apart. Red tape fell by the wayside in large basketfuls.

Armed with data from the back area, Forrestal flew up to the 'Canal on October 7, again unannounced.

His meetings with Vandegrift and Geiger were, of course, held in a completely different atmosphere. The generals on the line played it straight with him, were frank about the situation, and their visitor was all ears. There was a quick tour of the perimeter, and he was off again.

Within an hour of his arrival in Washington on October 9, Forrestal was closeted with Knox. He let him have it straight from the shoulder, as Knox had demanded. Finally, the two men sat back, silent, Knox toying with a tall Scotch-and-water. Forrestal, he thought, was close to exhaustion.

"What do we do?" he asked quietly.

"We shake 'em to hell up. Why goddamnit, the garrison needs action. It needs reinforcement. It needs help from wherever we can scrape it together." He paused. "It needs a new theater commander!"

The night crew of the Washington code room was soon watching, goggle-eyed, as Knox walked in and took over. In a direct order, not through channels, went the command to General Harmon to send the 164th Infantry, U.S. Army, to Guadalcanal "with all dispatch."

"To hell with that so-called 'weakening of our lines of communication' that has kept them on the sideline," Knox told Forrestal in an aside. "Another thing: we're going to challenge the Japs at night. As of right now."

The code room was by now operating at forced draught. It seemed to please the secretary. He linked his arm with Forrestal's. "In case I failed to mention it before, Jim—well done!" He paused a moment in the doorway of the code room. "What was the name of that admiral? Scott? Well, he's going to have his hands full."

Church services were brief on Sunday morning, October 11, aboard the United States heavy cruiser *San Francisco*, flagship of Rear Adm. Norman Scott.

There was an underlying feeling of urgency and purpose running through the ship. In the chief's wardroom you could feel it. Up in the chart house, where the navigator shared tight quarters with the new surface gunnery radars, you could almost hear the tension building. Something was up, that was for sure. Admiral Scott himself set the pattern with an unchanging demeanor of quiet optimism. It filtered down through ranks and rates. It was an intangible. Yet it bespoke something vibrant and new.

Perhaps it had something to do with the word "now."

It had galvanized the fleet—at least that part of it designated as Task Force 64.2. Three task forces were operating in the Lower Solomons that Sunday morning as the sun crossed the zenith and massive cumulus clouds piled to the east, white and fluffy. West of Guadalcanal, the aircraft carrier *Hornet* patrolled with her escort forces around her. East of Malaita, the battleship *Washington* and her supporting vessels were stationed.

The third force patrolled just south of the 'Canal. This was 64.2, commanded by Scott. There were nine ships in an arrow-shaped column: four cruisers and five destroyers. Their bows were up, their sterns down, and the long, white wakes on the calm surface of the sea stretched out far behind, indicating that they were making near flank speed.

In the van came the flagship, the *San Francisco*, with Capt. Charles McMorris on the bridge. She carried nine 8-inch guns in three turrets. Next came the light cruiser *Boise*, commanded by Capt. Edward Moran, with five three-gun turrets of 6-inchers. Behind her, clipper-bowed and with raked stacks and masts, with the low-hulled, beautiful *Salt Lake City*, with ten 8-inchers poking from four turrets fore and aft, and Capt. Ernest Small in command. The *Helena*, a fifteen-gun light cruiser, brought up the rear; Capt. Gilbert Hoover was her skipper.

The destroyers *Farenholt*, *Duncan*, *Laffey*, *McCalla*, and *Buchanan* provided the screen.

Up in flag country, the inscrutable Admiral Scott went over his orders, plotted his strategy, and considered his options. It was a fighting mission. The transports carrying the 164th Infantry into Guadalcanal were already at sea. They were due to arrive at the 'Canal on October 13.

Not explicit in his orders but certainly inherent in his mission was the need to assure the safe arrival of the 164th. The waters around Guadalcanal had to be cleared at least temporarily of enemy surface vessels. The moon would set one hour after sunset. That meant it would be a dark night. Plenty dark.

Admiral Scott had not been present at the debacle of Savo Island just two months earlier, but he had been close enough—barely twenty miles away—to have experienced that defeat as a personal calamity. There had been old shipmates of his aboard the vessels that rested now in Iron Bottom Bay. The tragedy stung. Almost as bad had been the intervening months of official indecision.

The face of Norman Scott, seamed by a thousand sea watches, wrinkled as he recalled, bitterly, the assignment of vessels to his command, and their equally quick withdrawal a little more than two months ago as COMSOPAC staff members played spin-the-bottle with their fears, real and imagined.

Now, at last, he had a mission to perform, and ships to do the job.

At 1345 hours, as the admiral was finishing a Spartan lunch, the intercom phone in his quarters rang. "Admiral? We've picked up a report that an enemy force of two cruisers and six destroyers has entered the two-hundred-mile zone."

"Are they coming down the Slot?"

"Affirmative, sir. Right at us."

It was what Norman Scott had been waiting for. His order to his operations officer had already been prepared.

"We will intercept. All ships prepare for action."

For the first time along the Slot, the Tokyo Express was about to be challenged.

Interception was set for Cape Esperance, the northernmost tip of Guadalcanal. The plot, based on estimated enemy speed and distance, indicated that the meeting should take place some time around midnight. The advantage, theoretically, would be with Scott's force. They had radar; the Japanese did not.

At 1810, Cactus Air Force search patrols made a final position-report on the Japanese fleet. The eight ships were 110 miles away. The curtain of night would cover their final approach.

Outside of the fact that two cruisers and six destroyers made up the enemy task force, little else was known to Scott as darkness fell and Cruiser Division 6 steamed southward at thirty knots. On the flag bridge of the Japanese cruiser *Aoba* was a veteran of many a Tokyo Express run, Rear Adm. Arimoto Goto. He had been second in command of Mikawa's fleet at Savo Island.

By 2145, Task Force 64.2 was only thirteen miles from Cape Esperance. Occasional flashes of heat lightning illuminated the skies. The seas remained calm. Scott ordered the speed of his column reduced to twenty knots. A floatplane on each cruiser was in its catapult, warming up. A pilot and an observer sat stiffly, awaiting the shock of their launch.

"Launch aircraft!" The catapult officer of the *Salt Lake City* gave the command, a dimmed flashlight swung through its prescribed arc, and the pilot opened his throttle wide.

On the flag bridge, Admiral Scott heard the catapult plane leave the deck of the *San Francisco*. It roared off into the darkness. The *Salt Lake City* plane, leaving at about the same instant, faltered in flight, sputtering and coughing as she headed downward, crashing into the sea about five hundred yards from the cruiser column. A fireball followed, illuminating the ships of the cruiser force. It was a tense moment for those on board. The shoreline was clearly visible by now. Japanese observers ashore must be watching . . . and reporting. Had surprise been lost? Worse, was it to be another Savo?

Scott continued on course. He reckoned the enemy force by now to be within twenty-five miles. At 2252, a visual sighting by one of the floatplanes aloft confirmed this estimate.

"One large, two smaller vessels observed," the pilot radioed back. "Will investigate."

A few minutes later a radar operator, deep in the operations room of the *Helena*, reported five blips on his screen. The distance plotted on its scanner was about fifteen miles. The *Boise*, also equipped with the latest radar, picked up the same five blips, and confirmed the distance: twenty-seven thousand yards.

It was the ultimate victory of technology over Japanese night eyes. Radar had now outstripped man, however well trained, and however powerful his telescopes.

The flag plot on the *San Francisco* crackled with radio jargon as the ship-to-ship TBS System was given the go-ahead. The *Helena*'s captain was requesting permission to fire. Iron Mike Moran of the *Boise* quickly followed suit. For those tumbling to battle stations, the only sounds were the sharp hiss of the bow wave and the deeper throb of the engines below as speed was increased.

In the plot rooms of the cruisers, enormous computers ingested a maze of figures being thrown into their maws: speed, windage, range, direction, charge. Topside, the massive turrets turned to starboard, and muzzles elevated. The radar blips continued on course. The range shortened. The Japanese fleet was sailing blithely on, unaware that a classic naval maneuver had been performed against them: Scott was crossing their T.

It was a moment to be savored.

"How many ships do you make out?" demanded Iron Mike on the *Boise*.

"Appears to be five."

"Pick out the biggest and stay with it."

"Aye, aye, sir."

Still no order to fire. The blips were there, and closing rapidly. Anxiety mounted as the flagship's silence continued. It was too much for Captain Hoover on the *Helena*. He thought he was in possession of enough facts to warrant a command decision.

"Commence firing!"

The Helena's fifteen 6-inch guns blazed forth. That was enough for the rest of the column. The *Boise* opened up, then the *Salt Lake City*. Finally it became the *San Francisco's* turn. There were four cruisers firing now, and still no word from the admiral. But he had placed his ships in position; he had crossed the T. It was by no means without precedent for subordinates to act on their own, when, in their judgment, communications might be at fault.

The *Aoba* was the biggest blip on the radar screens. Within minutes the flagship of Cruiser Division 6, the veteran of the Savo Island victory, was hit by forty large-caliber shells. She died, and Admiral Goto died with her. The cruiser *Furutaka*, which had fired 153 eight-inch shells and eight torpedoes on that awful night of defeat at Iron Bottom Bay, was holed repeatedly and sunk. The *Kinugasa*, like the others a 7,100-ton Kako-class cruiser and herself a veteran of the Savo engagement, was badly damaged.

In a matter of half an hour the final salvo was fired. The battle of Cape Esperance was over. Only two destroyers—the *Murakomo* and the *Natsugumo*—escaped unscathed, but their reprieve was short. Next day the Cactus Air Force pursued them up the Slot and sank them both.

It was a clear-cut American naval victory, one of the greatest in the navy's history. And coming on the heels of the Matanikau victory, it meant that the Japanese had lost a doubleheader.

The *Boise* had suffered heavy damage; the *Salt Lake City*'s wounds were less serious. The destroyer *Duncan* had been sunk and a sister DD, *Farenholt*, was heavily damaged. Some of the salt had been cleansed from the wounds of Savo, however. More importantly, the Japanese did not own the Slot anymore. From now on they would have to battle for it. It represented a turning point.

The point may have been considered moot by the marines, two nights later. "For Christ's sake, I thought our guys had won a sea battle or sumpin'," cracked one of the Cactus fliers, huddling at the bottom of his bombproof shelter.

"Not on your ass," popped back his buddy, digging even deeper. "What in hell are they throwing at us now, the Super Chief?"

It sounded like it. It was, in fact, Adm. Takeo Kurita with two of Japan's mightiest warships, the battleships *Haruna* and *Kongo*. They were standing off the perimeter, and for eighty very long minutes they

Gen. Alexander A. Vandegrift, whose steadfastness paid off in America's longest battle.

An American patrol wades across the Tenaru River to help deter Japanese forces landing down the coast in their buildup against the perimeter.

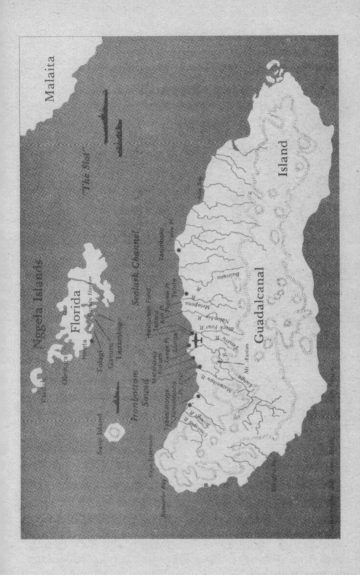

Malaita

Nggela Islands

"The Slot"

Savo Island

Florida

Tulagi
Gavutu
Tanambogo

Purvis Harbor

Sealark Channel

Tenaru

Ironbottom Sound

Guadalcanal
Island

A group of Melanesian natives, members of the Solomon Islands Defense Forces, with their commander, Capt. Martin Clemens, Royal Australian Army. This gallant band of men provided the Guadalcanal garrison with vital information on the enemy.

Gen. Archer Vandegrift (fourth from left, front row) sits surrounded by his unit commanders and staff.

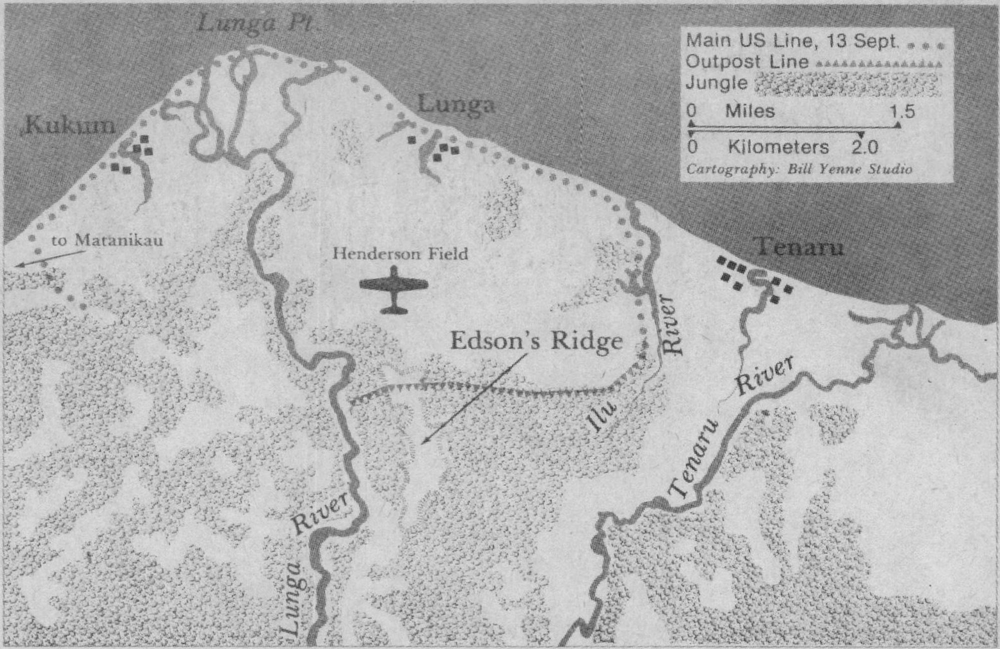

Main US Line, 13 Sept. ▪ ▪ ▪
Outpost Line ∙∙∙∙∙∙∙
Jungle ▲▲▲▲▲▲▲

0   Miles   1.5
0   Kilometers   2.0

Cartography: Bill Yenne Studio

Tenaru

Tenaru River

Ilu River

Ilu

Edson's Ridge

Henderson Field

Lunga River

Lunga

Lunga Pt.

Kukum

to Matanikau

When the marines captured the air strip, they held on to its Japanese-built operations building and renamed it "the Pagoda." It served as Cactus headquarters until Japanese naval fire reduced it to rubble during the "Night of the Battleship."

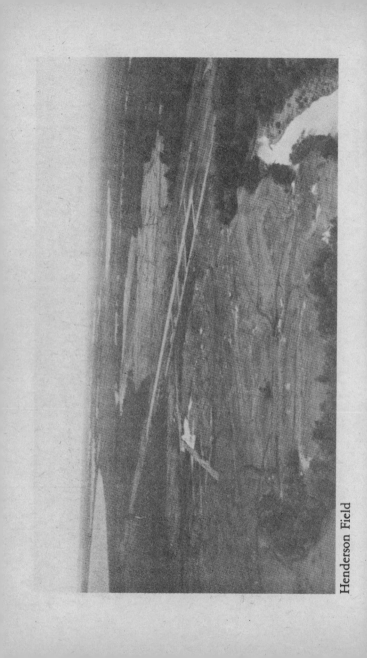

Henderson Field

Sergeant Major Vouza, who was honored by being made a member of the 1st Marine Division for his heroism, is congratulated by Capt. Martin Clemens.

Col. Kiyono Ichiki, who led the first counter-landing against the marines at Guadalcanal.

Maj. John L. Smith, who flew into Guadalcanal with the initial reinforcements to the Cactus Air Wing, is credited with the first downed Japanese airplane in the campaign. He went on to destroy a total of ten.

Merrit A. (Red Mike) Edson, the hero of "Edson's Ridge."

With September came the Seabees, who constructed this suspension span over the Matanikau River. It helped the marines control both banks of the often-swollen river, which formed the right wing of the perimeter.

Lt. Gen. Masao Muruyama, who commanded the prestigious Sendai Division and committed them to the envelopment and capture of Henderson Field.

A former Japanese construction barracks was turned into a makeshift hospital for the sick and wounded. Few among the 20,000 who landed initially escaped malaria, dengue fever, typhus, or a Japanese bullet.

"Pistol Pete" was the generic definition for the Japanese 105mm howitzer, which lobbed shells into the marine and army positions during the six-month campaign. Fortunately for the Americans, Pete's ammunition had to be hand-carried over the Maruyama Trail, a costly logistical problem for the Japanese and a godsend to the defenders.

The communication center on Guadalcanal shortly after a Japanese thousand-pound bomb scored a direct hit.

The famous "Blue Goose"—a Catalina PBY, command ship of Cactus Air Force chief, General Geiger. It was converted to the role of a torpedo bomber and destroyed an enemy transport, even though the 300-knot dive almost took her wings off.

Fleet Adm. Isoroku Yamamoto, an admirer of American
fighting men and the American tradition, takes out his
calipers to plot his one grand move against Admiral Halsey
at Santa Cruz.

The huge tree was a landmark during several early marine forays across the Matanikau River and later a point of reference along the ill-fated Maruyama Trail, near what the Japanese called Ippon Bashi. Japanese snipers hid in its interwoven roots and had to be blasted out by light artillery. Note the marine standing at its base.

Col. Gerald Thomas, chief of staff of the 1st Marine Division, conducts the final briefing before the First Battle of the Matanikau.

Capt. Joe Foss epitomized the fine qualities of the joint services which made the Cactus Air Force unique and victorious against superior numbers. He downed twenty-six Japanese planes.

A two-man marine artillery observation post on Sealark Channel relays information back to their batteries on the approach of a Japanese destroyer force coming down the Slot.

The workhorse of jungle warfare, the reliable Browning machine gun, water-cooled .30 caliber Model A-1, stands guard over a group of engineers who are enjoying their first bath in a week along the Matanikau.

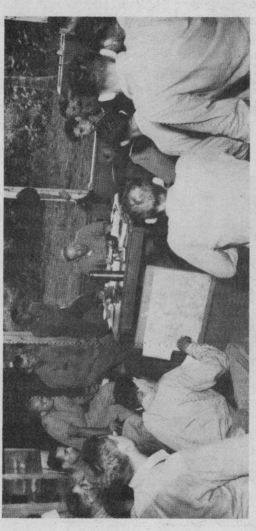

Col. Merritt A. Edson conducts a 5th Regiment battle briefing along the Lunga River in early November. The marines had moved outside the original perimeter by then and had taken the limited offensive. Intent on Red Mike's instructions were Lt. Col. W. A. Reaves; Lt. Comdr. Hopkins, USN; Lt. Col. W. Piper; Lt. Col. Guy Harter; 1st Lt. Ed Snell; Maj. Henry Turzke; and Major Barba.

poured nine hundred 14-inch shells into the airfield and its defense positions. The only opposition consisted of some newly arrived PT boats based at Tulagi, which buzzed around the giants like a swarm of gnats, and with about as much effectiveness. Who owned what? It was pretty hard to determine, the marines concluded, when you were ducking the Super Chief.

Despite the losses at Matanikau and Esperance, the Japanese kept coming. It was their persistence in the face of heavy losses that for once elicited an unusual note of pessimism from Chester Nimitz. Talking soberly to his staff at Pearl Harbor on October 14, the admiral shook his head. "It now appears," he said, "that we are unable to control the area around Guadalcanal." He was frowning at the map that showed how the tactical gains around the airfield had remained almost static for two months. "Our control of these positions can only be maintained at great expense to us."

He heaved what for him was a big sigh, and concluded his critique to an equally somber staff. "The situation is not hopeless, gentlemen, but it is certainly critical."

General Vandegrift and his marines, concerned with tactical successes and a few extra rations, were more pragmatic. Norman Scott and his cruisers had done their job of downfield blocking pretty well. At least they had opened the hole wide enough to allow a couple of well-remembered transports the luxury of safe passage. At Kukum dock lay the old Wacky Mac, the *McCawley*, and another invasion bucket-of-bolts, the *Zeilin*. And up from the holds came a very pretty sight, indeed.

225

"Doggies!" croaked a dockworker. "Hiya, dog face!"

The soldier-boys weren't shy in shooting it back. "What's it like here, shithead?" There was a lot more of the same. The 164th Infantry, U.S. Army, had arrived on the scene.

15

TASSAFARONGA

Twelve miles northwest of Matanikau Village on the coastal track toward Cape Esperance, the Bonegi River plunges swiftly between jungle ridges and goes out to meet the sea. From the shifting sandbars at its mouth, and extending northward toward Tassafaronga Point, runs a long, crescent-shaped beach. It was this beach that General Hyakutake had selected as the concentration point for his massive October offensive.

It was an excellent choice, he felt. Troops and supplies could be landed easily over gently sloping sand. Even the largest transports could be nosed into the shore and winched back into deep water after unloading.

Logistically, there were other advantages. It was only a little more than nine kilometers behind the forward assembly area of the Seventeenth Army. Everything was falling into place. Unload here, move north over improved, coral-packed roads, and attack.

The late afternoon sun of October 14 had dropped behind Tulagi. Savo Island, a conical pile of lava and stone, was shrouding itself in a purple mantle. The white trunks of the coco palms encircling the beach stood against the sunset, their graceful fronds moving gently in response to the soft urgency of the prevailing trades. And as Hyakutake beckoned his staff about him, he was animated, almost jovial. There was even a bit of restrained horseplay as the group moved into the coolness of the grove where canvas chairs had been grouped in a semicircle around a small podium.

General Hyakutake moved to the rostrum, adjusted his oversize black-framed glasses, and bowed politely to those seated about him. He was a little man whose sloping shoulders hardly filled his loose-fitting tunic. High boots took up most of the sag in his trousers. He looked, his few detractors said, like an undernourished owl. But his record as a warrior and an administrator was admittedly unequalled in the Imperial Army.

He had set up advance headquarters of the Seventeenth Army on Guadalcanal five days before. Now, with his feet on the ground and his study of the terrain completed, he would conduct his first critique of past performances, outline the information of the enemy, and detail the assignments of attack.

The men about him, senior commanders and staff officers, nodded with deference and approval. Major General Maruyama, commander of 2d Division, was there, smooth-cheeked, hard, and cool. Major General Kawaguchi, he of the lost breeches, was not. There had been a changing of the guard.

Past performances were taken up first, almost with a wave of the hand. The disaster to the Ichikis, the destruction of the Kawaguchi Brigade, and other such misfortunes were once more ascribed to poor planning, impetuousness, failure of the human spirit.

"Information as to our own strength:" Hyakutake

readjusted his glasses. The Seventeenth Imperial Army, on New Britain, was building to a fifty-thousand-man force. Admiral Mikawa's fleet at Rabaul was being further reinforced; the great Yamamoto himself had personally seen to that. And Yamamoto had had the war's most powerful naval task force assembled at Truk. This armada, the general said, would once and for all clear the seas around Guadalcanal and leave its defenders to the cat and his claws.

His audience, sharply inhaling its breath, produced a collective hiss of approval.

Hyakutake was a good "platform man." He paused to allow this expected reaction to take shape and character. But now his face grew stern. Matters closer to hand remained for discussion—such as the destruction of Admiral Goto's Cruiser Division 6 a few nights ago, in which Goto himself had been killed. The audience moved forward in its chairs. "This has not seriously interrupted our landing schedules." Another deprecating hand-wave. Despite Goto's unfortunate loss, the tenders *Chitose* and *Nisshin* had sailed through to Tassafaronga last night and had landed a thousand men. In addition, and most importantly, they had unloaded four 150mm howitzers, two field pieces, several antiaircraft batteries, and plenty of ammunition of all classes.

"And tonight," the general paused for proper emphasis, "or early tomorrow morning, we shall have tanks!" The announcement created a renewed buzz of approval. Hyakutake continued, acknowledging that the use of tanks in this terrain was somewhat limited. But their arrival demonstrated the Seventeenth Army's unlimited capacity for resupply.

229

He would let them in on a secret. Mikawa's Eighth Fleet was at that very moment on its way down from the Shortlands. With it were six transports, the biggest reinforcement column ever brought to the island. Included in the shipment, as the general ticked them off, were the 38th Field Antiaircraft Battalion, the 4th Heavy Field Artillery Regiment, the 7th Field Artillery Regiment, the 6th Rapid-Fire Gun Battalion, one company of the Independent Mortar Regiment, the 230th Infantry Regiment, and the 76th Hospital Force. In all, more than five thousand men.

Hyakutake let the figures sink in.

He pointed at the crescent beach, curling away toward Tassafaronga. "They will land here!" It was a dramatic moment, skillfully presented. "We are invincible!" His officers rose, to a man. Maruyama led the group in three *banzais*, then motioned them to be seated.

Hyakutake resumed. "We now have adequate artillery of all calibers," he told them. Its lack, he emphasized, had cost the Japanese heavily in the past. It was his only concession to the failure of the Kawaguchi Brigade.

"Some of you," he noted, "have not as yet met Major General Tadashi Sumoyoshi, responsible for the coordination of our artillery. Would the general stand up, please, and be recognized?" Sumoyoshi, grinning in embarrassment, shuffled to his feet. He sat down quickly.

Some of the guns, Hyakutake pointed out, had already been in action. They had joined the *Haruna* and the *Konga* in a bombardment which, on the night before, had thrown more than half a million pounds of steel into Henderson Field. "One-half million pounds! Do you gentlemen have any idea of the damage that weight of metal has caused the Americans, what havoc it has created?" He banged the podium with a clenched fist. "The airfield no longer exists. Its planes have been smashed, the petrol burned, the runways demolished." He spread his hands wide. "The navy has done its part. The rest is up to us."

Hyakutake wound up the critique, looking directly at Maruyama. "You were not as yet on the ground, my dear general, but . . ." There followed a casual reference to the 4th Infantry Regiment—which Chesty Puller's men had chewed up so badly south of the Matanikau—and a soft-spoken reprimand for "the first defeat of the colors of the Emperor's Own."

In the silence that followed, Maruyama fidged nervously. Hyakutake coughed.

"You will have ample opportunity in the days ahead, my dear general, to make good that loss of face." Hyakutake smiled benignly, but there was no mistaking the threat that was implied.

Far to the north, as the Tassafaronga conference was breaking up, the commander in chief of the Japanese Navy stood on the bridge of his flagship in the harbor of Truk.

Adm. Isoroku Yamamoto was presiding over a sight that would stir even a landlubber's heart. As he looked out on the magnificent roadstead, the marine guard in the companionway jumped to attention, and a visitor, in immaculate whites, returned the salute and passed through the hatch.

Vice Admiral Kakuta stood well over six feet. He

231

was, by Japanese standards, a giant of a man. His deep genuflection to his commander in chief was returned. On the battleship *Yamato*, mightiest dreadnaught ever built, such ritual was a time-honored custom. Then Yamamoto extended his hand, western-fashion. "I'm glad you've come," he told the taller man. "If only to see one of the most beautiful sights in the world."

Kakuta laughed politely. "It's really why I came, sir. I wanted to see . . ."

"What I'm about to see as you sail?"

"Yes, sir. And to thank you, personally, for your trust."

Yamamoto was touched. His battle orders to Kakuta had been characteristically concise. They had merely commanded him to "apprehend and annihilate any enemy forces in the Solomons."

Both men were silent as they stood at the rail of the bridge. In stately column the fleet was standing out to sea. Here, passing in review, signal flags snapping in the breeze, were the warships General Hyakutake had promised to his staff.

Already beyond the great coral barrier that encircles Truk, past the reef, where turquoise gives way to blue, darted the escort destroyers. They were followed by the cruisers, pagoda-like prows cutting huge bow waves. Their slanted masts and funnels, so favored by Japanese naval architects, added to the illusion of great speed. And finally, just getting underway, came the queens of the sea, the carriers, stately, tall, wide, and majestic. Semaphores blinked back an urgent message to the flagship. Kakuta, the giant, took in the signal.

"They want me, sir."

"It would seem so. Well, then, good hunting, Admiral."

"Thank you, sir."

Yamamoto stood watching as his guest was piped smartly over the side. The *Hiyo, Junyo,* and *Zuiho* steamed slowly past, bearing down on the small barge which had a single figure standing in its stern.

Yamamoto responded to its salute. He had assembled five carriers, five battleships, fourteen cruisers, and forty-five destroyers to form the Guadalcanal Supporting Forces. Vice Adm. Nobutake Kondo was in direct command. But Yamamoto's own eyes would follow the progress closely.

It was the vanguard of this mighty armada that had swung into action on the night of October 13. Yamamoto had noted the results with satisfaction. Henderson Field was a shambles.

This most powerful of Japanese fleets had a single mission: to seal off the Solomons area and allow the uninterrupted landing of ten thousand fresh Japanese troops on the night of October 14–15. Already down the Slot, en route from the Shortland Islands, was the rear echelon of the Sendai Division. The big push was scheduled for October 20.

It was 1400 hours on Sunday, October 18, when a four-engine Consolidated patrol-bomber lowered its flaps over Noumea Bay, some twelve hundred miles south of Truk. Among the passengers on the *Coronado* arriving from Pearl Harbor was the sturdy figure of Vice Adm. William F. Halsey. They called him "Bull," this man. He was built like one and he acted like one. He was, his shipmates would tell you, utterly sure of himself, gutty, wise, and—most important—lucky. Moreover, he was the kind of guy you would be apt to

233

find around when things were happening. He hated flying a desk, but he loved to fly fighters, and he had served as skipper of the *Saratoga* as far back as 1935. The year 1937 found him commandant of Pensacola, and later that same year, he finally earned his broad stripe. From then on, it was carriers all the way for the Bull.

A gregarious individual, Halsey had an intense loyalty quotient, both up and down the ladder. He gave praise generously, and it had earned him a reward in kind that amounted almost to reverence on the part of those who served under him. "The Old Man will listen; he'll argue with you half the night, on an even keel and with respect. But when he makes a final decision, that's it, bub. There ain't no talking back to him. He'll say, this is the way we're going to do it, son . . . my way."

Halsey had been sent out of the war zone some months back with a crippling skin ailment that the marines on Guadalcanal called "jungle rot." Now he was back, cured of the rot but lacking a combat assignment. That chafed almost as much. The inspection job that Nimitz handed him at Pearl was "just my meat," he had told the boss. But on the plane he'd "grumbled all the way down," according to Captain Browning.

The big props on the flying boat had barely stopped turning in the harbor of Noumea when a whaleboat pulled alongside. A flag lieutenant from COMSOPAC handed Halsey an envelope marked "Secret." Halsey flopped it over as he scrambled into the stern sheets. "It's from Nimitz," he told his companions. "Hell, I just saw him." He fumbled with the flap as the boat headed for the dock.

Halsey's remarks after reading the contents have been widely recorded. The look on his face as he finished has not been. "It was the look of a man reprieved," Captain Browning said. "The look of a man rescued from the backwaters of a war he wanted so much to fight."

"Jesus Christ and General Jackson!" The Halsey grin lit up his face. "This is the hottest potato they ever handed me."

The telegram was short. It read: "You will take command of the South Pacific area and South Pacific forces immediately."

Halsey loved every word of it.

There was also a letter. This was from an old pal and teammate on the Annapolis football team, Bob Ghormley. Bull had no comment on that one. His Adam's apple just bobbed a couple of times and he stuck the letter in his pocket.

By that time the whaleboat had docked.

William F. Halsey's first act as COMSOPAC was to set himself afloat. "Find me a ship and put my stuff aboard," he ordered. In the wee hours of October 19, Halsey's headquarters moved to the attack transport *Argonne* which was swinging at anchor in Noumea Bay.

Earlier, he had surveyed with evident distaste the rows of polished desks at base headquarters. After the brief courtesies attendant upon the change of command, he had plunged into a sea of paperwork. By midnight he had arrived at the only possible conclusion. Logistically, at least, his command was nearing bankruptcy. Henderson Field was out of gas, literally and figuratively. The field, reports indicated, was a junkyard. The buildings, revetments, and supply dumps had been reduced to rubble. Even the old Pagoda was down.

They called it "the Night of the Battleships." It might more accurately have been termed "the week." For there had been, since the *Kongo* and the *Haruna* had dumped their tons of destruction, seven continuous nights of bombardment by Japanese light and heavy cruisers.

There had been little opposition. Some of the torpedo boats, newly arrived at Tulagi, had made courageous forays to tackle the giants. There had been some unconfirmed hits. But the PT boats were too few in number to challenge the Japanese cruisers effectively.

By 0300 hours, Halsey groaned, pushing the papers aside. "I've seen enough. Let's hit the sack." On the ride out to the *Argonne*, the sea air had helped him get the details of what he had read into some measure of perspective. Guns, planes, tanks, and ships? They can be replaced. But how about the guys who man them? Have they shown the guts, the will, the pride to fight?

The admiral's barge bumped the *Argonne*'s gangway platform. Halsey wearily climbed the ladder, saluted the quarterdeck, and headed for flag country, where a steward had already turned down his bed. The sounds of the ship and of the sea were all about him. This is more like it, he thought.

"Coffee, sir?"

The admiral brightened. "Thank you. Yes, they'll fight."

"I beg pardon, sir?"

"Our men, steward. I think they want to kill Japs."

In the days before the Halsey takeover and immediately following the Night of the Battleships, a new menace had appeared on the Guadalcanal scene: Pistol Pete.

Pete was not really singular. It was the marine designation for a group of heavy six-inch howitzers that had been brought forward, as promised, by General Sumoyoshi, and emplaced along the southern and eastern rims of the perimeter. Cleverly camouflaged in caves and deep valleys to avoid counterbattery fire, Sumoyoshi's guns were beginning to lob shells with increasing frequency onto the new fighter strip, which had miraculously escaped serious damage by the naval barrages.

The guns were in action on October 14, four days before Halsey assumed command. It was a report of General Geiger's on that day which had confirmed Bull's optimism that the marines on Guadalcanal still wanted to "kill Japs."

Twenty-nine fighter planes had been wired up, patched up, and declared "operational."

Geiger had rubbed his eyes when the morning report had been handed him. "It's hard to believe," he told an aide. But at 0930 hours, when a coastwatcher alert came in, all twenty-nine planes scrambled, dodging around the bulldozers that were already out to repair the shell-holes in the tarmac.

In an hour, all twenty-nine were back. They had seen no approaching bombers, the pilots reported by radio. But they had hardly clambered out of their cockpits when twenty-six Bettys buzzed overhead, bombing the field unopposed. The Japanese squadron leader reported the results: "No activity here. No opposition raised to meet us." At the other end, where this report was received, there was jubilation. Henderson Field was presumed dead.

An hour later came a second Bonzo alarm, and again the Cactus fighters went aloft. This time eighteen Bettys were intercepted. The Japanese probably had been lulled by the earlier report into a false sense of security. Nine of their bombers and three escorting Zekes were shot down.

Search planes, late that afternoon, spotted a new peril. Two groups of Japanese ships—six transports and eight destroyers—were north of Santa Isabel, well within the two-hundred-mile radius. Then Admiral Mikawa's Eighth Fleet, identified by the now-familiar silhouette of the *Chokai*, was observed on its way in support.

There was a grimly purposeful meeting in General Vandegrift's tent. The general led it off with a wry smile and a wisecrack. He poked the solemn Geiger in the ribs. "I see you've removed that eyesore at last." The Pagoda had been vaporized by the battleship salvos. Geiger had long suspected that it was a prime aiming-point for the Japanese. "Good riddance, I say."

It was tough trying to pump a little humor into the meeting. But the head man kept pecking away. "You've got the wireless going again?"

"Yes, sir. Patched up and working." Along with the Pagoda, the Cactus radio station had been demolished. "We were out three hours."

"There wasn't much to say anyway, was there?"

"No, sir."

"Well, let's have the bad news."

For General Geiger, it was a relief to lay it out on the table. Forty-one of his men had been killed. Virtually all of his aviation gas supply had gone up in flames. Only seven SBDs remained operational; thirty-two had been destroyed. "We've got twenty-eight fighters left. Lost one this morning." Geiger's face lightened. "But our guys shot down twelve planes in that last bunch."

"How's the fighter strip?"

"Pretty good shape. Surprisingly so. It beats me how they missed it."

The talks continued. Admiral Fitch at Espiritu Santo was trying to help. He had nine aircraft but nobody to fly them up. The only SBD squadron not on Guadalcanal, Lt. Comdr. Ray Davis's Bombing Six, was on the way and should be in shortly with eight planes. Could Colonel Bauer furnish pilots to ferry back the nine planes? Can do.

It was a bit like sweeping back the ocean with a broom.

Two PAB barges carrying aviation gas had left Santo four days ago. But would they get through? Meanwhile, the only gas left was being salvaged from the inoperational planes and the wrecks. And six fat Japanese transports would be arriving sometime that night. The staff made some rapid calculations: that would put Seventeenth Army strength at around twenty-five thousand men. The meeting closed on that note, and General Geiger went back down the hill, shaking his head.

That night, under a single 60-watt bulb, General

Vandegrift sent two stark dispatches to COMSOPAC. Their very brevity suggests the immense strain under which the fortress-keeper labored: as though words, of themselves, were incapable of expressing the crisis his beleaguered garrison faced.

"Urgently necessary," the first read, "this force receive maximum support of air and surface units." And almost as an afterthought, the second: "Absolutely essential aviation gas be flown here continuously."

As night closed down on the island, so did a sense of impending doom. Apprehension, the handmaiden of fear, hung heavy over the perimeter, in the dugouts, and in the wrecked revetments where flight crews patched bullet holes and dumped the last five-gallon tin into the tanks of a half-filled fighter.

"That's all there is, buddy, there ain't no more," a flight chief croaked, tilting up the empty can of high-test and tossing it away.

What sleep there was on the line was fitful. It was like waiting for the other shoe to drop. Guadalcanal was Zombieland. Finally it came, almost as a relief.

At 0200 hours, a mosquito-like buzz could be heard clearly from far out over Sealark Channel. The ack-ack along the beach opened up. A floatplane passed by, leaving a green-white flare over the field. The flare swayed slowly down, bathing the ground below with pitiless brilliance.

Two old nemeses, Capt. Mikio Hayakawa and Capt. Masao Sawa, gave the commence-fire order from the bridges of the *Chokai* and *Kinugasa*. The combined weight of their ordnance descended once more upon Henderson. Between them, they launched 752 eight-

240

inch high-explosive shells in half an hour. By comparison, the same two ships had used less than five hundred rounds in annihilating a U.S. cruiser fleet off Savo Island, a little over two months ago.

No American planes would fly this night or tomorrow, predicted Admiral Mikawa, the victor of Savo, so he cruised the few miles west to Tassafaronga Point. Along the crescent beach, half-hidden by the headland, six transports could be seen moving slowly toward shore. Blinking semaphores along the beach were already relaying instructions from the awaiting beach parties.

Mikawa's job had been done. The rest was up to a watchful, owl-eyed lieutenant-general who stood silently at the water's edge, awaiting his shipment of men, artillery, and tanks. The bulk of Savo Island loomed to port. It had been a good talisman for the admiral. He acknowledged it gravely as he swept by, heading up the Slot.

Back at the Cactus Air Force headquarters there was great excitement. Someone on the staff recalled that Louis Woods had cached quite a few drums of gas out in the boondocks some weeks before. "It's hidden around somewhere, General."

"By God, find it!" roared Geiger.

Engineers, air crews, grounded airmen—everybody joined in. The supply major organized the search. It turned up 465 drums of good high-test, unluckily forgotten, providentially remembered.

Division was on the line. "What can you send up to hit those arrogant bastards?" It was the D-3, Merrill Twining. "They're just sitting there."

"Yeah, I had a look at 'em." It was just before

0600. "Duke Davis is warming up on the line now. We got most of the holes filled, we hope. Maybe they can get off. We'll try."

The whine of five F4Fs could be heard over the line. They took off on a strafing mission. Smokey Stover, one of the pilots, met a Japanese floatplane head-on. He shot it down with a couple of bursts but pulled up just a little late, his right wing scraping across the floatplane's top. It was a near thing. But Smokey flew on, expended his ammo, and returned to the field.

"What in hell have we got here, Smokey?" his crew chief asked when the fighter bumped to a halt and the canopy slid back. The chief was holding a piece of a "meatball," the standard Japanese marking. Smokey's wing had torn off a piece of wing fabric, and it had stuck.

Back at Cactus this was considered a good omen. The newly found cache of high-test had added to the general optimism and to the improvisations that were buzzing, the latest of which concerned the Blue Goose.

The Blue Goose was a PBY-5A amphibian, the personal plane of General Geiger. During palmier days, she had been the "fat cat" of the Cactus force, flying in everything from Class VI liquor supplies, when these could be found, to mail sacks and toilet paper. In short, the Blue Goose was Cactus's morale booster.

Now she was destined for a more serious task—if the plans of Maj. Jack Cram, her pilot, and of Lt. Bill Woodruff, in charge of SBD maintenance, could be put into operation. They were going to make a torpedo bomber out of a fat, ponderous, ninety-knots (manufacturer's assigned top speed) amphibian. Like kids with a new toy, the mechanics and crew of the Blue Goose went to work. Geiger's aide, Toby Munn, organized the fighter protection, and they too joined in with enthusiasm.

Manual devices were rigged for release of the two torpedoes being slung under the amphibian's wings. Woodruff and his flight crews patched up a twelve-plane flight: three P-39s, four F4Fs, and one old P-40 would provide fighter cover. The old Blue Goose and three remaining SBDs, still operative, became the attack group.

It was nearing 1000 hours when, planes ready, the final briefing took place. Cactus being what it was, there was a committee decision covering the strike plans. Jack Cram, Al Cooley, and Duke Davis laid out the tactics. It was high drama, made even more so by the knowledge of all present that if the Blue Goose got through with her two fish, it would be a miracle.

The SBDs, the sturdy Douglas bombers, were to be the decoys. They would rendezvous east of Henderson, then swing around to attack the transports off Tassafaronga from the west. Got it? Heads nodded.

"Okay. When Cram, here, sees the first bomber go into his roll, he starts his dive from out by Savo. He's at six thousand feet. You fighter guys move down and ahead of him. You gotta keep the ack-ack occupied. He's coming in parallel to the beach, right across those transports, so that if he misses one, maybe he'll get the next. Remember, he's got to come in at two hundred knots. That's damned slow for a torpedo attack. Any faster, those big parasols they call wings will just go . . . blop, off."

The Blue Goose crew was silent. They were all

determined to go on this run. Cram couldn't talk them out of it. But they gulped a bit, bow gunner, flight engineer, two waist gunners and a tunnel gunner. Only the copilot's seat was empty. Nobody flew in that seat but the general himself, and he'd been grounded—by none other than Archer Vandegrift.

"Out of the question," had been the stiff reply to Geiger's guarded inquiry.

The dark blue bulk of the grotesquely loaded PBY swallowed up its pilot and crew, and lumbered off down the pockmarked strip, dodging bulldozers, its nose- and turret-guns swinging in their sponsons like antennae on a butterfly.

When the Blue Goose was off the strip and circling, Tassafaronga came into view. There they were, six on the beach, calmly unloading their cargo like a fleet of copra schooners. And off to both sides were the escorting destroyers, leaving long circular wakes in the blue of Sealark Channel.

Cram banked over Savo and looked back. He had his six thousand feet. He levelled his yoke, and for what seemed like an eternity watched for the signal to attack. He and the nose gunner saw it at almost the same instant.

"There she goes, sir. They're going in."

A flash of silver against the sky. The Douglas had started its dive. There was another and then another. Cram shoved the yoke forward. As he approached, white puffs appeared on the decks of the six transports. The ack-ack had spotted the incoming SBDs.

Cram was now in a steep dive, the tableau below coming closer and taking form. There was an ominous rumble from the Goose. Her wings were flapping like a mallard. Great God, the airspeed indicator stood at 240 and climbing. He eased back on the yoke and flashed over the outlying Japanese destroyer screen at two hundred feet. He was by them before they spotted him. The transports were directly ahead. He released one torpedo, then the other. The Goose shuddered as the weight left her. The first fish ran true, and as Cram banked left, both he and the crew looked: she boiled home. There was a terrific explosion. The second torpedo porpoised up and down and did not find a mark.

Observation time was over. There was Zeros on the Goose's tail, like a hive of angry hornets. The PBY's waist- and tail-gunners got into the act now. So did Duke Davis and his fighter cover. Even as the strip came into view, one Zeke still hung in there, his guns chattering. Fighting 121's Roger Haberman made a fortuitous entrance on the scene at this moment. Wheels down, badly shot-up, he was approaching the field when the Goose shot up, pursued by one meatball. Haberman never even bothered to retract his wheels. He hadn't time. He put the Zero in his sights and squeezed. The Zeke disintegrated and the Blue Goose was home free.

Geiger sent for his pilot. "I understand you got my plane shot up?" he growled at Cram.

"Yes, sir."

"How bad?"

"One hundred and seventy-five bullet holes, sir."

Geiger proceeded to chew him out, threatening court martial for destruction of government property. Major Cram, too recently removed from the world of grim reality, failed to appreciate the general's badinage. Why, you crummy old son of a bitch, he thought, very much to himself. Toby Munn recognized his red-faced anger and gave Cram a broad wink.

"Jack, that was a damned fine job," the Cactus chief said with feeling. "Let's go to lunch."

Things were looking up. There was gas for another attack by the SBDs. Another transport had been torpedoed. And word had it that eleven B-17s were on the way up from Santo. As Geiger and Cram broke out their mess gear and lunched at the new Book Cadillac, the Flying Forts got through, registering three bomb hits. By 1330 hours, three of the six Japanese transports—the *Kyushu Maru*, *Sasako Maru*, and *Azumasan Maru*—were beached and burning. By 1600, the convoy commander, Rear Admiral Takama, pulled anchor with the remaining three. He had, he told the Seventeenth Army commander, safely landed eighty percent of his cargo.

It was a supply victory of the first magnitude for the Japanese. But Cactus was by no means dead, and neither was Henderson Field. That much was relayed back that night to Pearl Harbor in a "send us more Japs" message that impressed Admiral Nimitz and the bull-necked man who sat beside him reading the dispatches.

"What do you think, Bill?" he asked Halsey, who ostensibly was being sent down to inspect the wreckage.

"Goddammit, they've got guts."

Next day, all along the perimeter, the marines, the dog-faces of the 164th, and the rifle-carrying fliers who had joined them, listened with good-natured derision to the radio broadcast of a Washington press conference. Secretary of the Navy Frank Knox was conducting it, and the subject was Guadalcanal. Frank Knox was a tough guy to pin down. But this time he stubbed his toe on one sharp question. Answering it, Knox said he "hoped" that Guadalcanal could be held. That was a slip that made the headlines.

"Will ya listen to that? The guy 'hopes' we can hold!"

"Yeah, but he ain't real sure. And get this: he says we're all goin' to give 'em hell, ashore or afloat. That's what the man said." There was a chorus of loud hooting.

Halsey had his first team pegged right.

16

YAMAMOTO'S GAME PLAN

Isoroku Yamamoto looked sharply over the ornate chess board. He searched for signs of discomfiture in his opponent, Lt. Masao Okada, his personal aide. He found none. The younger man's eyes studying the board betrayed no emotion. But the trap was baited. Should he move the knight to queen five. . . .

A knock interrupted the concentration. The fifty-eight-year-old admiral gestured for Okada to carry on and moved with cat-like grace to the cabin door. It was a routine message. The admiral absorbed its contents at a glance, his attention remaining fixed on the board.

The lieutenant moved tentatively, one hand extended. What piece? Yamamoto craned for a better look. Ah hah! He moves the knight! Still on his feet, the admiral's countermove was a blur.

"Check."

"It's a checkmate, sir."

"Ah, yes, so it is." The admiral beamed. "But you have played well."

Okada was duly flattered and returned the compliment in full measure. Later on that October evening in Truk he confided to his diary: "A most wily chess player is His Excellency. He calculates with geometric precision and serene logic.''

It was this fundamental logic which years ago had prompted Yamamoto, then a young naval attaché assigned to the Japanese Embassy in Washington, to become a serious student of the American wars. The American Civil War, in particular, fascinated him. He became, over the years, a veritable buff. In round-table discussions at the Army and Navy Club across from Farragut Square, where he was a frequent guest, he amazed his Yankee hosts with his knowledge and depth of understanding. The tactics and strategies of Lee, Grant, Longstreet, Sherman, Sheridan, Jackson, and Meade were familiar to him. And he openly admired the qualities of the American fighting man.

Unlike many of his peers in the Japanese command echelon, Yamamoto had the deepest respect for the United States and its people. From this knowledge, he felt, would come a better judgment of an opponent's character should, heaven forbid, the United States ever emerge as an enemy of his homeland.

He had agonized with himself when it happened. Now, on October 19, with the morning chess game over, he would use that source material to his advantage. In the months since Pearl Harbor, the chess master was certain he had detected the presence of an historic American flaw. It had appeared before, in other battles and campaigns. It would appear again, he felt sure. He had studied and trained for this moment. Now he would exploit it.

And just in time.

Outside flag quarters there was a shuffling of feet in the companionway. A conference had been scheduled

249

for 10 A.M. His guests were here and the fatal flaw would be outlined.

As his staff filed in, Yamamoto glanced out the porthole to where the battleship *Musashi*, sister ship of the *Yamato*, swung at anchor. Together they were the mightiest battlewagons ever launched.

He turned to the seated men. First it would be well, he announced, to review our own mistakes. Many blunders have been made. The most tragic of all? He looked around the cabin, eliciting several responses. To each he waved a professional finger: no, no, not even close.

His chess partner of that morning has provided history with a documented précis how Yamamoto described the greatest Japanese error up to that point in the war.

We have underestimated the strength of American resolve. They too have Bushido, of a different sort. We must never overestimate our own *seishan* and denigrate theirs. It will not work to our advantage, for they too are warriors and they will fight hard.

The annihilation of the Ichiki Detachment, the slaughter of the Kawaguchi Brigade, the entrapment of the 4th Infantry of the Sendai Division along the Matanikau . . . all are examples. Such operations, conducted with disregard of the American spirit, are wasteful, criminal, unacceptable.

All future operations of this command are to be closely coordinated, and piecemeal commitments discontinued.

Word has just come in from Seventeenth Army headquarters that General Hyakutake's attack, originally scheduled to be launched tomorrow, has been postponed until 21 October. I have approved this postponement so as to assure the very coordination of which I speak.

The position in regard to comparative land strengths is acceptable. Reinforcements landed the past three days have been effected to bring our forces to approximately twenty-seven thousand. The marines are estimated to have somewhat less than that, despite the appearance of new army units of untried worth.

But the most important ground statistic is this: while the marine garrison is battle-weary after two and a half months of constant action, more than half of our battalions are fresh. Two marine parachute battalions, our intelligence reports, have been evacuated, mere skeleton forces. Malaria has filled the marine hospitals, we are told. More than seven hundred new cases were reported last week, and further evacuation by air has been slowed by the condition of Henderson Field and the shortage of gasoline.

Yet none of this is to be taken as a serious impairment of the fighting resolve of the remaining garrison, however weakened. Such an evaluation would only repeat a mistake that has been made too many times before. Still, it will be difficult for the marines to receive replacements and to be resupplied—we must see to that. And we ourselves will be able to make good our battle losses.

Let us explore, gentlemen, that strategic flaw I spoke of before. In each instance since the invasion of August 7, the American navy, particularly its carrier force, has always executed a withdrawal to the south and east. I have asked myself why, and I shall ask you this same question. Clearly they are very much concerned about their base at Ndeni, in the Santa Cruz Islands. Is that where the raw nerve of the enemy high command lies most exposed? Is it like the hand which is drawn instinctively to a sore tooth?

Consider this: do they so fear a thrust on their right flank, their line of communications Noumea-Fiji-Samoa, that they would risk the recapture of Guadalcanal?

The evidence, Yamamoto concluded, confirmed this rationale. He then turned historian to shore up his conclusion. Three times during the American Civil War, he related, President Abraham Lincoln had been disturbed by the threat to Washington. It had happened first following the first battle of Bull Run, and again after Second Bull Run, when General Lee crossed the Potomac and invaded Maryland. It happened yet a third time when Early's ragged columns moved north from the Shenandoah Valley, late in the war. Each time Lincoln had reacted the same way, disrupting Union grand strategy.

"There is a historical parallel here," the admiral explained. "My American opponent, Admiral Ghormley, has demonstrated that same diffidence on three separate and distinct occasions. Now there is to be a fourth."

For the task at hand, Yamamoto believed he had the muscle. He had five battleships on station. The Yanks had two. Japanese heavy and light cruisers outnumbered the enemy's, fourteen to nine; the imperial destroyer force had a numerical superiority or forty-four to twenty-four.

"As to carriers, the disparity is even more important, with yet another factor in our favor: the reluctance of the American commanders to keep them on the scene. However, the *Enterprise*, our informants report, is no longer at Pearl Harbor. We must assume that she is headed our way. That gives them two against our four."

The odds were right. And so the area of greatest sensitivity, Santa Cruz, became the meeting-place of the adversaries. That would leave the marine garrison on Guadalcanal unsupported during its moment of greatest need.

It was, as any football coach would have conceded, a good game plan. But it overlooked one major historic parallel. In the War Between the States, Lincoln had finally called in a man named Grant, and Grant had a single-track mind. He believed in attack; he held that the best defense of Washington lay in a good offense. He persuaded the president to his view.

Chester Nimitz also had made a substitution: Ghormley out, Halsey in.

Out of the huddle came Halsey's first "audible." It passed through the fleet. It hit all stations and depots. It was repeated on the line at the 'Canal: three sharply barked words.

"Attack, repeat, attack."

Game time at Santa Cruz was only a few days away.

To the men on the Big E, the *Enterprise*, just arrived from Pearl, the order had a familiar ring. They knew the man well. "By God," the word went around the wardrooms, "it looks like we're going after 'em now."

There was no cheering in the foxholes. Along the perimeter they didn't know Halsey from Adam's off ox. But if the three-word order had bought them some time, well and good.

Unknown to them, however, a lonely, giant chess-game was underway across thousands of miles of the vast Pacific. Two not-dissimilar opponents had lined up their pieces. As Bull Halsey waited aboard the *Argonne* at Noumea Bay, Yamamoto moved the first pawn.

All through those late October days and nights, signs of a massive Japanese buildup were unmistakable. Far down the coastal road the rumble of tanks could be heard on occasion. Heavy Japanese artillery, manhandled far back into the bush, opened up with renewed intensity. Pistol Pete now ringed the perimeter. Against this weight of metal, the five-inchers of the marine 3d Defense Battalion, under Col. Bob Pepper, were used as counterbattery weapons and succeeded in silencing several of the guns. Maj. Sam Taxis, the battalion 3, estimated them to be of 155mm caliber.

The dramatic order of Admiral Halsey—"Attack, repeat, attack"—was being translated along the perimeter into "Dig, repeat, dig." Casualties of all types mounted steadily, from artillery, air strikes, naval bombardment and, most of all, from disease.

Jitters were developing. At the divisional meeting on October 19—the morning following the transfer of command from Ghormley to Halsey—General Vandegrift could feel the tension in the air as his commanders sat down on ammo boxes, ration cases, and the few campstools that served as headquarters furniture.

They were all there, his battle-tested, weary veterans: Gerry Thomas, Ed Buckley, Merrill Twining, and Randy Pate from division; Clifton Cates, Red Mike Edson, Sims, and Chesty Puller from the line regiments.

Vandegrift made his summary after all the staff reports had been detailed. "Across the river-line to the west, the enemy is getting into position. This appears to be a new tactic. We can expect an attack at any time. Maybe tonight, maybe tomorrow night. We're as well set defensively as we can reasonably hope to be, all things considered. That's about it, gentlemen. Thank you and good luck."

He asked General Geiger to stay behind, and when they were alone Vandegrift motioned the Cactus chief to sit down. A message from the new theater commander had just come in. Vandegrift held it aloft.

"Halsey wants me to come to Noumea," he said softly. "My going is apt to make it a little tougher on you for a few days."

"I can take it, General," Geiger said, rubbing his jaw.

Vandegrift smiled. "I know you could. In essence, my absence means that you'll be the ground commander here."

"Aw, f' Christ's sake, no! How about Rupertus?"

"I considered that, Roy, but I need him where he is, on Tulagi, ramrodding the aviation gasoline problem, getting the fuel to Henderson. He'll, of course, be technically in command, but you're here on the ground. Besides, the tactical dispositions are as complete here as I can make them. Now, when can you get me out?"

"Get your hat, General. I'll find you something."

It was to be a short conference at Noumea, Vandegrift explained. "Just keep this chair warm for me," he grinned, patting the Cactus chief on the shoulder. "I hope they don't hit us tonight. But if they do," he shrugged, "you've heard it all. You know exactly what we've got and what we haven't got."

Geiger got on the phone. "Get the Goose ready," he said.

Later, looking down through a porthole in the Blue Goose as she circled for altitude, Vandegrift shook his head. There had been sniping at his back, he was well aware of that. He'd caught the zings from several quarters ever since the August 7 landings. Why hadn't the perimeter been extended? Does Vandegrift have the offensive potential? Should we have a guy in there who can motivate? He'd heard it all, and he had shrugged it off. Maybe today's the day when I lose the command, he mused. Well, that's okay, if they want it that way. I did my best.

In the fight game, there are punchers and there are counterpunchers. Archer Vandegrift was a counterpuncher: patch a window here, close a door there. A sandbag general with a shovel. The conservationist at work.

He had battled many an enemy besides the Japs in the past eleven weeks, he reflected. From his battered briefcase he took out a dog-eared report submitted by his divisional surgeon. He intended to lay it on the conference table at Noumea.

The psychological factors resulting from the terrain and climate are tremendously important. After a man has subsisted for days in a wet slit-trench, or in a swamp, his physical stamina diminishes materially. This serves to make him extremely nervous, and causes him to attribute to any unfamiliar jungle noise the spectre of Japanese activity. Such reactions prey upon his mind until he may be reduced to a pitifully abject state, incapable of aggressive action.

Constant high humidity lessens combat effectiveness, sapping human energy and will. Dengue and malaria fever are widespread, and there has been a large increase in the number of cases of fatal blackwater fever and scrub typhus. Both amoebic and bacillary dysentery are common within the command, despite the most vigorous precautions, and tropic ulcers and "jungle rot" develop frequently at the slightest break in the skin.

Casualties from hookworm, ringworm, and yaws were listed. The battle against insects was detailed: despite the tightest medical precautions mosquitoes, leeches, chiggers, and fleas continued to flourish. Giant ants, the marines had already learned, could remove the flesh from a corpse overnight, leaving only white bones and a grinning skull.

Guadalcanal, the general mused, was a place where those in command must learn to husband their strength. He had become a wary fortress-keeper, enclave defense his specialty. But was that good enough? Halsey would want to make sure.

Vandegrift thought back to his fury over being left "bare-ass naked" when the Navy sailed away on August 9. That one still rankled, way deep down. If anything like that came up again, he might let it all out. One more time. For the final time? Well, maybe fifty-five was old enough to cash in the chips. He felt older, a lot older.

The council of war convened aboard the *Argonne* later that evening. Halsey presided, beetle-browed, gruff, decked out in fresh, open-necked suntans. There was a lot of brass on hand. Maj. Gen. Alexander M. Patch, commander of the army's American Division, was there. He would want to know how his 164th Infantry Regiment was doing. Vandegrift wondered if he were waiting in the wings. Maj. Gen. Millard Harmon, the senior army officer in the theater, was at the table, a long yellow tablet at his elbow. From Marine Corps Headquarters there was the Commandant himself, Lt. Gen. Thomas Holcomb, out to get a look-see at what was going on and to help resolve the natural "growing pains" resulting from this first major amphibious operation. Maj. Gen. Clayton Vogel, commander of the 1st Marine Amphibious Corps had come along with General Holcomb to add his expertise in solving some of the problems besetting the participants.

Of course the navy was fully represented, staff officers of COMSOPAC filling in the gaps. And at one end of the table, directly opposite Vandegrift, sat Richmond Kelly Turner, slim, cool, reserved, his gray-thatched hair cropped closely, almost nothing detracting from his appearance of self confidence.

If there was to be a confrontation, these two were admirably placed for it.

The meeting seemed to be routine—those present had been through it many hundreds of times. There were summaries by staff on the situation of friendly forces, information of the enemy, status of troops, supplies, materiel, planes, ships. There were discussions of the facts and figures, and logistics based accordingly.

At last the maps were rolled up, the notes initialed and tucked away. The decks had been cleared for the ultimate decision. Halsey moved to the issue with characteristic bluntness. Looking Vandegrift squarely in the eye, he asked, "In your opinion, General, should we evacuate or hold?"

There it was, laid out cold on the table. Vandegrift was just as succinct. "I can hold, Admiral." After a pause, he slowly shifted his gaze to the man directly across the table, as though to indicate the man for whom the weight of his further remarks was really intended. Kelly Turner stared back at him, shifting uncomfortably. "But I'll tell you this. We've got to have one helluva lot more support than we've been getting." The voice was conversationally subdued, but the clenched fists on the edge of the table added eloquence.

Turner took this hard, it was noted. He could not accept the implied criticism from a former subordinate without a reply.

Halsey waved him on. "There are always two sides to a coin," he said. "I want to see both. Then I'll make the final decision, and I'll expect everybody to abide by it. I hope that's understood."

Turner complained about his bases, which had admittedly proven inadequate for handling the problems of supply. "We have fewer ships than the Japanese and must of sheer necessity conserve those we have. Moreover, the waters around Guadalcanal do not allow for the freedom of maneuver we need for the proper disposition and protection of surface vessels and carriers," he pointed out. "We must live within the restrictions imposed upon us by the enemy. He can operate on interior lines of supply. He has excellent harbors, Rabaul, Kavieng, Truk, and a string of subsidiary bases, Buin, Bougainville, the Shortlands. It follows that our line of communications is longer and in constant danger."

It had all been said before, many times, during the past eleven weeks. From the standpoint of pure naval strategy it certainly had validity. But to Vandegrift, the fortress-keeper, the words were unacceptable.

There was silence as Turner came to a close. All eyes were on the Bull. He thanked them for their attendance and promised an early decision. That was his way. He held up one finger: "There is one decision, however, that awaits no postponement, gentlemen. This man," he pointed at Vandegrift, "remains in command on Guadalcanal."

Halsey's brows shot up, in a gesture which his officers recognized as the question, "Is there any further business?" Then he smiled and pushed his chair back, and the assemblage came to its feet. Walking around the table, he draped his arm over the shoulders of his reaffirmed division commander. They moved quietly toward the companionway and the guards stepped back.

"I promised you the meeting would be short, General," he said. "You've got work to do . . . and so have I. Right now, I can only tell you one thing: you'll get everything I've got. And that's a promise!"

It was 0500 hours on Wednesday, October 21, when the field telephone rang at division headquarters on Guadalcanal. Geiger appeared, with tousled hair and rumpled fatigues, but wide awake. He was tending the store.

"General, Bill Stickney here. Sorry to get you up, sir, but it looks like it's starting." Stickney was the light colonel commanding the 3d Battalion, 1st Marines. His position was along the Matanikau, near the river's mouth.

"What ya got, Bill?"

"Tanks. It sounds like ten or more of 'em. They're heading for the sandbar on my right."

"You got the 57s in place?"

"Yes, sir. But we might need some help."

"You'll get it. I'll call for artillery on the sandbar." Orders started flashing around the perimeter. The Cactus Air Force chief was behind the counter, opening shop. The counterpuncher wasn't back yet. But word from Noumea was that he soon would be.

This time he'd have a new man in his corner: Bull Halsey.

17

THE HORSESHOE

The threatened tank attack against the river-mouth failed to materialize in the early morning hours of October 21. Stickney's forward observation posts, he reported to Geiger, had actually counted nine. But like the king's men in the nursery rhyme, they had marched up the hill . . . and marched back again. Their mere presence on the field, Stickney said, had created an atmosphere of apprehension among the troops, which he deplored.

There had been, Geiger noted at breakfast, a lot of backing and filling of late. There was an unmistakable note of indecision in the enemy's stop-and-go tactics. At staff meeting later in the morning he ventured a guess that "somebody was catching hell" over on the other side of the Matanikau.

As a man wearing two hats, Geiger's own position as Cactus Air Force boss had been considerably relieved. The elderly oiler *Southard* had safely run the gauntlet on the previous night with a precious 175 drums of aviation gas. Even better, a PAB barge with 2,000 drums, towed by the tug *Seminole*, had got through to Tulagi, whence its cargo could be ferried across to

Kukum dock in smaller vessels. Henderson Field was still closed, but the fighter strip remained operational, and now it had gas—for a few days anyway. Meanwhile, Pistol Pete kept up a sporadic bombardment, some of the shells falling uncomfortably close to the strip.

The general had been right in his guess that someone was catching hell. Down at Tassafaronga Point, the latest object of Lieutenant General Hyakutake's wrath left the headquarters tent pale and shaken. Colonel Oka and his Imperial Engineers had run into unexpected roadblocks. The Maruyama Trail, so neatly laid out on the maps, was turning into a morass.

It was a pity. For the Seventeenth Army commander had pinned his highest hopes on an early completion of the Maruyama Trail. When fully completed, the trail would carve a broad track around the marine defenses. Its route ran along the Matanikau to a spot upriver named Ippon Bashi—literally, "One-tree Bridge." On Yank maps this spot was identified as "Nippon Bridge," and Chesty Puller had used the crossing himself when he set a death trap for the 4th Infantry.

Colonel Oka had reported that work was more or less on schedule up to that point. But from Ippon Bashi southward around Edson's Ridge, the trail petered out into a single-file jungle trail. On October 21 the Japanese moved over it with agonizing slowness. Manhandled artillery blocked the right-of-way; ammo carriers slipped and fell in the treacherous footing. Infantry units moving up were halted for hours on end at blind crossings. The Maruyama Trail was fast becoming a logistical nightmare. Once more, Japanese strategy and Japanese tactics had met head-on. On the unfinished Maruyama Trail, preparation fell victim to an unyielding field order. Already the problems on the trail had caused a day's postponement of the original attack. Now there would have to be additional delays, a trembling Oka had told his superior.

Unthinkable. There could be no further postponement. In his field order already issued, Hyakutake had decreed that all troops moving into position would carry fifty pounds of ammunition in addition to their regular field packs. Ippon Bashi groaned and shook under the load. Equally shaken, Colonel Oka had left headquarters with the exhortation of his general to redouble his efforts.

Late in the afternoon, a runner from a marine forward observation post hustled into division headquarters with a field message for the D-2, Lt. Col. Ed Buckley. A Japanese officer had been spotted studying the airfield with field glasses from a position on Edson's Ridge, scene of the great September battle. Buckley read the report and handed it to the D-3, Lieutenant Colonel Twining. "Bad news, Merrill. They're at our back door again."

Colonel Thomas, the chief of staff, joined them. He had just received fresh and disturbing reports of a new landing down the coast to the east. Native scouts were describing units, identified as belonging to the 38th Imperial Division, landing near Tasimboko. That knocked the defense posture of a single front into a cocked hat. A double envelopment was shaping up.

"We'd better get hold of del Valle," Thomas said.

Pedro A. del Valle commanded the 11th Marines. He had made the landing as the division's senior colonel, and it had been his 105s and pack-75s that had turned the tide at Bloody Ridge, now called Edson's Ridge. One of the Corps' most respected artillerists, del Valle had received his first star on October 9. He was now Brigadier General del Valle. And the brigadier had problems of his own.

He was going over these with his executive officer, Lt. Col. Bob Luckey, when the call came in from Division. Del Valle, hurrying over, brought with him an armload of maps and overlays. Geiger, Luckey, Thomas, and Buckley got their heads together over them. "We've got twelve batteries in position," del Valle explained, "all but one on the periphery of the airfield." The lone battery position outside the periphery was just west of the Lunga River; it was the only battery capable of laying down concentrations of fire along the Matanikau. "It's not enough, gentlemen, at least not the way I see it. I recommend that we displace nine batteries of 105s and 75s across the Lunga to these points. The bridges across the Lunga are not too strong, so I've already positioned amphibian tractors here," he indicated on the map, "and there, to drag the guns out should the log bridges collapse. The rain isn't helping any either."

The new brigadier went on. "We've studied the terrain maps, and it seems certain that an assault on the Matanikau will require the Japs to use severely restricted assembly areas. Not only that," he continued, "but they seem intent as well on extending their right in an encircling movement. And it's bunching them up even deeper, like the small end of a funnel. In short, they're going to be stacked pretty thick right here, and here—where the ridgelines

265

impinge on the coastal track—during their approach march.

"Now, we know the ranges, and we've divided the area into strips paralleling the line of fire. Each battery has been assigned one strip, which it can cover by increasing or decreasing range."

"They used to call that 'laddering' in World War I, right?" General Geiger made the point.

"Exactly. We've gone back a war for this one. I never thought we'd use it in the jungle, but it'll work." Del Valle covered another concern. "Remember, this is not tank country. They've got a dozen mediums over there. But there's only one way for them to come." A big bony finger pointed at the mouth of the Matanikau. "Besides the antitank guns up front, we've got this battery . . . and this one . . . zeroed in on the sandbars."

Geiger nodded in approval. There was one thing bothering him, however. "What about this new poop we've got? How about the Tenaru, and this area in back of the ridge?"

The marines' newest one-star shrugged. There was a certain amount of resignation implied. "I think it's diversionary. I believe they're going to make their main effort here." Again he indicated the Matanikau.

Geiger shifted in his seat. He wished nothing more than that Vandegrift would get back. His staff, and del Valle, were looking at him expectantly. "How soon can you get moving?" he asked.

"Oh, hell, we're already on the way. Trying to beat the rains." There was a hearty chuckle all around, at Geiger's expense. He shook it off with a grin as if to say, if you can't beat 'em, join 'em. The marines hadn't yet lost their sense of humor.

They had lost some men, however, down by the mouth of the Matanikau. As the late afternoon turned into brief tropical twilight, Company I of the 1st Marines had come under heavy artillery fire. Stickney, the battalion C.O., again came on the wire. ''They're throwing a strong combat patrol against our positions, and we can hear the tanks again,'' he reported. Division kept an open line to the forward command post. Before dark it was all quiet once more. One medium tank out of the nine that had poked a tentative nose across the sandbar had been shot up, its hull blackened. The battalion turned back the combat patrol. The action had cost six dead and twenty-five wounded.

All through the night, del Valle's gunners were busy, moving their batteries up and preparing—with the World War I tactics of Château Thierry and Saint-Mihiel—a box barrage.

On October 22, the Old Man still hadn't returned from Noumea, but he had been in touch and had been filled in. Aside from Pistol Pete and the counterbattery fire from the marine 5-inchers, the day passed quietly. Duke Davis, Joe Foss, and Fred Payne led small flights of F4Fs out to see what the Japanese were up to in the area around Cape Esperance. The jungle hid most of the movement, but an occasional and ominous glint of steel came through between the rain squalls.

It was nearing 1800 hours and mess was about over when the peace of October 22 was disturbed. Along the eastern sector of the perimeter, now called ''the Horseshoe,'' another heavy Japanese bombardment got underway. Once again most of it was leveled at the positions of the 3d Battalion, 1st Marines. It waxed in intensity until darkness fell. Then tanks were heard approaching as the Japanese artillery ceased fire.

A forward observation post of the 3d Battalion, 7th Marines, called back to its command post. "We can see 'em, Colonel! There's a million of them following the goddamned tanks!"

"Get out quick. Fall back to the main line of defense." Lt. Col. Bill Williams passed back the word to Regiment. "They're coming at us," he told Col. Amor Sims. "We're laying down an 81 barrage."

The mortars of the two adjacent battalions started coughing. At the front, their yellow H-E explosions bloomed, twelve barrels putting 108 rounds into the air every thirty seconds. The automatic weapons of the visually engaged battalions began their deadly chatter.

Back at Division the tumult of battle rolled in through the night. Pedro del Valle's phone rang. He had anticipated the call. "On the way," he told Geiger. Ten batteries were going into action on del Valle's prearranged plan to ladder down from Point Cruz to the river-line. Counting the 75s, 105s, the 81- and 60mm mortars, and the antitank guns, there were close to a hundred pieces blasting away at the narrow approach-trails through which the Japanese attack had to be channeled.

The first enemy wave was stopped cold. The burning hulks of several tanks lit up the sandbar over which they had vainly attempted to penetrate.

As the Sendai Division regrouped, del Valle's gunners laddered back to its assembly areas. It was an artilleryman's dream: the ocean on one side, the hills on the other. No way to go save forward. Again and again they came, the Emperor's Own. Again and again they were thrown back.

At the gun positions, ammunition passers collapsed by the trails during the lulls of what was to become a six-hour cannonade. Gunners sweated and yelled for more ammo; the trucks bringing it forward roared back and forth through the night. Battalion commanders, on the line to their forward observers, checked and rechecked their coordinates. Directing the mechanical maw were Lt. Col. Manley Curry, 1st Battalion; Maj. Forest Thompson, 2d Battalion; Lt. Col. Jim Keating, 3d Battalion; Lt. Col. Mel Fuller, 4th Battalion, and Maj. Noah Wood, Jr., 5th Battalion.

"Jesus Christ, how can they keep coming?" That was Noah Wood's reaction as his observer noted wearily that another wave was forming.

"What time you got?" queried the voice on the other end.

The major looked at his watch. "Straight up twenty-three hundred."

"Better get ready . . . here we go again! For God's sake, how many times does that make?"

The major didn't know. His firing orders had become routine. He called them out, and the noses of the howitzers that were lined off to his right rose in unison as the wheels were spun. The front lit up again. Out on the sandbar, tanks appeared once more; behind them, a shadowy wave pressed forward in the dim light of other tank hulls still on fire. *"Banzai!"* it shrieked over the clatter of the treads. But this time the sound, to those who had heard it too often before, sounded less menacing.

One lone tank made it across the sandbar. From its

turret, machine-gun fire sprayed the bushes, back and forth. It was in defilade; the marine antitank guns could not depress far enough to reach it.

"Get him, get him, get him!"

From a nearby machine-gun position, one of the loaders detached himself and crawled forward. He tossed a grenade between the treads. The tank, buzzing and chattering, spun in a crazy circle at the water's edge, like a big bug with only one wing. A dark silhouette moved out from the cover of the trees. Its long tube belched four times, and the tank was suddenly ablaze. A marine half-track with a flamethrower had provided the *coup de grâce.*

It was all over at midnight—all over save for the moans of the wounded and dying on the far side of the Matanikau. Sixteen blackened tank-hulls stood on the sandbar against the backdrop of the sea and distant Savo. Already the incoming tide was splashing over broken treads and limply dangling ordnance.

The big PBY carrying General Vandegrift back to his command from the Noumea conference banked ponderously over Sealark Channel and commenced its descent. Heavy cloud formations hung over the island, and sight contact with the escorting F4Fs was quickly lost in a line of rain squalls.

The general stumbled forward from his seat and tapped the pilot on the shoulder, pointing down. The pilot nodded, then altered the plane's approach a few points to starboard.

Vandegrift wanted to take a look at the Horseshoe, that portion of the marine perimeter which faced the Matanikau.

Now the PBY slid under the low cloud-bank that had hidden the river from above. And there, upstream, sat Nippon Bridge, with the extension of the Maruyama Trail curling away like a muddy thread to the east.

There was not much to see after all, the general conceded to himself. He returned amidships to gather up his gear when the plane touched down on the fighter strip and taxied up to the Cactus command post.

Colonel Joe Bauer peered out of the Operations shack at the new Fighter Strip No. 2 and watched as Geiger's jeep, returning from division headquarters, sloshed to a stop. In the deluge, Bauer couldn't see across the runway. As a matter of fact, he couldn't even see the runway itself. To Joe Bauer's eyes the strip was a solid muddy lake.

"It ain't a fit day out for man or beast, W. C. Fields would say," he joked to the general.

"Yeah, but look at those doggone Seabees. Nobody's told them."

The newly arrived naval construction battalions were a tough breed, both had to conclude. They were an all-weather group if ever there was one. Today they had their blades, tractors, big trucks, and earth-moving equipment chugging along and looking more like Mississippi river-barges than like what they were. The monsoon season, Pistol Pete, and the Tokyo Express might make the working lot of the Seabees miserable, but the Seabees got the job done. Some of the damage from the Night of the Battleship still remained, but it was fast disappearing; and, although it was behind schedule, the emplacement of metal landing mats was being pushed forward. With these "Marston mats," Fighter Strip No. 2 would soon be an all-weather strip.

The two men were still watching from the doorway of the shack when a geyser of mud and water rose noisily less than a hundred feet away. They ducked, and Bauer cursed—Ol' Pete was at it again. It was damned lucky, Geiger observed, that those bastards had to hand-carry every round.

"Suppose they had ammo trucks" said Vandegrift. "What we gotta do, Joe, is see that they never get them. What they can hand-carry, we can take. So it's up to us to see that they don't get a road net built."

The Seabee crews had constructed the underfooting of No. 2 very well. They had dug coral rock at Lunga Point and hauled it in. Coral provides magnificent drainage. Bauer was amazed by its porous quality. "You know, General, if the rain stops for just an hour, there's dust flying out there."

The fighter command boss was happy to be relieved as Cactus chief. Bauer had been as glad to see Geiger as Geiger had been to see Vandegrift.

Now Bauer and Geiger huddled. "Not much action the past two days," Bauer said. "A lucky thing, too. The field doesn't look like much, but under all that water it's fully operational again."

"Joe, how do your guys feel about the Zeke pilots they've seen lately? Has there been any change in their performance?"

Bauer's face grew serious. "Yeah. We've pretty well knocked that around in bull sessions the past couple of days. They sure aren't getting any better. Maybe it's because our guys are better trained. And don't forget, Jack Smith's gang [Major Smith had been rotated home in September] blew away as much as half of their first-line people. We dogfight 'em these days, every chance we get."

"How's their maintenance?"

"Not so good either. It's like you see on the backstretch at the Indianapolis 500. A car goes sour, there's a puff of black smoke from its tailpipe. We see that, too, and then they just pull out and head for home."

"Interesting."

"Yeah, you wonder why."

If the two men could have been present at the inspection of Japanese airfields outside Tokyo following the surrender ceremonies aboard the *Missouri*, they would have noted some eight thousand imperial planes grounded because they were missing just a single part or two. But on October 23, 1942, they had as yet no hard proof of this already growing attrition, although Joe Bauer and his boys had an inkling of it.

By 1030 the rain had stopped, and Bonzo was reporting bogeys on the way. The field galvanized into action. At 1100 Bauer's promise of "dust within an hour" came true, and Duke Davis, Joe Foss, and Fred Payne took off, with their squadrons behind them. The F4Fs pushed back clouds of coral dust in their slipstreams.

The long barrels of the 3d Defense Battalion's ack-ack swung skyward.

The Cactus Air Force, so nearly out of gas after the pounding by the *Kongo* and the *Haruna*, put up twenty-four F4Fs and four P-39s for the intercept. The fighters spotted the incoming Zeros, and the dogfight was on.

Far below, the newly arrived army boys saw their first Zeke go down. Soon there were other planes spinning down in flames, the smoke darkening the white cumulus. Theirs or ours? Impossible to say. The 90s of Bob Pepper's and Dave Nimmer's ack-ack batteries had opened with a full-throated roar against the incoming Japanese bombers. Five of the Bettys exploded in midair on the approach. Five more broke away short of their bombing run and headed north. They would be picked off, one by one, by Davis, Foss, and Payne and their squadrons. Only six of the sixteen Japanese bombers who made their appearance that day returned to base.

Geiger and his fighter chief watched the "count-back." The fighter intercom linkup behind them had ceased its mumbo-jumbo of the melee. They were coming in, all twenty-eight of them, one 'cripple' leading the circling pack. The cripple turned out to be Joe Foss's F4F, which later had to be 'dozed off the end of the runway, a pile of junk.

Foss got a jeep ride back to Ops where the pilots were assembled. Geiger stepped forward. "This is getting to be a habit, Joe." It was the fourth shot-up plane Foss had managed to bring back, safe but unsalvageable. The kidding was merciless, all around. It was a jubilant group.

The debriefing was a hectic affair. A clear picture was never collected from the interrogation. Banked hands simulated snap-rolls and pullouts as their owners vied with each other in the excited clamor. Clearly, it was Cactus's finest showing yet. Geiger let the kettle boil over and got on the wire to Division.

"I don't know how many, Arch. We probably will

never get it straight. Looks like we shot down seventeen out of twenty-eight Zekes, and we got ten or twelve of the sixteen Bettys. Yeah, thanks. Thanks a lot. I'll pass the word to the boys. We're sure happy down here."

Far to the south, Admiral Halsey received the relayed report with grim satisfaction. It was his kind of show. He himself had scheduled a rendezvous below the New Hebrides; Task Forces 16 and 17 were forming. For a month, the *Hornet* had been the only carrier on station in the South Pacific. She and her escort, the battleship *Washington*, made up one task force under Rear Adm. Tom Kincaid. Joining her this day from Pearl was the *Enterprise*, supported by the fine new battleship *North Dakota*.

True to his promise, the Bull was about to give all he could to the embattled marines. The two carriers and two battleships, plus their escorting cruisers and destroyers, were to head round the Santa Cruz Islands, then set a northwesterly course to cover Guadalcanal.

Through the night of October 23 the Japanese were on the move, their axes ringing through the jungle, clearing trail. All the way up past Nippon Bridge, marine outposts reported the forward movement of troops and supplies.

From Tassafaronga Point, Lieutenant General Hyakutake had requested another day's postponement of his main attack. Yamamoto, reluctantly entertaining the request, had discovered a newly found impatience. Yet it had been he who, only four days ago, had cautioned against attack until all the pieces were in place.

But now there were the navy's fuel tanks to be

considered; and as the gauges dropped, the admiral grumbled about landlubber generals who seemed to believe that his ships were sailing on a sea of oil.

The 164th Infantry, late of the American Division, had also been up through the night of October 23, waiting for a call to move into line along the Matanikau. It had not come. But on the night of October 24, it did. The soldiers of the American, the only division in the U.S. Army without a numerical designation, would be going into action. They were National Guardsmen, these men of the 164th and their unit was a by-product of the triangulation of the old "square" divisions of the Guard shortly before the start of the war. Shipped to New Caledonia for staging, their new designation as the American Division had been a contraction of 'America' and 'Caledonia'.

They had already bedded down for the night when, at 2130 hours, the 3d Battalion field phone jingled to three rings of the crank.

"Colonel Hall? This is Merrill Twining. Are you ready?"

"Yes, sir, we're standing by."

"General Vandegrift is sending you in. No, not along the river. You're going in on Sector 3. Get your men in motion, we'll send guides to pick 'em up. You better shoot right over to Division and we'll fill you in."

In minutes the bivouac was turned into organized bedlam. Canteens were topped off, combat packs slung, tripods shouldered, ammo belts looped over sloping shoulders. The last letter from home was carefully folded and slipped into the wide combat pocket, along with K-rations and cigarettes. The jumble of men formed in an orderly column and stood silently, awaiting their guides. At the head of the column there was a quiet conference. Then a barely audible "Move out." The 164th was going into the line.

At division headquarters Lt. Col. Robert K. Hall joined the meeting already in progress. Twining, the operations officer, beckoned him to the map. "It looks like what we're up against in Sector 3 is the Koli Detachment of the 38th Imperial Division. That's the outfit the scouts reported landing last week down here, to the east of us. They have moved up the coastal track toward the Tenaru. Yeah, that's where the Ichikis and the Kawaguchis came at us. Puller's 1st Battalion of the 7th Marines is in position there.

"Now, about half an hour ago, one of Chesty's forward platoon positions was overrun. The outpost had orders to fall back if they were attacked in force. All except one man came back into the lines. We don't expect the main attack on Sector 3. But Chesty is stretched too thin to handle what we expect they'll throw at us. The terrain from the ridge to the Tenaru is lowland jungle country. You'll move your outfit in on Chesty's left flank, and extend it toward the Tenaru as far as you can. Right now there's a big hole there. The Japs might well try to pour through it."

Artillery concentrations were falling as the 3d Battalion, 164th Infantry, moved toward its assigned positions. Small groups of Japanese had already penetrated the front. One rather large salient had been pinched out by Puller's men shortly before dark.

Once more what looked so easy on the map became a nightmare on the ground. Hall's men, numbering almost a thousand, had to be committed piecemeal. The first unit stumbled into the left flank of the 7th Marines and proceeded to extend it further to the left; the next arrival moved blindly forward and extended another fifty yards. And so it went: grope forward, extend. Not exactly a textbook solution, but the 164th got in place.

Commitment was completed around midnight. By then it was raining buckets, and the massing of the enemy along the ridgeline was clearly audible. The 81mm mortars of the army troops quickly set up and joined the artillery fire. Within twenty minutes came the first *banzai;* it was an attack mounted on a narrow front of not more than a hundred yards. It would have outflanked Puller, but by now the army boys were in place, and their automatic weapons opened up, full throttle. From the rear the 105s and pack 75s reduced the range and increased the tempo of their fire. The first Japanese wave faltered and perished on the wire. Other waves arrived, right at the same spot—on the hour, every hour.

By 0700, in the light of early morning, the 164th could see what havoc it had administered. The Japanese were stacked up in windows along the wire. They had attacked a sector that their early-evening scouting had found unmanned; their tactics had never changed after it was fortified.

Mop-up operations began; prisoners were taken. By daylight, too, the defense posture of the Americans could be analyzed. The two commands were hopelessly intermixed. A light machine-gun section on Puller's left peered across a few yards and there, beside them, was a .30-caliber heavy, manned by the army. The two crews looked at each other in disbelief and amazement.

"Hey, were you the guys making all that racket last night?"

The gunner of the heavy stood up and shook off the rain like a Labrador. "Yeah, buddy, it was just us chickens."

"Oh, well. There goes the neighborhood."

That the enemy would be back was quickly confirmed in the early morning hours of October 25 as the marines and army troops disentangled and reorganized. Three Japanese regiments had participated in the attack on Sector 3. Their losses had been heavy, but last night's battle had to be marked down as the repulse of a reconnaissance-in-force. The Japanese high command had been looking for a soft spot, and they had been willing to pay the price for that information. Examinations of papers and diaries taken from the dead established that the force from the east had included units from the 29th Infantry, the 16th Infantry, and the 230th Infantry. There were also parts of the decimated Kawaguchi Brigade.

At the compound near division headquarters—a small wired-in area surrounding a few pyramidal tents—prisoners were being interrogated. There were few prisoners on Guadalcanal, and fewer still who could be persuaded to talk. When taken, most of them gave the *hari-kiri* sign, drawing an imaginary knife across their bellies. Most were surprised that they had been allowed to live. Some pleaded for knives so that they could end their disgrace in the traditional manner.

Among those who didn't was a sergeant of the 29th. Would he enjoy a cigarette? He bowed and hissed his pleasure. His own had been completely soaked last night. The division interpreter provided the match. Unique rapport had been established. "Tell me, why did you repeatedly attack on the same narrow front? Why, can you tell me, was there no attempt to probe for some weaker spot in our lines?"

The sergeant looked at his questioner with some amazement. He shrugged his narrow shoulders, puffed the cigarette reflectively, and launched a long, uninterrupted discourse.

"What did he say?" the division intelligence officer asked.

"Well, sir," the interpreter summarized, "he says the Japanese orders for battle had been oh so carefully worked out in advance, there was no question that they had to be followed, to the letter. No one, he says, from the top to the bottom of command, would have dared to improvise. If such a thing had been done, he says, it would have caused the general to lose much face."

Later, with the summary before him, Vandegrift shook his head in disbelief and looked across the planning table at his chief of staff.

"I guess I'll never understand these people."

But he didn't have to be hit on the head, he reasoned aloud. Sector 3 would catch it again. So would the Horseshoe. He allowed himself a moment of reflection. "They had a Mule Shoe once in the Civil War," he said to Jerry Thomas. "In the wilderness, remember? It cost Grant a helluva lot of men."

18

DUGOUT SUNDAY

Capt. Toshio Takama was awakened from a fitful slumber by a gentle tug on his shoulder. By instinct he looked at the luminous dial on his watch. "It is time. Takama-san," the voice above him said softly.

It had rained heavily during the three hours he had slept on the ground on the reverse slope of Mukade Hill. But it had not been the tropical downpour that had disturbed his sleep, for he had curled his slight five-foot-two-inch frame well within the perimeter of his generous rain coat, and he had been dry. No, it had not been physical discomfort, he thought. It was a sense of impending doom. Not for himself, he confided with the meticulous care of the confirmed diarist, but for his comrades of the 29th Infantry.

"For myself," he wrote, "I feel a curious immortality. It is as though I had been here before."

As Takama struggled to his feet, the horizon to the east of Lungo Channel lightened almost imperceptibly. Dawn of October 25 was only minutes away. The assistant adjutant of the 29th hurried to the command post, where he found his commanding officer, Col. Juro Hiroyasu, already awake.

" 'Ah, there you are, Takama,' he said to me with one of his rare smiles. 'We are witnesses to the dawn, perhaps my last.' "

The captain's diary of October 25 continued with this entry:

> I, of course, remonstrated with the colonel, pointing out that this was destined to become a glorious day of assured victory for our regiment, but I don't think he heard my words. Instead, he turned away, looking slowly from left to right. It was as though he wished every object to be engraved in his mind's eye for all time.

Hiroyasu bowed to the east, his adjutant wrote,

> and when he faced me again his countenance was animated, the tension and apprehension gone. He told me he wished me to accompany him to the division meeting where we would get our final briefing. This was unusual, for only high-ranking staff members attend such events. But I did not question the reason. His radiance carried me along.

At 0600 the officers had assembled under a huge tarpaulin. Maruyama nodded, and the division intelligence officer arose to give the estimate of enemy strength. "We are faced," he said, "by an enemy who is tired and battle-weary after nearly three months of action. Seventeenth Army intelligence puts the joint effective strength of marines and soldiers at ten thousand. They are well entrenched from the mouth of the Matanikau River to a distance upriver of almost a mile." The officers followed his pointer on the large map. "At this point, the American positions curl back along the line starting at the Matanikau River, going through Mukade Hill and then moving eastward toward the Tenaru. It is not," the intelligence officer emphasized, "a continuous line. Rather it is one of strong points and redoubts; Operation 174, which you have before you, carefully evaluates the strong points which protect the airfield. We have detailed the routes to be followed in attacking the marine lines."

The attack would have air support, the unit commanders were told. One of the heaviest bombing missions, covered by fighters, would be launched from airfields at Rabaul and Buin. Also on the way down: the Eighth and Second cruiser-destroyer fleets of Admirals Mikawa and Kondo.

There were hisses of approval from those who remembered the devastation wreaked on Henderson Field during the Night of the Battleships.

Major General Maruyama took the podium. He could now, he said, confide in them yet another strategic operation which would guarantee the success of the night attack of October 25–26. Far to the southeast of Guadalcanal, off the coast of Santa Cruz, Admiral Yamamoto had stationed a powerful force that would assure that no United States carrier or surface vessels would interfere with the operation. Commanded by Admiral Nagumo, the imperial force included four carriers—the *Junyo*, *Shokaku*, *Zuikaku*, and *Zuiho*—supported by the battleships *Kongo*, *Haruna*, *Hiei*, and *Kirishima*.

"The imperial forces on the sea and in the air," proclaimed Maruyama, "are united in the support of this great effort. Within the hour our artillery will commence its registration. The step-by-step coordination of all units of the Seventeenth Army is included in Operation 174. It will be followed . . . to the letter! One quick blow tonight and the airfield will be ours!''

An aide handed Maruyama his ceremonial sword. He bowed low and the officers scrambled to their feet and returned the bow.

The meeting had taken an hour. It was now 0700.

In Seventeenth Army headquarters at Rabaul, Lt. General Hyakutake studied Operation 174, which had been forwarded to him earlier by his ground commander. A marginal note in Maruyama's handwriting appeared opposite the following paragraphs:

1. In case the enemy forwards a surrender, the following demands should be made as to the intentions of the commander-in-chief, Japanese forces: The whole [American] force will immediately stop fighting and disarm.

2. After the enemy commander has transacted the terms of the first item, he shall be accompanied by the necessary side-guards and interpreters, head toward the mouth of the Matanikau River by way of the coastal road, and agree to the terms of the surrender to the commander of our force.

Maruyama's notation read: ''I hope, my dear general, that the details of the surrender ceremonies will prove satisfactory.'' Hyakutake nodded his head. Some four hundred miles to the south, the day to be known as Dugout Sunday had begun.

Father O'Brien was conducting early-morning mass

at divisional headquarters when Maj. Gen. Tadashi Sumiyoshi's artillery units began pumping out their sporadic registering fire. One of the rounds landed in a jungle ravine less than twenty-five yards away.

The concussion shook the small congregation, but not the padre. "I think," he said softly, "that we had better take communion underground." They headed for the divisional bombproof.

By 0800, at the morning briefing, it was becoming clear to General Vandegrift that something big was afoot. Unusually heavy intelligence reports had been filtering forward from Noumea, Pearl Harbor, and Washington. The air-waves had been humming for more than two hours. An extraordinary volume of fleet transmissions had been intercepted. The summation indicated that "a major Japanese offensive was about to be launched."

The telephone network to the forward OPs had been jammed for an hour. Gerry Thomas, the chief of staff, had been inundated with messages. He broke off to update his general.

"Sir, the artillery guys tell me the Japs have at least ten new battery emplacements. Maybe as many as twenty."

"Have we started counterbattery fire?"

"Not yet, sir. They say they're harder than hell to locate. They've got the high ground, you know, and they're in defilade. Del Valle wants to know whether Cactus can give him a hand with some spotter planes."

"Check with Geiger."

"Sure thing," the white-thatched Cactus boss shot back, on hearing the request. "We'll have a couple of P-400s up there when del Valle's ready. I'd suggest that we wait an hour, however, and see if this damned cloud cover lifts.''

''Thanks, General, I'll pass the word.'' Thomas relayed the intelligence about the almost quadrupled Japanese fleet intercepts of the past twenty-four hours and wondered whether the Cactus dawn patrol had spotted anything.

''Just a minute, Ger . . .''

The intercom at Cactus crackled.

''Fighter 2 . . . this is Red One.'' It was the squadron commander of the flight of six SBDs that had gone up earlier.

''Can you hear that, Gerry?''

The distortion increased, but the words were audible. Thomas grunted: ''Five by five.''

''Red One, what have you got?''

''We've got three Nip destroyers thirty-five miles out and headed your way at twenty knots. Cloud cover: one thousand feet. And now . . . as luck would have it . . . we've lost 'em! Over.''

''Continue search, Red One. Roger and out.''

Geiger put the phone to his head. ''Get it?''

''Got it, sir.''

Two hundred miles up the Slot from where Red One had spotted his advance destroyer force, Admiral Kondo was finishing a leisurely breakfast. The commander of the 2d cruiser-destroyer force was enjoying rice-cakes and a second cup of tea. Kondo's ships, together with Admiral Mikawa's veteran Eighth Fleet—which was steaming over the western horizon on a parallel course—would rendezvous that night off Guadalcanal. They were to shell the airfield in preparation for its capture.

Several disquieting intelligence reports had been broadcast to him in code from Yamamoto's fleet, which at this moment was to his east, sailing a southward course toward the Santa Cruz Islands.

"The whereabouts of the battleship *Washington* and her cruiser-destroyer screen cannot be pinpointed. The possible presence of this force in the area of your assigned mission cannot, repeat, cannot be ignored."

Kondo sighed and pushed his teacup away. If this were indeed so, there appeared to be one strategic error in Yamamoto's thrust toward Santa Cruz: it had not drawn off the entire weight of U.S. metal as had been anticipated.

Other pressing questions came to mind: Was the American airfield still alive? Would it be feasible to land Japanese planes there next day, when the island garrison had surrendered as General Hyakutake had assured him it would? He hoped he would have more concrete evidence of that surrender within the hour.

To get the hard facts, Kondo had authorized a daring mission. A big, two-engine reconnaissance plane had taken off two hours ago from the new airfield at Buin. She was loaded, not with bombs, but with the latest photographic equipment, including wide-angle lenses, zooms, and the most advanced cameras—gifts of a friendly Third Reich.

Word just back from his advance screening force indicated the most favorable weather conditions for the mission: low cloud cover all the way to the airfield. The reconnaissance plane and its eight escorting Zeros, flying at fifteen hundred feet, should make the trip unobserved.

Precisely at 0815, eight "bogeys" were heard through the one-thousand-foot ceiling that covered Henderson Field. Condition Red was flashed along the line. A big Japanese two-engine plane dropped out of the clouds that covered the end of the runway. It was Kondo's photo-mission plane, and she flew the entire length of Henderson at treetop level, cameras grinding away.

By the time the reconnaissance plane banked left toward Fighter 2, she had a welcoming committee. Every cook, baker, office pinkie, pilot, and mechanic on hand had grabbed up a weapon and was firing. The arsenal included Springfields, M1s, BARs, carbines, Thompson submachine guns, .45-caliber automatic pistols, and light machine-guns. It made for quite a racket.

With sheer bravado, the plane completed a full pass, cameramen dangling like monkeys from every angle of the opened plastic canopy. But she carried her luck about one hundred yards too far. The furious fusillade from the ground caught up with her, and just over the end of the runway a puff of white smoke blossomed out. The ship went into a steep wingover, both engines still at full throttle. There was no pulling out. She dove straight into the trees with a shattering roar that could be heard over the crash of artillery shells on the Horseshoe, four miles away. A giant fireball rose over the jungle.

Up above, the drone of the escort planes could be heard circling the field. That sound was drowned out as Joe Foss and a flight of four F4Fs roared down the runway to tangle with the Zekes.

Foss and his wingmen could apply their new "scissors technique." In bull sessions the past week Cactus pilots had adopted the scissors as the best tactic for fighting the Zero. "You turn into them—either from below or on top, it makes no difference," Foss had explained to newly arrived fliers. He worked his two hands back and forth as though he were operating a pruning shears. "Just meet 'em head on . . . and scissor them."

The technique worked splendidly. By 0900 the flight of Cactus interceptors was touching down on the runway. They had been aloft only twenty minutes. Foss taxied to his revetment. He pushed back his canopy, grinned down to his ground crew, and held up five fingers. The crew let out a cheer.

Behind Mukade Hill it was approaching 1000 hours as four generals put down their teacups and arose. They had been in close consultation for nearly three hours, and now the presiding officer, Maruyama, believed the full scope of Operation 174 was completely understood by all, and the final delegation of responsibility for its success clearly outlined.

There would be three attacking wings. Maj. Gen. Tadashi Sumoyoshi, the artillery commander, would be in command of forces attacking the Matanikau positions. The marines identified their works as the Horseshoe. There would be a frontal assault against the river redoubts, but the main effort would be a turning movement farther upstream to envelop the marines' left.

Maj. Gen. Yumio Nasu commanded the center. His task force would drive straight for the airfield, penetrating the marine strongpoints drawn across Mukade Hill. Japanese intelligence reported that the marines had named this sector Bloody Ridge.

Command of the third attack-force, reaching from Nasu's right to the mouth of the Tenaru River, would fall to Major General Kawaguchi. Maruyama had violently opposed the choice, but he had been overruled earlier by Lieutenant General Hyakutake, the Seventeenth Army boss.

"Give him a post of honor," Hyakutake had gently but firmly insisted. "He has earned the right to redeem himself."

Maruyama considered himself made of sterner stuff. There was no place, he argued, for an officer who had acknowledged defeat. The Kawaguchi Brigade had been slaughtered and dishonored. His protests had been to no avail, however, and Kawaguchi had been assigned to command the right wing. It was the smallest of the forces. Its major mission was to threaten and demonstrate against the Yankee left—to assure that no reinforcements could be drawn from that quarter to bolster the other two threatened sectors.

The details for the night's attack were completed. The artillery from the hills kept up its sporadic harassing fire. As the three general officers left their superior, Sumiyoshi drew Kawaguchi aside. The two were friends, comrades of other, happier occasions.

"It will come out all right, Kawaguchi-san. There will be honor enough to go around."

Down below them the clouds had lifted so that Sealark Channel was clearly visible. Several black dots appeared on the horizon. From one appeared a quick tiny flash of fire. Sixty seconds later the low rumble of gunfire, ten miles away, could be heard.

"I wonder if they are ours?" Kawaguchi asked.

"Let's hope so. And good luck." The two shook hands solemnly.

The sound of naval gunfire had taken only half a minute to reach the decks of the old four-stacker *Trevor* heading out of Tulagi harbor. The *Trevor* was a relic of World War I and a part of the "mothball fleet" that had slumbered away the time between wars in San Diego. Her Guadalcanal assignment was to carry torpedoes, ammunition, gasoline, and "goodies" across the channel from Tulagi. Now she was once more called to action—her decks piled high with cargo, and two new motor torpedo boats in tow. Lieutenant Commander Agnew called for flank speed, and the weary, rusted boilers responded.

There had been a warning from Cactus two hours earlier that three Japanese destroyers had been heading this way. And here they were, bearing east past Iron Bottom Sound. At a range of five miles and closing, the Japanese opened fire, salvos straddling the overladen Yank ships.

These had cut loose their tows. On the bridge of the *Trevor*, Agnew barked out his orders: to his gunnery officer to return fire, and to the helmsman to sail a more northerly course down the shoal-ridden Ngela Channel, which under ordinary circumstances he would have avoided like the plague.

The ship shuddered, engineers of the black gang getting an incredible twenty-nine knots out of her straining boilers. His three-inchers, Agnew knew, would not effectively carry the four miles now separating them from the onrushing Japanese ships. Short or not, the ship was being fought. The barking of the 3-inch barbette-mounted guns continued. Down below, the boiler casings burned clear through.

At 1030 hours, a half hour after action had commenced, Agnew ordered another sharp turn left. On the bridge of the nearby *Zane*, Lieutenant Commander Wirtz acknowledged the signal and executed. Then his ship staggered under a bracketing enemy salvo. One of her guns disappeared in the act of firing. Three of its crew were killed.

Salvation appeared in the form of four fighters out of Henderson Field. Cactus had come to the rescue. Abruptly, the *Akatsuki* put her helm over, and the *Ikazuchi*, the second Japanese destroyer, did likewise. The *Shiratsuyo* followed in line, fighting off the air attack as the course changed 90 degrees.

"Omigod," Lt. Carl Rasmussen said. "They're heading right for us." Up until now Rasmussen, skipper of YP-284, one of a collection of ragtag vessels that made up the Cactus Navy, had been just an interested spectator to the action. Now the three powerful enemy destroyers were heading straight for Lunga Point, where Rasmussen's "Yippie" had just finished unloading. At 1050 hours the hapless vessel was dead in the water and aflame. Minutes later she sank, carrying three marines to the bottom.

Out of the clouds a flight of forty Zekes appeared as cover for the attacking Japanese destroyers. This drew off Jack Conger and his flight of F4Fs, leaving the Japanese armada to prowl unopposed.

The tug *Seminole*, with a cargo of aviation fuel in tow, became the next target. Twenty minutes later she was bracketed, straddled, and sent to a blazing end.

By now the Japanese task force had completed a full 180-degree turn and was heading back down the channel. The warehouse and dock area at Lunga Point came under fire. Shore batteries took on the destroyers, and hits were registered on the *Akatsuki* at 1055 hours. Ten minutes later the destroyers called off the fight and disappeared under a smoke screen in the direction of Savo Island.

The battle of the Cactus Navy was over.

It was nearing noon when Lieutenant Colonel Timboe's battalion of the 164th Infantry took its first break of the morning. It had been a tough night for Timboe and his men. Their assigned position on the perimeter had been south and east of Fighter Strip 2. "Coffin Corner," as they called their sector, had been hit hard by the combat patrols of General Nasu. But the 164th had been ready. They had cleared fields of fire through the seven-foot *kunai* grass, sited their weapons for interlocking fire, and covered the "dead spaces" with mortars. They had also set up a crude but effective warning system. Two jerks on a strand of barbed wire strung with tin cans meant "the Japs are coming."

To the right of Timboe's battalion were Chesty Puller's marines. And out in front, three thousand yards in advance of the main line of resistance, had been posted a forty-eight-man detachment of marines on a little grassy knoll. At 2130 hours this detachment had been overrun, the marines retreating after a sharp firefight. A half hour later, Coffin Corner caught it. A torrential downpour at the height of the midnight attack further confused the outcome, but in the end the line was stabilized as Col. Bob Hall committed the reserve battalion of the 164th.

Infiltration and penetration of the marine sector along the Matanikau, although not as heavy, had continued throughout the pre-midnight hours of October 24. An observation post on the Horseshoe was swamped. Companies E and G of the 7th Marines were subjected to intense artillery bombardment, while Company F of the same regiment was forced to the limit to prevent a lodgement. By dawn it was evident that enemy patrols had completed an encirclement of the 7th Marine positions.

As an aftermath of the night attacks, marine intelligence concluded: "The Japanese efforts of October 24 must be regarded as a reconnaissance-in-force to (a) seek lodgements within our perimeter and (b) develop approach routes for a breakthrough on the night of October 25–26." Lt. Col. Ed Buckley, the D-2, had hit the nail right on the head.

Rear Adm. Tamotsu Takama stood on the flag bridge of the destroyer *Akizuki* and watched the clearing skies to the south with apprehension. It was 1250 hours, and the lean *Akizuki* was cutting through the waters between Malaita and Santa Isabel at a smart thirty knots. She was fifty miles northeast of her target area, Henderson Field.

Three ships of Takama's Destroyer Division 4, designated as the assault unit, had completed their assignment earlier this day by sinking a United States tanker and an auxiliary craft as well as scattering two old four-stack destroyers. They had been blessed by low clouds, and were now en route to their base in the Shortlands.

The cloud cover, unfortunately, was being dissipated. He sighed. It was too bad, for it would make his mission more difficult. That mission, assigned to him by Vice Admiral Mikawa, commander of the Outer South Seas Forces, was the daylight shelling of the American air field.

That, in itself, was unique. But implicit in his orders was a secondary and perhaps even more important mission: to determine, if possible, the presence in the Guadalcanal area of major U.S. surface units, particularly the super-battleship *Washington*.

If he were lucky, Mikawa had told him, the *Washington* would not be there. It was something, Mikawa had emphasized, that Admiral Yamamoto needed to know at all costs. In short, Takama was told, Division 4 was being employed as a decoy.

Takama interrupted his search of the skies to look past the boiling stern of his sleek flagship. Four destroyers—the *Harusame*, *Yudachi*, *Murasame*, and *Samidare*—followed in his wake. A fifth and larger vessel, the light cruiser *Yura*, brought up the rear. She had been sent along to add muscle to the bombardment.

At 1300 hours the air-alert signal on the *Akizuki* blasted out. The admiral spun around. His gaze followed a pointing finger to the southern horizon. Five tiny dots grew in size. From the waist, bow, and stern of the ship, crewmen spilled topside in answer to the call to general quarters.

Signal flags snapped aloft at a word from the admiral. They spelled out "take evasive action." Division 4 began a serpentine dance.

Lt. Comdr. John Eldridge had been in the air forty-five minutes when he spotted the lead ship of the Japanese column. Almost immediately the pattern of six S's appeared on the surface of the sea below him.

"Get the big one," he radioed to the four SBDs who were vectored in behind him. His pilots waggled their wings in acknowledgment. The five-thousand-ton light cruiser had been singled out as the principal target.

Eldridge throttled back. Secondary targets were assigned. And then he "split his flaps," the wing-mounted brakes screaming as the scout bomber went into a near-vertical dive.

Like Joe Foss and other Cactus innovators, Eldridge did not always fly by the book. Long training had taught him the limitations of his regular bombsight against a twisting, turning target. Instead he sighted the cruiser over the leading edge of his cowling; a little left rudder first, then a touch on the aileron. The airspeed indicator climbed. The altimeter dropped. When it read under three thousand feet he pulled the bomb release. There was a jolt as the thousand-pounder left its rack, and he eased the plane up, feeling the force of the four Gs pressing him against his seat.

As Eldridge levelled off, his rear gunner waved excitedly, pointing down. They had made a direct hit. Seconds later, Eldridge's wingman dropped his bomb just off to the side of the cruiser, buckling her thin plates. By the time the flight had completed its chore, the *Yura* lay dead in the water, steam and smoke billowing from forepeak to stern.

Admiral Takama's flagship *Akizuki* was near-missed and believed damaged, a jubilant Eldridge reported to Geiger.

"What was the fleet course when you left?" the Cactus general asked.

"North, sir. They were heading back up the Slot."

The battered old clock above Geiger's situation map read 1400. In the next few hours it would register more activity than for any comparable period in the history of the Cactus Air Force. The MAG-23 War Diary summed it up with classic simplicity:

Enemy fighter planes were over Cactus at irregular intervals throughout the daylight hours. Our Grummans were almost continuously in the air, landing, refueling, reloading, and taking off again, time after time.

Eldridge was barely back when Geiger sent out three P-39s to shadow the retreat of the Japanese column. They reported that the damaged cruiser was listing badly but underway. They registered several near misses.

At 1500 hours, Lt. Comdr. Ray Davis was over the stricken *Yura* with a flight of four SBDs from Bomber Six. With him were lieutenants (jg.) Coit and Doughty, who had gone out with Eldridge in the first strike. They scored a couple of damaging blows and radioed back that the cruiser was apparently flooding fast.

Eldridge led another strike at 1630 hours that included four Scout bombers, four P-39s, and three F4Fs. They mauled the *Yura* heavily, one of the army planes registering another direct hit with a five-hundred-pounder. A half hour later, six B-17s from Espiritu Santo hove into sight and gave an exhibition of precision high-level bombing, claiming two hits.

Clearly, this was the end of the *Yura*.

But her end required an epilogue of its own. Admiral Takama provided it late in the day off Cape Astrolabe near the southern tip of Santa Isabel.

"Finish her off," he signalled. Two Long Lances from one of the destroyers hissed true on course. The *Yura* shuddered under the dual impact and quickly went down by the bow.

Aboard the heavy cruiser *Chokai* somewhere up the Slot, Vice Admiral Mikawa, the victor of the first battle of Savo Island, pondered the odds. His screening force had not determined the presence of the battleship *Washington*. But all evidence indicated that she and her task force must be lying in wait somewhere to the south and west of Savo Island or the Russells. That was his gut feeling.

Mikawa had earned a record as a stand-up brawler who neither asked nor sought quarter. But surprise had been lost in this instance, he felt. He would scrub tonight's projected bombardment of Henderson Field by his forces. As the *Yura* went down, the wireless crackled with the coded message to his fleet units: "We will reassemble our forces in rear areas until the capture of the Guadalcanal airfield is definitely reported."

It was up to the Imperial Army now.

Guadalcanal was pitch-black. Another storm was brewing, blotting out the last faint pinpricks of the Southern Cross. A light rain began to fall, bringing a deep lassitude, almost like a narcotic, to the fifteen infantry battalions manning the perimeter. Like Puller's battalion in Sector 3, they had withstood the tensions of the day of October 25. They had dug in, strung wire, improved their positions, coordinated their fire, and settled down. Now, except at outpost positions and the posts of gimlet-eyed sentries who scanned the jungle to the front, sleep claimed the field.

Herman Hanneken was awakened at 2100 hours by a tug on his shoulder.

"Sir, I've got the forward OP on the line. They say something weird is going on."

The commander of the 2d Battalion, 7th Marines, rolled over and grunted into the phone. He sat up and blinked. "Well I'll be damned. Yeah, I'll take a look. Hang in there, we'll get you some artillery."

Hanneken had visited the observation post just before dark. It had been shelled heavily, suffering three casualties. It stood on high ground, on the left face of the Horseshoe. From the OP to the Matanikau, where Lt. Col. Bill Williams's 3d Battalion, 7th Marines, was dug-in, there was a five-hundred-yard gap in the line. This was admittedly a critical danger-point. The Japanese had filtered through it the night before, overrunning one of the outpost positions. Hanneken and Williams had discussed the gap at great length during the daylight hours of Dugout Sunday as the front had been restored and the infiltrators had been smoked out. Col. Amor Sims, the 7th Regiment commander, had joined in.

"We haven't got the troops to fill the gap," Sims had told his battalion commanders. "We've 'singled up' to the very limit. It's just something we've got to live with. But we'll register the hell out of it with artillery. And get your mortars into the act as well."

The two men had done that. It was not a textbook solution; open flanks can lead to disaster, they knew.

But it was a necessary field expedient.

Hanneken put down the phone, pushed back the blackout curtain, and climbed out of the headquarters dugout. "Come on, Art," he called out to Capt. Arthur Sherwood. "Let's take a gander at this light-show they're talking about." He paused at the top, slinging a pair of binoculars over his shoulders. "Better bring along a couple of men from your section."

The five men who made up the detail slithered down the trail that led along the ridge to the OP. It was slow progress, with many challenges and countersigns from the wired-up positions to the rear of Company G and Company E.

"We don't want to get shot-up by our own guys," Hanneken kept repeating. Several times they did draw fire, despite their caution. The detail crawled along. It took a half hour to go six hundred yards; finally they were at the tunnel to the rear of the observation post.

"What do you make of it, Colonel?"

"It's the damnedest sight I ever saw," Hanneken said in disbelief. Below him, approaching the gap and continuing for more than a half mile to the other side of the Matanikau River, were hundreds of lights. They appeared to be in single file—reds, blues, greens—flickering like glowworms as they disappeared and appeared again along a jungle trail. Heavy rifle and automatic-weapons fire arose from the Japanese side of the river, as if on cue, as the light show blinked on and off.

From the OP, Hanneken could see the answering fire swell in intensity as the 3rd Battalion opened up. He reached for the phone and rang his regimental commander. "We'd better get the artillery in on the act," he said to an equally puzzled Amor Sims. "I don't know what kind of lights they are, Colonel. Flashlights, I guess. They're coming upriver, crossing at Nippon Bridge and heading right for the gap."

Within minutes, batteries supporting the Horseshoe began placing ranging shots along the strange column. The lights blinked off, then on again. Now the marine howitzers fired for effect, the multibursts of the barrage falling along the river of fireflies undulating through the jungle.

Just as suddenly as it had appeared, the light-show ended. With its disappearance the Japanese automatic weapons stopped chattering. The answering fire from the marine side of the river sputtered to a halt. There was silence.

Then, far back in the jungle, tucked away in caves and ravines behind Mukade Hill, the Japanese artillery responded. In the momentary quiet that lay over the field, the men in the OP could hear the first muffled cough of a high-angle artillery piece being fired fifteen hundred to two thousand yards away. The sound swelled like corn in a popper, and suddenly the shriek of incoming shells and the blast of their detonation tore through the observation post.

"Let's get the hell out of here," Hanneken yelled over the din. As he crawled into the night he could see bursts falling all across the line of his entrenched battalion. Getting back was going to be tougher than coming out.

High up Mukade Hill, General Maruyama looked at his watch and nodded approval. Operation 174 was proceeding on schedule. Within ten minutes the artillery barrage would lift and the first assault phase of the operation would be put into effect.

General Sumoyoshi's forces along the Matanikau were poised for a frontal attack across the river. Sumoyoshi had extended his right, crossing Nippon Bridge. Units had already infiltrated into the gap that existed in the marine positions.

In the center was Major General Nasu's command. The 29th Infantry, Maruyama's trusted shock troops, was already moving forward. They would penetrate the long ridge that led up from the airfield. Behind them would come the 16th Regiment. They would consolidate the breakthrough.

On the right was General Kawaguchi, whose zone of attack continued eastward to the mouth of the Tenaru. The 230th Infantry, Kawaguchi's main force, was already in position.

Three red arrows dominated the map. They converged on the airfield.

Suddenly, activity at the switchboard came to an abrupt halt. H-Hour was sixty seconds away. Maruyama's Charlie-Chaplin-like mustache quivered as the silent countdown began. Then he bolted through the blackout curtains.

Off to his left some four miles, orange and red flashes blinked at a slow tempo. Directly below his darkened OP they had already sputtered out, like the thunder of a passing storm.

And in their place came a new phenomenon: a sound, terrifying in its intensity. It was the *banzai*. It swept up Mukade Hill like a wave. It was echoed in back of them at the artillery positions. It came with the distortion of shortwave from the banks of the

Matanikau. Finally, it even roared through his own command post. And the general joined in.

Bushido had reached its high water mark.

To the commanding general of the U.S. forces on Guadalcanal, the next hour was an eternity.

Right or wrong, he had committed his troops to battle. The dispositions having been made, there was little he could do but wait. Night defense in the jungle was a static thing. Each unit, even the smallest, wired itself for all-around defense. There was no front, no rear. The enemy could come at you from any side . . . or from the rear.

General Vandegrift had heard the *banzai* and the lifting of the Japanese artillery fire on his forward strong-points. Now Sumoyoshi's batteries searched inland, interdicting a series of prearranged targets. The airfield was catching it; so were the docks. A terrific blast just outside the dugout tore down the blackout curtains, scattering mud, dirt, and splinters. The single 40-watt bulb, which provided dim illumination, spun crazily on the end of its connecting wire. Division troops, too, were receipting for their share of the Japanese fury.

The switchboard at the far end of the revetment stood silent. Were all the lines shot out? Had there been a massive breakthrough? Or did everybody just have their hands full?

The general looked around. Quick hands had restored the curtains. Others scraped off the blobs of mud that had spattered the big situation map. One of the radio operators had sustained a scalp wound, and a corpsman dabbed it, slapping on a sulfa pad.

"That'll teach you to keep your helmet on," the medic said without feeling.

"And just what do I do with these? Wear 'em on my ass?" The wounded man held up a pair of earphones.

Outside, the rounds kept pouring in. The dugout shuddered. Vandegrift could stand it no longer. He turned to his chief of staff.

"Get me Geiger," he said. "And Gerry, you better start calling around."

The switchboard lit up.

Sgt. Mitchell Paige's heavy-machine-gun squad was well-disciplined, and had been fully briefed on what they might expect this night. They had withstood heavy patrol attacks on the night of October 24, when the Japanese had filtered through the lines of the 2d Battalion, 7th Marines.

"They'll come at us again from that ravine out there, you can make book on it," Paige had told them. One of his gunners had squeezed off a burst of six earlier that evening, when Herman Hanneken's detail had slithered forward to view the light-show from the forward OP. Paige's unit had not seen it. But through the jungle telegraph they had heard about it.

"Keep your butts down," Paige had shouted as the artillery bombardment crashed down around their position. "When it lifts, watch out."

To Sergeant Paige, whose marines had never experienced a bombardment of such intensity, the minutes seemed to stretch into hours. Out in front of the nest, barbed wire was chewed up, strands of the torn wire whistling overhead with a banshee scream. Others screams, human ones, echoed back. An incoming shell had scored a direct hit on an adjoining position, and a grisly exhibit of its effectiveness whirled in, landing on his parapet: a bloody field-boot with a severed foot still in it.

The bombardment slowly petered out, one final burst of red and yellow arcing in to Paige's right. The sergeant's handsome face, lean and stubbled, turned to the squad behind him. "Man the gun," he called. In the silence that followed, only the sound of the tropical downpour could be heard. Then out of the night, directly to their front, came the shriek of the *banzai*.

Sergeant Paige's gun began stuttering. Out of the ravine swarmed a horde of Japanese. Screaming, falling on the tangled wire, pushing forward over the bodies of their comrades, they came on and on, and the Browning A-1 cut them down.

Sheer numbers alone dictated that some of the attacking wave would push past as the gun crew changed belts. Yet the men were scarcely aware of anything except what was happening in their immediate front. To their right and left the staccato of the battalion's machine-guns blended with the rapid fire of semiautomatics and rifles.

Paige's men did not hear it.

Nor did they consciously hear the cough of their own 60- and 81mm mortars as these poured hundreds of rounds into the dead spaces and into the enemy assembly-area to their front. The blasts of high-explosive shells from those weapons only served to illuminate the fleeting figures of the attackers.

Hanneken's 2d Battalion was being pushed to its limit. The artillery began pumping out death and destruction. Marine 105s were called in by their forward observers. Just to the front of Paige's position, not more than twenty yards away, an entire Japanese squad disappeared in a shell-burst. They had been in the machine-gunner's sights, but they had vaporized in one blinding flash.

There was a cheer along the line as the first wave faltered. There had been lodgements made, however, and the Japanese seemed to be regrouping. You could hear them out in front, Paige said, chanting and yelling across the line.

"Babe Ruth eats shit!"

A moment of unaccountable silence. "Did you hear that?"

"Yeah, buddy, I heard it."

From off somewhere to the left, came a retort. "Blow it out your C-Bag, Jap!"

And with total irreverence: "The emperor eats shit, too."

The first test had been met.

19

NEW HOPES AND OLD FEARS

It was nearing midnight when "Manila John" Basilone slumped wearily over the receiver of his machine gun. For almost a minute, the tableau within the emplacement was frozen in a single frame.

Then, as though filmed in slow motion, the scene dissolved. The sergeant's right hand moved from the traversing mechanism where it had been locked for almost an hour. It sought the left hand, which had been welded to the trigger assembly. Together they joined in prayer.

"Oh God!" was the brief supplication.

The perimeter had withstood the savagery of yet another Japanese attack. In the comparative quiet that stole over the field, the sound of the monsoon quickly reasserted its dominance, but it was punctuated by the awful cries of the wounded and dying.

Self-preservation, the primal law of the battlefield, worked its way into the consciousness of Manila John. In front of his position was a mound, varying in height from two to four feet. It had not been there when the attack began. It masked the emplacement. It had to be removed.

Basilone's strong jaw began to move. Orders poured out, filtering through the numbness of his gun crew. A half-dozen quick blasts circled the gun pit. Grenades did their grisly work. Then Basilone's men moved quickly forward to remove the mounds from their field of fire . . . to spread the bodies of the Japanese lest corpses, like sandbags, become the final rallying point for yet another attack.

Manila John felt there would be one.

So did Archer Vandegrift. His staff had been on the phones, shortly after midnight, assessing the damage of the second major Japanese thrust. Colonel Thomas, Colonel Kilmartin, Lt. Col. Merrill Twining, and Lieutenant Colonel Pate all had participated in the round robin.

The assembled information was boiled down into diary form:

> Mouth of the Matanikau—3d Battalion, 1st Marines. McKelvy reports heavy pressure and infiltration by small units. Lodgements neither deep nor strong.
>
> Upriver—3d Battalion, 7th Marines. All major frontal attacks thrown back. Williams worried about infiltration to his rear. The gap between Third Battalion and Second Battalion is lousy with Japs.
>
> Left face of the Horseshoe—2d Battalion, 7th Marines. Hanneken's position most vulnerable. The F Company position on his left has been hard-hit and overrun.
>
> Sector 3—Puller not in any serious trouble, he says. Japs keep coming at him in the same places.

He has built up positions against the approach routes, and they have been holding fast.

Coffin Corner—164th Infantry. Lots of infiltration by small units. Major assaults turned back with surprising ease, Hall reports. He thinks main attack has not as yet been launched.

Tenaru—Sector fairly quiet save for noisy demonstrations. Some infiltration.

The commanding general put down the summary and looked around at his staff, his gaze settling on his supply officer.

"How's the ammunition, Pate?"

"No shortages, sir. We've got two units of fire at every position."

"Good. Ed, how do you shape up?" He looked at his intelligence officer. Ed Buckley moved to the wall map. He elaborated on the sketchy summary, citing the two most probable danger spots for breakthroughs: Sector 3, and the left face of the Horseshoe. In his judgment there would be a third Japanese attempt to penetrate, perhaps within two hours.

"We've got something going for us, General. Something I don't quite understand, but it's there. It's real, it's something I think we should pass on."

Vandegrift nodded at him to continue.

"I think they'll be coming back at us from the same old rat-hole. I think the failure of the first two attacks was the result of faulty terrain intelligence. The attacks, I believe, were intended to establish a lodgement here," he pointed to the map, "and here." The D-2's pointer had indicated Hanneken's and Puller's positions. "From these lodgements the breakthrough was to be launched."

"You don't think they have the initiative to strike elsewhere in force?"

Buckley shook his head. "I think they're locked in."

"Gerry?" Vandegrift turned to his chief of staff.

"I think Ed's right."

"Okay, I accept the premise. Get the word down to expect the main effort at 0200 hours. And to shore up those positions that caught it worst in the last two attacks."

The D-2 was wrong in only one respect. At 0200 nothing happened. The rain had eased during the past hour, and the only sounds between the lines were the intermittent rattle of small-arms fire and an occasional awful moan from the wounded, though death had mercifully silenced some of that.

Now and then, taunts were thrown back and forth:

"Hey, Yank. Japanese drink blood of Eleanor!" The president's wife, the president's little dog, Fala, and even the president himself, shared the indignities.

There were rejoinders, of course.

"Hey, Jap. Marines drink blood of emperor!" At the shouted suggestion that the marines had better retreat, one man paraphrased Captain Lloyd Williams's response to a French officer during the battle of Belleau Woods, almost a quarter of a century before: "Retreat, hell! We just got here!"

At some points on the perimeter, the shoring-up process was proving difficult. Sergeant Basilone's crew had shoveled out thousands of empty shell-casings from their pit. They had tidied up the fields of fire. But the ranks of supporting riflemen to their flanks

310

remained painfully thin.

To the rear of Sergeant Paige's sandbagged gun, a battalion runner slithered forward on his belly with a message.

"Shore up, hell. What with? We're out here by ourselves!"

It was to be the night of the machine-gunners. Within the hour, Basilone and Paige would stand, like two boulders in a creek, against the fury of the flash flood. And both would earn the Medal of Honor for their steadfastness.

At 0300 hours the attack came.

The pattern, as predicted, was the same. First came the rolling barrage that crept over the crests of the defense lines, deafening in its intensity. Then, when it lifted, once again screaming hordes swept forward to hit the identical spots they had attacked twice before. This time, however, American artillery and front-line mortars concentrated all their fire within those sectors.

The scream of the *banzai* was quickly drowned by thousands of rounds of high explosives dropped along the canalized thrust-lines. The Yanks had made a calculated bet that the Japanese would return. The "rat-hole" theory had been proven valid. Like salmon against a fish ladder they came on, in twice the numbers that had come before.

Some spilled past the marine positions, thrusting their way, screaming, toward the airfield and the docks. Hanneken's left trembled and gave way, the surviving riflemen of Company F drifting back dazedly to the rear. A corridor had been punched into the extreme left of the Horseshoe. Company G, on the right, swivelled its guns around to enfilade the attackers. But within a half hour, three machine-gun emplacements had been captured and 150 Japanese infantrymen had secured a lodgement.

Along Sector 3, farther to the left, the carnage was repeated in all its brutal intensity. The second prong of the Japanese thrust died in its tracks, stopped by massed artillery and by an overwhelming concentration of automatic-weapons and rifle fire.

By 0330 the news of the Japanese break through the 2d Battalion, 7th Marine position reached division headquarters. There was deep concern. The updated situation-map offered no consolation.

"We've only got a couple of machine-gun positions standing in their way, sir," Vandegrift's chief of staff said. "If they throw in a battalion of shock troops right now they'll be on the beach within the hour."

But the shock troops never materialized.

The first light of dawn saw a marine patrol moving cautiously toward that section of the line of the 2d Battalion, 7th Marines, which had been overrun a few hours earlier.

Maj. Odell Conoley led the patrol. He was the executive officer of 2d Battalion, and he had rounded up a strange collection of troops from regimental head-quarters—a mixed bag of cooks, bakers, mess sergeants, company runners, and office pinkies. Initially they numbered seventeen; but as Conoley combed the rear, word spread, and he added to his ragtag combat unit by enlisting volunteers from headquarters and service companies. It was perhaps the strangest "battalion reserve" ever assembled. Many had not operated the weapons they toted since basic training.

When the patrol was a half mile up the trail from regimental headquarters, the mists lifted. And there, walking about in the open, were some of the Japanese who had cut their way through the perimeter, captured three machine-gun nests, and established a lodgement. To the men who came upon them, they seemed dazed, uncomprehending, quietly mad.

"For Christ's sake, why don't they pull out?"

Conoley's question went unanswered. To the left he sent his light machine-guns, to the right his collection of BAR men and Thompson submachine-gunners. Behind him the lone 60mm mortar was plopped down. On signal, the scratch combat-team opened up. The fire was terrifying.

"It was like shooting ducks in a rain barrel," one of the cooks said. "They didn't know which way to run. In ten minutes it was all over." There were 150 soldiers of the emperor stretched out dead. They had been too exhausted to fight back . . . too shocked to even flee the bloodied field. From them, Bushido had extracted a terrible toll.

Monday, October 26. The marines, the army, and the Japanese did exactly what soldiers of all ages had done after the exhaustion of battle: they slept on their arms.

Nightfall witnessed a few flare-ups, as Japanese patrols probed Chesty Puller's 3d Sector lines. The largest and by far the most aggressive of these patrols was headed by the assistant adjutant of the decimated 29th Infantry. As senior officer on the field, he enlisted his force almost exclusively from the ranks of surviving officers and NCOs.

"Ours is an honorable mission," wrote Capt. Toshio Takama. "We hope to recover our regimental colors." Their flag had been lost within the marine positions in the attack of the night before. Captain Takama commited his remembrance of that attack to paper:

About 2300 [25 October] we finally had an encounter with the enemy. On the way there was a heavy rainstorm. The unit's advance was greatly delayed.

When the unit encountered the enemy, the terrain and enemy situation were completely obscured, and it was necessary to advance along a trail made by the enemy.

To make matters worse, the enemy had excellent detectors, and there was intense machine-gun and mortar fire. Artillery fire followed. Even though it was night, the enemy had good plots and was able to inflict extremely heavy losses in this way.

However, the 3d Battalion commander, with strong determination, strove to break through. Each company, in accordance with its orders, began the assault, but because of the heaviest mortar and machine-gun fire the breakthrough was delayed.

About that time the regimental commander (Col. Juro Hiroyasu) arrived with the 7th Company, which guards the regimental colors, and entered the enemy positions.

The colors entered the position, but the 3d Battalion assault made no progress. Three times assaults were mounted, and each time the enemy fire became more and more intense. Finally the dawn came and our survivors withdrew to the rear. Singly, in twos and threes, I watched them pass. Their faces were haunted and pale. Bushido was gone. Colonel Hiroyasu had been right when he said that our intelligence had been faulty. We had been led into a trap. His premonition of death, which I had sought to dispel, had been proven true.

Maj. Gen. Yumio Nasu and my colonel died honorable deaths in battle. Since the regiment did not know the whereabouts of the colors or its commander, the division, as also the Seventeenth Army, were most concerned. The regiment did its utmost in searching for Colonel Hiroyasu and his colors, but to no avail.

The 3d Battalion was practically annihilated in the assault. In round numbers our regimental losses at this Mukade Hill battle were 1,050 casualties.

What other regiments suffered, I do not know. But ours is decimated. We have been ordered to recover our wounded and take them back across the Matanikau as quickly as possible. There are so few of us left it is sad.

By midnight, October 26, as Captain Takama guided the last of his walking wounded across the Matanikau, bits and pieces of information began filtering into the wireless room at marine headquarters. Fragmentary coded wires from Pearl Harbor and Noumea tentatively suggested that American naval forces had scored a pivotal victory over the Japanese off the Santa Cruz Islands on October 25–26.

If true, it was pretty heady stuff.

Vandegrift and his staff were joined by Geiger and some of the Cactus brass. They fitted the jigsaw pieces together as these drifted in. By 0300 a clear picture began to emerge.

Yamamoto's grand strategy had misfired. The three-day air, sea, and land assault which was to have sealed the fate of Guadalcanal had failed. Bull Halsey had kept his promise. And at this hour three naval columns of the Japanese combined fleet—the Advance Force of Vice Adm. Nobutake Kondo, the Striking Force of Vice Adm. Chuichi Nagumo, and the Outer Seas Force of Vice Adm. Gunichi Mikawa—were in full retreat up the Slot.

It had cost Halsey the carrier *Hornet*, a fearful price. The destroyer *Porter* had also been sent to the bottom, victim of a submarine attack. The rest of his fleet was afloat, albeit heavily mauled.

The *Enterprise*, the redoubtable "Big E," with Capt. Osborne B. Harrison on the bridge, had suffered extensive damage to her superstructure, flight deck, and elevators. Capt. Tom Gatch's *South Dakota* had been repeatedly hit in her defense of the *Enterprise*. The cruiser *San Juan*, which under Capt. Jim Maher had been credited with firing the first round in support of the August 7 landings on Guadalcanal, was likewise seriously hit.

Under Capt. Charles Mason, the *Hornet* had fought well before she had gone under. And some of her air groups under Walt Rodee, Hank Sanchez, Jim Vose, Bill Widhelm, and Ed Parker would be sent to the "unsinkable flattop," Henderson Field, for future air-battles with the Japanese.

There was another grim bill to pay: seventy-four planes—from Adm. Thomas Kinkaid's Task Force 16 (*Enterprise*), and from Task Force 17 under Rear Adm. George Murray (*Hornet*)—had been shot down.

Japanese losses were thought to be heavy. Two big flattops, the *Shokaku* and the *Zuiho*, had been knocked out of the action. The heavy cruiser *Chikuma* and the destroyer *Terutsuki* were believed sunk. American pilots, in debriefing sessions, were claiming upwards of ninety kills.

As dawn came on Tuesday, October 27, there was one man who knew the real figures only too well. As units of his combined fleet scurried north, Adm. Isoroku Yamamoto had the figures spread before him. Santa Cruz had cost him 100 front-line pilots. During the past two weeks 203 fliers had been lost attacking Henderson.

And here was the communiqué from Seventeenth Army headquarters: "Our forces are regrouping behind the Matanikau River line."

The man who had never wanted this war in the first place, but whose advice had gone unheeded, rose wearily from his desk aboard the *Yamato*, which was still anchored at Truk.

He began dictating a message to higher head-quarters. Soon it would reach Premier Tojo's desk. The words came slowly, but the advice they conveyed was clear: We must abandon the effort to recapture Guadalcanal.

From that moment, the Japanese had lost the initiative. They would never regain it.

317

Admiral Yamamoto's assessment of the battle of Santa Cruz, and his recommendation that the attempt to recapture the airfield at Guadalcanal be abandoned, produced a predictable reaction within Tokyo's high councils of war.

There were voices in the Imperial General Staff that called for his immediate removal. To others, however, the Yamamoto paper pointed up a bitterly disappointing fact: the two-pronged pincer movement against Australia and the Antipodes had failed.

Its right jaw, reaching for Port Moresby, had on this very day been blocked on the Kokoda Trail. General Horii, who had slogged over the towering Owen Stanley Mountains to within twenty miles of his goal, had been stopped cold. His report, now before the war council, told of a steady buildup of enemy forces. His own troops were exhausted, and intelligence indicated the probability of a strong amphibious attack on the Japanese base at Buna Mission, on the northeast coast of New Guinea.

General Horii's fears were well founded. Douglas MacArthur would soon launch an amphibious end-run on Buna in the first of his island-hopping operations, which the world press would herald as "innovative" but which were, in fact, as old as warfare itself.

As November 7 wound up the eleventh month of the war, the Japanese high command had become enmeshed in the trivia of tactics. It seemed powerless to accommodate its strategy to such reversals.

Limping home to their bases in Japan were three carriers that had been victims of the battle of Santa Cruz. Into drydock went the *Shokaku*, the *Zuikaku*, and the *Zuiho*. They would be out of the war for several months. Still on station were the *Hiyo* and the *Junyo*, the latter with only a handful of operational planes.

Pilot losses were becoming a critical factor. Admiral Nagumo's air groups had numbered 242 before Santa Cruz; they now had 84. Most of his experienced squadron commanders were dead.

The official Marine Monograph summarizes the changes in Japanese strategies that evolved as November opened:

> Only late in the campaign had the Japanese been forced to realize that the marines were determined to hold Henderson Field, and that, in holding it, they were prepared to risk all the planes available at the field and to employ to the maximum possible extent the task forces afloat in the area.
>
> This realization led directly to the Japanese decision to send to the island (on November 7) a large convoy of transports, heavily guarded by strong surface forces.

At church services one week after Dugout Sunday, Father O'Brien's brief sermon touched on his discernment of a rebirth of hope among his parishioners. The padre was observant. With new hope had come renewed resolve. Front-line squads had tidied up their positions, restrung wire, and buried the dead. Bathing details splashed in the Tenaru and the Matanikau. Work by the Seabee battalions on Henderson Field and Fighter Strip 2 was stepped up, the Marston-matted runways lengthened.

At Division, old maps were torn down. New ones

appeared; and on them, bright red arrows pointed in new directions, extending beyond the Matanikau, thrusting on to Cape Esperance.

"Just putting those arrows up there for our guys to see is half the battle," Gerry Thomas said. "Now they'll say: 'Maybe we can beat these bastards after all.' "

Vandegrift nodded approval, himself well aware of the change in morale. "Maybe it will lead somewhere, Gerry." He tapped the far end of the island map. "Maybe all the way."

The red arrows on Guadalcanal became inside-page news on November 8. Events with even more important implications for the folks back home were taking place. Montgomery's Eighth Army, approaching Tobruk, was heading for the "shores of Tripoli." Simultaneously, three American spearheads were landing on the beaches of North Africa.

No shoestrings were in evidence in this campaign; no shortages of equipment and supplies of armor and landing craft. No planes or warships were held back. The troops were green, but they had everything, including ample reserves and capable, resolute theater leadership behind them.

It was just as well, for they would soon be meeting the Desert Fox, although the crucible that was to test their mettle, Kasserine Pass, was still more than three months away.

These were the dog days on the 'Canal.

They were welcomed. There was the impending arrival of the 8th Marine Regiment to be considered.

Col. Richard Jeschke's advance party, including Capt. Wilmot Spires, the regimental intelligence officer, and Maj. Dixon Goen, the R-3, was already on the scene.

With the 8th Marine's three infantry battalions, support troops, and attached 75mm howitzer batteries on hand, veteran units could be freed from perimeter duty and made available for probing attacks.

The Engineers had completed three bridges across the Matanikau now that the entire west bank was under American control. The rear guard of the retreating 2d Division, the once invincible Sendais, had been brushed back all the way to Point Cruz. In one of the actions to clear the field, a reinforced marine combat patrol had taken part in the only bayonet charge of the campaign, wiping out a small pocket of resistance with cold steel.

What had been a no-man's-land west of the Matanikau was becoming Marineland, U.S.A. This was mop-up time. And with it came a flood of scuttlebutt. The Japanese, driven from the perimeter, were about to be evacuated. General Maruyama would surrender and then commit *hara-kiri* to save face. No one knew where the rumors came from, or how they started. Division headquarters heard them all and shook its collective head.

There was yet another rumor, this one more substantive. It had been coming in from Noumea and Pearl, with backup from code-breakers in Washington: Tokyo was going to shoot the works. A full infantry division was being dispatched. They would be landed at Cape Esperance, join the Seventeenth Army forces in place, and drive down the coastal road.

Day by day, the information built up. The threat

could no longer be ignored.

During the mop-up days, the 1st Battalion, 164th Infantry, and the 1st Battalion, 5th Marines, joined forces and within one pocket of resistance killed 239 Japanese; including 28 officers and one full colonel. These were believed to be the remnants of a full Imperial regiment which had once numbered 3,500 men. Captured were a 70mm field piece, twelve antitank guns, and thirty-four Nambu heavy machine-guns.

Action reports carried a lot of familiar names at the bottom of the pages: Bill LaBarba, Gordon Gayle, Lewis Walt, and Chuck Nees.

To the east, there was the Koli Point action. Intelligence from native scouts indicated that a Japanese buildup was taking place here which could threaten Aola, where a new U.S. airstrip was being prepared. Accordingly, as the 8th Marines moved in, the 2d Battalion, 7th Marines, was pulled out of the Horseshoe, loaded up on trucks, and moved eastward to meet the threat. They had a short ride; the road ended at the Tenaru River. They de-trucked, amid groans, and settled into marching column, Lt. Col. Herman Hanneken at their front and Maj. Odell Conoley at the rear. The major had new troubles: his radios. Two days out of the perimeter they conked out, soaked and inoperable. The column was twenty miles from home. It went into sodden bivouac.

At midnight, November 2, Hanneken was awakened in his pup tent. Three Japanese ships—a destroyer, a light cruiser, and what looked like a small troopship—had been spotted standing offshore. The marine command was alerted and Hanneken moved forward from his prepared positions to observe the landings. The Japanese were a mixed bag, he noted as they came noisily ashore. It would be folly, he deduced, to oppose their landing: that cruiser and the destroyers packed too much muscle. By 0200 the unloading was completed and the convoy moved away. Even without the naval guns, the Japanese force was much too strong for a decimated marine battalion to take issue with, the commander felt.

His estimation of enemy strength was later proved correct. The invaders, fresh from Bougainville, consisted of elements of the 228th Infantry and the 230th Infantry.

"They've got us four or five to one, and I don't like the odds," he told his exec. "What a time to have the radios out. Have you got any of 'em dried yet?"

"Not yet, Skipper. The boys are trying everything, including putting them in their jocks."

At dawn Hanneken began a slow withdrawal westward toward the Metapona River, whose left bank offered the best defensible position. The retrograde movement was soon unmasked, and Japanese patrols became aggressive. By mid-morning, when the Metapona was reached, the affair had grown to a hotly pressed rear-guard action, and Hanneken's wounded numbered twenty-five.

The left bank was quickly organized, and the firefight grew as the Japanese built up their line. Hanneken sent two runners to the rear. With luck, word of the battalion's plight would reach the perimeter before dark. Hanneken wondered to himself if he could hold out until then. There was a shout of triumph to his rear. The commo section had persevered: one of the radio sets was now working. He was soon on it. Division had been worried stiff. What had happened? Where was he? Hanneken filled them in. The general wanted to know if he could hold until reinforcements could be forwarded by land?

"Negative, tell him. There's just too goddamned many of 'em."

There was a pause, while the crackle of fire along the Metapona filtered through the open mike.

"Keep your line open, Herm. Small conference here." His ear glued to the receiver, Hanneken took it all in. "Who have we got? How soon can he move? Okay. How about an air strike? Good, good! Let's get moving. Fill him in."

Col. Gerald Thomas passed on the full scoop. Puller's battalion was being trucked to Kukum, where they would embark in landing craft and head east. They would arrive around 1100 at a beach just west of Hanneken's position. General Geiger had been filled in and was organizing an air strike. It should be on the way shortly. The radio snapped off.

Along the east bank of the Metapona, the Japanese fire quieted down to desultory exchanges. The marines had dug in. To the rear of the river-line, marine corpsmen now were treating thirty-four wounded, in a defiladed aid station out of danger from flat-rejectory fire.

Off in the direction of the perimeter, one of the corpsmen picked up the drone of planes approaching. Ours, I hope, he thought. Within seconds the roar became louder and a white star caught the corpsman's eye. Something black tumbled down, flip-flopping as it hit the top of a palm, not twenty-five yards away. A blinding flash of orange and red erupted, followed a millisecond later by the ear-shattering detonation of a fifty-pound high explosive antipersonnel bomb.

"Good God, they're plastering us!"

It was true. Jungle bombing is an inexact science, and Cactus fliers, trying to be helpful, would learn that lesson with tragic finality.

Major Conoley switched the radio on after the first squadron had unloaded its lethal load. There were more casualties brought back to the aid station. "Get me Colonel Thomas. Gerry, your guys from Cactus just flew in and bombed the hell out of us. Sure, we've got casualties. What the hell did you expect?"

Thomas sought to soothe the irate exec. "I don't know how they messed up. The exact coordinates of your position went out of here."

But communications in war is another inexact science. And somehow, on this day, even the first correction was not duly noted. Twenty minutes later another flight made its appearance. Once again there was a good solid working over of the marine positions, this time with fewer casualties because the men had buttoned up at the sound of approaching planes.

Bad as it was, the attack had one salutary effect: it had shaken up the Japanese on the far bank of the river, taking some of the fight out of them.

Incredibly, in spite of the blistering deluge of messages to Cactus, a third strike was mounted at 1900 hours. Had there been ground-to-plane communication, the fliers' ears and tails would have been peeled bare with invectives.

One further benefit accrued from the bombing, however. About half an hour before the final mission,

Japanese units had been seen crossing upriver in an obvious move to encircle the marine position. Fortuitously, several of the bombs dropped to the rear and right of the river positions. The Japanese skedaddled back to their own side.

"It's time we got out of here," Hanneken told his exec. And so in the dying light of day the battalion moved down the coast to its rendezvous point, carrying its wounded and fighting its way through several enemy pockets.

On the sandy beach near the Nalimbiu River, the marines set up a new defense perimeter, four hundred yards long and one hundred yards deep. Communications were reopened, and over the wireless came apologies from Cactus, none more abject than those of the pilots who had flown the afternoon's mission.

General Geiger himself got on the horn. "Tell 'em, Christ we're sorry," he told the battalion commander. "It's all our fault. And our boys all say they'd have a lot rather had it happen to us than to you."

It was not the happiest moment of the war to the rock-hard old airman, who was distraught on yet another score: in a few days he would be relieved by Col. Louis Woods, ten years his junior. The old warrior had been furious when told of his loss of command. He thought he had been betrayed by his friends. But he was tired, fought-out, and bone weary. He had given it his best, and he had brought Cactus through the night, to a point where a faint glimmering of light could be seen at the end of the tunnel.

Geiger's apologies in behalf of Cactus were accepted throughout the ranks, and Hanneken's men blinked out recognition signals at 1130 when the landing craft carrying Puller's reinforcements arrived. The entire command settled down for the night. At first light they moved forward down the coast, battalions abreast.

During the night of November 5–6 the enemy continued to withdraw, offering little resistance. By then, Vandegrift called it quits. He had learned enough. The battalions were returned by boat to the perimeter.

There was some reorganization to be effected. Vandegrift had probed and assessed the enemy strength on both his flanks. Information of a fresh threat from the north kept filtering through channels. Was there to be a massive new attack upon the airfield, spearheaded by a reinforcement of division strength? Had Japanese strategies changed?

Signs pointed almost unmistakably to that conclusion. And amid all the guidelines of enemy intelligence that kept pouring in, there was one reappearing word: Hiroshima.

20

THE HIROSHIMA DIVISION

At 1000 hours on 10 November, Lt. Masao Hirokawa stood at the forward ladder upward from A deck to the bridge of the *Arizona Maru*. Despite her wartime gray, she was still a handsome ship, he thought. He looked down at the deck below, where the taffrail of the former merchantman was packed solid with troops.

Other gray transports swung at anchor in Simpson Harbor, and between them plied smaller vessels, tugs, lighters, and gigs, their signal flags snapping in the light trades. Since early morning they had been moving about with frenetic energy, loading aboard the final items of ship's stores. And now the transports lay heavy in the water, their Plimsoll marks almost submerged.

Already aboard were 13,500 troops, most of them topside and waving to each other as the hawse lines were cleared and the anchors hoisted. Below them, deep in the holds, was their equipment: heavy-artillery pieces, tanks, trucks, shells, ammunition, medical supplies. They were fully combat-loaded for their mission, the first massive reinforcement in the three-month battle for Guadalcanal.

Falling into line behind the *Arizona* came ten more

Marus. There were the *Brisbane* and *Canberra*, both of which had seen service in the pre-war Japan to Australia run. Then came the *Kumagawa*, *Sado*, *Nagara*, *Nako*, *Kinugawa*, *Hirokawa*, *Yamaura*, and *Yamatsuki*. All had been earmarked to carry troops for the final mopping-up that was to have followed the surrender of Henderson Field. Santa Cruz and the ground action of Dugout Sunday had washed out that plan.

Now, in the wake of the frustration that had followed those setbacks, the eleven transports and the entire infantry division they carried would be committed to a battle that the Japanese high command refused to concede. Many in high council, including Admiral Yamamoto, had urged such a concession. But to no avail. It was still within their power, the majority had argued, to unlock the hold the marines had on this most vital airfield.

Other efforts to bolster General Maruyama's badly decimated battalions had continued apace. Between the 2nd and 10th of November, sixty-five destroyer-loads of troops had been ferried down from the Short-lands, most of them landing on the western end of the island. Several cruisers and small transports had taken part in the night forays which by now had become the standard Japanese tactic. Most of these reinforcements came from the 38th Infantry Division, which had been relegated, in effect, to a replacement-pool status.

With the 2d Division losses made good and a fresh division on hand, the attack could be resumed. That was the rationale as the transport column moved out to join its escorts, eleven sleek destroyers under the command of Rear Adm. Raizo Tanaka.

Ahead ranged units of the Combined Fleet, under the flag of Vice Adm. Hiroaki Abe with the battleships *Hiei* and *Kirishima*. There was the Attack Group built around the heavy cruisers *Atago* and *Takao* and comprised of three light cruisers and ten destroyers. There was Admiral Mikawa's Support Group, two heavy cruisers, one light cruiser, and four destroyers, led by that old Savo Island nemesis, the *Chokai*.

Finally, there was the Carrier Support Group of Vice Admiral Takeo Kurita, with the battleships *Kongo* and *Haruna*, the heavy cruiser *Tone*, and eight destroyers. Kurita would provide support for Rear Adm. Kakuji Kukat's carriers, the *Junyo* and the *Hiyo*. There was one ominous note. As a result of Santa Cruz, both carriers were undermanned, the *Junyo* with only forty-eight operational planes of all types, the *Hiyo* with but forty-six.

From his place by the bridge ladder, Lieutenant Hirokawa noted a quick procession of messengers moving past him from the radio shack. "There are many messages coming into our ship," he wrote. "I note our captain's face as he reads them. It is not a happy face, and I am glad the responsibility is not mine. Curiously, I am at peace, now that our course is set. Tonight when things quiet down, I shall visit my troops in the hold. I shall pray and ask my company to join me."

There had been a prayer of another sort a week earlier in the code section of the U.S. Department of the Navy in Washington. Cryptologists, working around the clock for months on end, had finally broken the Japanese naval code. For the last several days, section heads had been dealing systematically with the flood of intercepts that had been pouring out of Truk, Kavieng, and Rabaul.

As night darkened the holds of the *Arizona Maru*, the lieutenant prayed with his men. Hirokawa's company, indeed the entire body of troops aboard the *Arizona* and her sister ships, were townsmen, neighbors. They had all been recruited from the city of Hiroshima. Their division bore that name.

Now, as they were praying, a message flashed out across the International Date Line. The message, flashed to all concerned headquarters, ashore and afloat, carried this fateful notation within its context: "The Hiroshima Division is on its way."

Admiral Halsey's promise to General Vandegrift that he would give the marines everything that was in his power to give had not been an idle boast. To counter the new threat, the Bull had moved with characteristic boldness.

On Armistice Day, November 11, he had forwarded three attack cargo ships (AKAs) to Lunga Point with troops, ammunition, and supplies. They unloaded under the protection of Rear Adm. Norman Scott's heavy cruiser *Atlanta* and four destroyers. Four other AKAs waited their turn at the docks, lying off San Cristobal under the wing of Rear Adm. Daniel J. Callaghan and his task force built around the heavy cruiser *San Francisco*.

This was not nearly enough, Halsey told Miles Browning, his chief of staff. He had before him a message from Admiral Nimitz, dated November 10, which read:

There is every indication that a major operation, assisted by carrier striking forces, is slated to support movement of army transports to Guadalcanal. While this looks like the big push, I am confident that you and your forces will take their measure.

Halsey pushed in all his chips. The battleships *Washington* and *South Dakota*, under the flag of Rear Adm. Willis Lee, were ordered into the combat area. As for the *Enterprise*, Halsey shrugged. "It looks like we'll have to go in without her," he said to Browning. Two days earlier he had forwarded a combat-readiness report on the ship to Nimitz. "The carrier will not be available for 25 knots or even minimum air action until 21 November." But her presence would be felt, Nimitz was assured. Her squadrons had joined the Cactus Air Force. They would be led by Lt. Al Coffin and Lt. Cols. Jim Finley, Jim Thomas, and Jim Lee. There were eighty Dauntlesses, Wildcats, and Avengers ready for the showdown.

Despite an almost total commitment, Halsey's forces were nowhere near as strong as intelligence reports had pegged those of the Japanese. He had one crippled carrier, two battleships, four heavy cruisers, four light cruisers, and twenty-two destroyers. Even the *South Dakota* was not at full strength: one of her sixteen-inch turrets was out of commission as a result of bomb damage at Santa Cruz.

But they would all be in the fight. He was giving 110 percent. He pushed the Nimitz telegram across the desk to Browning. "It's good to know that the old man has so much confidence in me," he said wryly.

* * *

The sixteen-day hiatus in the air action over Guadalcanal ended abruptly on Armistice Day.

It had been interrupted from time to time by forays against Japanese surface vessels, which had become unusually active in ferrying troops down from the Shortlands. In one of these actions, Joe Sailer had led a flight of seven SBDs in a strike against eleven destroyers, each carrying one hundred troops, some 125 miles north of Henderson. Twelve P-39s provided cover. As action was joined, in flew Maj. Joe Foss with twenty-two F4Fs. The sun had just dipped behind the horizon. The Japanese DDs fought valiantly, sending up ten float Zeros and reconnaissance biplanes to help them buy time. Six of the Zeros were on the tail of Major Fontana's Scout bomber squadron when Foss and his fighters vectored in; all six were shot down, Foss marvelling at the sight as their pilots bailed out.

It was now almost pitch-black. Two of the destroyers, the *Naganami* and the *Takuanami*, had been badly damaged, and Foss himself was far to the north, pursuing one of the remaining biplanes. Darkness and maneuverability saved the little Japanese plane, its tail-gunner even retaliating by getting a burst into the marine ace's fuselage.

Foss glanced at his fuel gauge; the needle was moving toward E. There would be little margin for navigational error. In the darkness, however, and with rain squalls covering familiar landfalls, Foss made just that one little error. Out of gas, he ditched the fighter in the surf off the coast of Malaita.

A coastwatcher sighted the ditching, picked Foss out of the drink, and entertained him royally that night on roast pig, yams, and a tumblerfull of Scotch. The

Malaitan mission people, not to be outdone, then serenaded the downed pilot with renditions from the mission hymn book. It has not been noted whether these details were forwarded via radio to Cactus. But next morning the Blue Goose, Jack Cram's torpedo-packing PBY, picked up Foss and flew him back to Henderson, where General Geiger headed the large delegation that was drawn up to greet him.

"You're out of uniform, Major," he cracked.

And sure enough he was, with bellbottom sailor whites, a fat cigar between his teeth, and a grin as wide as all outdoors.

"War is hell, General," said Foss.

Next morning at 0830 hours Condition Red sounded. At the docks at Kukum, the last troops on the *Zeilin* hurriedly disembarked. The big AKA, one of three in the roadstead, had brought units of the Americal Division to join their buddies of the 164th Infantry Regiment.

Capt. Pat Buchanan stood on the bridge, watching the cargo handlers tend the big booms that swung oversides.

"How much time have we got?" he asked.

The dockmaster looked up. From Henderson Field he could hear the distant sound of planes warming up. "About an hour, maybe less," he said. Buchanan winced. Cactus planes began taking off, and from the deck of the *Zeilin* you could spot them, circling for altitude, awaiting the intercept.

The dockmaster's estimate proved accurate. At 0930 hours nine Val bombers from the carrier *Hiyo* appeared overhead, escorted by eighteen Zekes. A dogfight immediately broke out as the Vals flew in with great determination to attack the shipping. The *Zeilin*'s plates were buckled, the damage control officer reported to the bridge, "but our pumps are handling it."

There were near misses on the *Betelgeuse* and *Libra*, two other AKAs standing by, before the bombers flew out. Condition Red continued, and at 1030 hours a second strike was mounted, this time with fifty planes: twenty-five Betty bombers and an equal number of Zeros. Again the damage to shipping was minimal; most of the weight of this attack was hurled at the dock and storage area, where huge fires burned out of control.

A far more serious matter was the ratio of American to Japanese plane losses. Brig. Gen. Louis Woods, who had just taken over the Cactus Air Force from Jiggs Geiger, shook his head as he went over the stats an hour after his birds had returned and Condition Green had been set. He felt, he said, like the new manager of a baseball club that had been shellacked 10-zip on the day he had taken over the reins. The averages had gone the other way. Discouraged, he called Vandegrift.

Seven of his planes had been shot down, he told the general, and four pilots killed, all from Duke Davis's Marine Fighter Group 121. The Duke himself had been wounded. Nine of the attacking bombers had been shot down. But here was a disquieting statistic: the Japanese had lost only four Zeros.

Vandegrift sought to console the new Cactus boss. No, he did not think the turnaround significant. No, he did not think Geiger's departure had created a morale problem. "He was the best there was, Louis.

335

There'll never be another. But he was tired. Now go get 'em, Colonel. They'll be back.''

Capt. Charlie McFeaters was no stranger to the waters around Guadalcanal. He was the captain of the "Wacky Mac" and had participated in the first landings on August 7. The *McCawley* was now the flagship of Task Force 67.1, the sometime home of Rear Adm. Richmond K. Turner, and on the afternoon of November 12 was nearing Kukum dock area to await her turn to be unloaded.

She had been sent in company with three other AKAs as part of the reinforcement column promised by Admiral Halsey. Off her bow were three other veterans of the landings: the *Crescent City* and two ex-president liners, the *Adams* and the *Jackson.* Aboard the ships and lining the rails were the 1st and 2d Battalions of the 182nd Infantry, Americal Division. Packed in with the dogfaces were members of the 4th Marine Replacement battalion.

Around 1330 the semaphores blinked between ships, and a short time later the Condition Red klaxon blared through the companionways and along the *McCawley*'s decks. Coastwatchers at Buin had sent word: bombers and fighters were on the way.

Admiral Turner quickly broke off the unloading and the ships got underway, the transports falling in line between parallel columns of men of war. They set a snake-dance trail toward Savo. At 1405, with the *McCawley*'s sides shaking and her troops tucked below, the lookout picked up nineteen incoming attackers diving down from twenty-five thousand feet.

Seconds earlier, Major Foss had seen them too, from

four thousand feet higher. Foss had seven F4Fs behind him as he dove on the Japanese bombers. Foss's air-speed indicator crept by the red line of three hundred knots and his canopy blew off. He caught the Bettys just as they began their torpedo run. By then the sky was black with antiaircraft bursts and the transports weaved wildly, moving across the white wakes of the twenty-seven ships of war committed to the transports' preservation. Now quick bursts of flame and long black smoke trails appeared, larger than life, among the ack-ack. Foss had been joined by Major Fontana and a second flight of Grummans. The Bettys started dropping like mallards at a duck shoot.

It was all over in eight minutes. All but two of the attackers had been brought down. Eight P-39s took after the survivors and got one of them. When the all-clear sounded, the troops below came up for a breather. The air had been as hot in the buttoned-down holds as the action had been topside. There were still reminders about as they headed back for the unloading area. A crippled bomber had crashed into the after control-station of the cruiser *San Francisco*, knocking out her fire-control radar and causing fifty casualties, including the ship's executive officer, Comdr. Mark Crouter.

The destroyer *Buchanan* had been severely damaged topside by friendly but misdirected antiaircraft fire. In the waters as they passed, soldiers of the Americal saw several of the twin-engine Bettys, tails still afloat.

They had received their baptism, McFeaters noted, but they had bounced right back. "Jesus! Mother told me there'd be days like this."

By nightfall he and his mates were ashore. And the

Wacky Mac, along with her sister transports, was headed back to Espiritu Santo, from a job well done.

At 0001 hours on Friday, October 13, Vice Adm. Hiroaki Abe's Combat Group 11, heading south toward Guadalcanal from Santa Isabel, reversed its course. The ships had run into a squall. Visibility fell to zero.

Group 11 had a mission that night: to bombard Henderson Field, to reduce the dock area to rubble, and to shell the marine positions. It was to be a repeat performance of the Night of the Battleships, and cocky little Abe, a barroom fighter, had the muscle to do it.

Admiral Abe's flag was aboard the battleship *Hiei*, which followed the battleship *Kirishima* in a tight 180-degree turn. In the van were seven destroyers; off to the flank was the light cruiser *Nagara*. Bringing up the rear were seven more DDs.

For the mission, shell hoists on the two battlewagons had been crammed with thin-shelled, high-explosive, quick-fuse projectiles, ideal for shore bombardment but of little use against naval armor. As the battleships marked time, precautionary orders sped down the line: Prepare to change from HE to armor-piercing ammunition. Groans went up from the hoist crews as they awaited the execution order. It would be heavy, backbreaking work.

Forty minutes later, a cheer went up from the ammo-passers. "Cancel precautionary order." Admiral Abe had received word that Guadalcanal was clear. Group 11 once more headed south.

Abe's force had rendezvoused that afternoon seventy miles north of Indispensable Strait. He had intelligence

338

galore of the presence of American cruisers. But the fact that other Japanese task forces were in the area, plus the knowledge that American fighting ships usually left with the sun, had once again influenced Japanese strategy.

That all the converging Japanese columns had been sighted and reported, he had no doubt. And in this he had been accurate. The day before, an amazed coastwatcher in the Buin-Faisi station had radioed the following to his contact station: "Never seen so many bloody Nips in me whole life. You're not going to believe this, old fruit, but I counted sixty-one frigging ships. Must be the whole damned Jap Navy."

The report had since been refined somewhat. Passed forward it read like this: "Sixty-one enemy vessels bearing south from Buin, including positive identification of six cruisers, thirty-three destroyers, and eleven large transports."

Admiral Abe sailed on. The time for the bombardment of Guadalcanal had been set back to 0130. His presence was first noted at 0124 by a tiny blip on the radar scope of the *Helena*. In seconds, two more traces appeared and the warning went out: "Contacts bearing 312 and 310. Distance 27,000 and 32,000 yards."

The opposing forces were closing the approximate fifteen miles separating them at a collective speed of forty knots. The initial advantage of radar was being diminished: the American force would soon be within view of Japanese nightglasses.

There was some confusion as the range narrowed. The *San Francisco*'s radar, unfortunately, was not providing sound information, so Admiral Callaghan had to rely upon TBS, or ship-to-ship shortwave, for relayed information from *Helena* and the destroyer *O'Bannon*. The airwaves soon became jumbled. Finally at 0145, twenty-one minutes after the initial detection, Admiral Callaghan gave the open fire command. The Japanese column, which by now had rounded Savo Island, was still caught by surprise. But the advantage quickly dissipated. Japanese searchlights added to the confusion, and the *Atlanta*, the leading cruiser, was taken under fire. Her participation in the fight was brief. One salvo hit the misnamed "Lucky A" on the bridge, killing Admiral Scott, the victor of the battle of Cape Esperance, and all but one member of his staff. Two torpedoes, fired by destroyers at close range, shook the ship to its beam ends, and she lay dead in the water.

Another fire order went out from the *San Francisco*: "Odds ships commence fire to starboard, even ships to port." In the twisting, rodeo-like melee that followed, that order became meaningless. There was no port, no starboard, no direction to the attack. The center of the field of action had become a maelstrom in which destroyers took on battleships at point-blank range.

The destroyer *Barton*, launched only five months before, had a total combat life of just seven minutes. Two torpedoes broke her in half and she plunged to the bottom like a rock, taking with her all but a few hands.

The *O'Bannon* was more fortunate. She had just launched two torpedoes at the *Hiei* when the battleship blazed back with her 14-inchers. A split second later, an enormous broadside whistled overhead, sounding like a freight train moving across a steel bridge. The

O'Bannon avoided instant oblivion because the dreadnought could not depress her muzzles sufficiently.

The *Laffey* lay further away. That sealed her doom. Two salvoes from the *Hiei* and a torpedo in her stern ended her life quickly. There were those who survived the broadside but perished minutes later when the burning hulk exploded. A fourth destroyer, the *Cushing*, was caught in the pitiless glare of searchlights, brought under fire quickly, and reduced to a sinking wreck.

In only minutes, one cruiser and five destroyers in the U.S. van had been lost. And now a second puzzling order was sent from the flagship, even as the cruisers went into action: "Cease firing own ships." No record of ship positions at that exact moment exists. But it is clear that the vanguard of the American column had penetrated to the very center of Admiral Abe's force. The *Portland*, the *Juneau*, and four destroyers in the rear were close behind, their batteries blazing. The *Hiei*, the focus of all, was bearing the brunt of increasingly accurate fire.

As the cease-fire order was given, the *San Francisco*'s main-battery control officer had the Japanese battle-wagon in his cross-hairs. He closed the firing keys and blasted away. The *Hiei* shuddered under the impact. A survivor from *Laffey*, swimming in the water a half mile away, saw a sheet of incandescent fire envelop the Japanese ship.

Moments later an incredulous inquiry was directed to Admiral Callaghan. The TBS crackled on the bridge of the *San Francisco*. It was Capt. Laurance DuBose of the *Portland*.

"What's the dope?" the amazed DuBose shouted over the din of the *Portland*'s main battery. "We're not engaging our own ships. Did you want us to cease, repeat cease, fire?"

There was a pause while the TBS operator checked the flag bridge. He was back in a few seconds. "Affirmative!" he said. An uncomprehending DuBose shook his head in disbelief.

What the intent of the order really was will never be known. Suddenly, up ahead, the *San Francisco* was illuminated in the brilliance of thousands of candlepower. Powerful searchlights etched her familiar silhouette against the darkness of night, bathing her superstructure, main batteries, and clipper bow in their glare.

The *Kirishima*, with her mighty fourteen-inch batteries, had entered the battle. A full broadside crunched into the American heavy cruiser. The topside damage wrought by the thin-cased high-explosive shells was awesome. The bridge was a shambles. Admiral Callaghan had given his last order.

The *Portland* had ceased fire briefly, but she renewed it again as the *San Francisco* burned along her entire length. It had become clear to DuBose that few had complied with the admiral's final order. Now, as the *Portland* steamed past the stricken ship, her gunnery officers picked up the *Kirishima*. Before a salvo could be fired, a terrific explosion rocked the cruiser's aft section. A torpedo had ripped off a large section of *Portland*'s stern, and she was unable to answer the helm. As the crippled ship steered lazily in wide circles, the *Hiei* was unmasked and both of *Portland*'s forward turrets, loaded earlier for the

Kirishima, were turned on Admiral Abe's flagship. The battlewagon shook under the direct hit, the second one it had taken in a matter of minutes.

It was enough for the admiral. It had now become obvious that he would not be able to complete his primary mission, the bombardment of Henderson Field. And he had not come out loaded with the proper armor-piercing shells to bring this fight to its proper conclusion. The admiral scanned the damage control report handed him. The *Hiei* had been badly mauled. The *Kirishima*, fortunately, had suffered only superficial damage. The light cruiser *Yudachi* had been badly hit, and one destroyer had been sunk. It was time to leave the field.

At 0203 hours, just eighteen minutes after action had been joined, Abe ordered his course reversed, the *Kirishima* leaving by the channel to the left of Savo Island, the *Hiei* limping by the channel to its right.

Henderson Field had been spared its second Night of the Battleships.

As dawn of Friday the 13th broke, there wasn't a man on Guadalcanal who was unaware of the great sea battle that had taken place in the wee hours of the morning. They had heard the rolling cannonade of big guns, they had seen the skies light up in the fury of fire and explosions. Fragmentary action reports had been filtering in to division headquarters via Noumea since 0200, and as they were pieced together it became evident that despite heavy losses, the navy had turned back two battleships.

Vandegrift, who remembered only too well the devastation inflicted on his field by two other Japanese dreadnoughts, offered a warrior's prayer for the navy's intercession and a sincere, heartfelt vote of thanks to Bull Halsey for keeping his word.

He was on the phone to Louis Woods through the night, exchanging bits and pieces of information and intelligence. Now at first light the Cactus Air Force, which had been spared through navy sacrifice, would sally forth to avenge the losses.

"There are two battlewagons out there, General," Woods said, "and we're going to get 'em both."

Vandegrift silently noted the renewed confidence of his new air boss and merely said: "Attaboy, Louie."

Woods's first strike left the field at 0600. It was commanded by Maj. Bob Richard, with five dive bombers carrying thousand-pounders. The mountains of Guadalcanal turned from black to purple and then to green as VMSB 142 climbed off the field and circled for altitude. The sight and smell of the jungle below was new to the squadron; they had just arrived the day before. Now they were on top and the panorama of Iron Bottom Bay unfolded before them.

Down below, off Lunga Point, they saw the crippled *Atlanta*, fighting to stay afloat, her admiral's body shrouded. Just off to her right was the *Portland*, still steaming in wide circles, still fighting. As they watched, a broadside belched from her sides, appearing like tiny smoke-rings from a cigarette.

Seconds later, seven miles away, the *Yudashi* erupted. The *Portland*'s salvos had hit the Japanese destroyer's magazine as she lay dead in the water. By the time the flight passed over, she was out of sight, headed for the bottom of Iron Bottom Bay. Two smoking Yankee hulks, the abandoned destroyers

Cushing and *Monssen*, lay off to the starboard. And all about them, the surface of the sea was covered by the flotsam and jetsam of tragedy.

Now Savo Island was raised. And on its northern side, away from Guadalcanal, lay their target: the *Hiei*, smoke from uncontrolled fires below still climbing in the skies. Her engines had broken down shortly after she retired from the fight. She lay close to Savo, as though searching for cover, the destroyer *Yukikaze* standing by like a terrier guarding its fallen master.

Major Richard waggled his wings; it had taken only fifteen minutes to reach his target. He called that information back to base and headed down. There were a couple of near misses; then a thousand-pounder landed amidships. The squadron headed home, leaving the *Hiei*'s forward guns dangling at crazy angles and leaving also a new plume of black smoke to guide others in the attack.

In the end, the *Hiei* sank, taking with her some of the best-laid plans for the recapture of Guadalcanal. There followed a hurried reorganization of fleet command; Admiral Abe was relieved in disgrace. He had transferred his flag to another ship when the *Hiei* had broken down. Now, as he left the field, he pondered the wisdom of having left the old battlewagon.

If the attack were to succeed, it was argued, Guadalcanal must be bombarded, the airfield neutralized for at least forty-eight hours. The decision was arrived at hastily, and the search for a force to do the job quickly narrowed to one man—Admiral Mikawa. Here was the veteran, the victor of the first battle of Savo Island. A man to be trusted.

All well and good, it was argued back; the field had to be hit and Mikawa was ideally fitted for the assignment, admittedly. But his heavy cruiser force, headed by the redoubtable *Chokai*, had been originally assigned to support the eleven Marus, the transports carrying the Hiroshima Division and its 13,500 troops. How about them? They were the raison d'être for the entire operation, were they not?

As darkness fell on November 13 the air-wave traffic between Truk (and a reluctant Admiral Yamamoto) and Onrong Java, headquarters afloat of the Combined Fleet, became overloaded. A not-so-reluctant Admiral Kondo, poised with his Advanced Force only 250 miles north of the action, won the final round. The attack would continue.

From the *Atago*, Kondo's flagship, the orders went out. Mikawa, with four heavy cruisers, two light cruisers, and six destroyers, would bombard the airfield. Support of the transport column would be left to Rear Admiral Tanaka. There was one final argument against this decision presented by staff officers at Truk. "But Tanaka has only eleven destroyers." Yamomoto, who could countermand, did not choose to; he merely shrugged.

The combat-loaded Hiroshima Division, which had been forwarded to Faisi, would discharge its troops on Guadalcanal after sunset on November 14. Air cover would be provided by the *Hiyo* and the *Junyo*. It was so ordered.

Dawn of November 14 found a strange collection of cripples beating their way southeasterly down Indispensable Straits on a course toward New Hebrides, out of the war zone. The evening before, they had patched up the damage suffered at Savo. And now, jerry-rigged and pumps going, they limped along at eighteen knots, heading for the barn and the repairs they all so desperately needed.

Captain Hoover of the *Helena*, the senior officer present, commanded the wounded. The column had left the cruiser *Portland* at Tulagi harbor. "Ol' Sweet Pea's" shot-out rudder could not be fixed in time. In Hoover's column were the *San Francisco*, her bridge still a bloody shambles; the *Juneau*, last in line and least injured; and the destroyers *O'Bannon*, *Sterrett*, and *Fletcher*.

At 0950 the *Sterrett*, riding shotgun, sounded a submarine alert. She followed with a depth-charge attack. An hour passed without further incident and then two torpedo wakes streaked across the *San Francisco*'s bow, heading toward the *Juneau*, a thousand yards off the Frisco's starboard beam. *San Francisco*'s TBS had been shot out the night before when "Uncle Dan" Callaghan had been killed. From the jerry-rigged bridge, her deck-watch now followed the progress of the torpedo wakes as they sped toward the ship on their flank. It was like watching a disaster in slow motion. There was little that one could do save follow the tangents and hope for the best. But the best was not in the *Juneau*'s destiny. Her Friday the 13th came one day late. Torpedo and ship came slowly together and there was a blinding crash as the Long Lance detonated against her port side, just abaft the bridge.

Horrified, crewmen aboard the *San Francisco* saw the light cruiser disintegrate completely. Within seconds she was gone except for a tall pillar of black smoke that marked the spot as the column moved on. There was scarcely a trace of debris.

Captain Hoover did not pause. The safety of his column was paramount. To a B-17 from Espiritu Santo, which had been attracted to the rising smoke, he dispatched a Mayday request for help to the survivors. There were American submarines in the area, he knew. Unfortunately, the message never got through.

Seven hundred sailors of the ship's complement perished in the blast. Of the hundred men who survived and clung pitifully to wreckage, awaiting rescue, only ten survived. Signalman 1st class L. E. Zook was among the ten. His graphic account of shark attacks, which took the lives of many of the wounded and dying, is chilling. Among those lost were the five Sullivan brothers.

News of the sinking was duly forwarded by the Japanese skipper of the I-26 to Vice Adm. Teruhisa Komatsu, commanding submarine patrol groups of the Advanced Expeditionary Force in Truk. "Have this date sunk the United States heavy cruiser *San Francisco* at .10 degree, 30 minutes south, long. 161 degrees, two minutes east."

It was the wrong ship, but the I-26 duly recorded the place where *Juneau* rests.

21

REQUIEM FOR A SAMURAI

There had been changes in American strategy, too, as the result of the early-morning action of Friday the 13th off Guadalcanal. With a penchant for putting neat, tidy labels on things, keepers on the naval combat log at COMSOPAC in Noumea had been tentatively identifying the engagement as either the third or fourth Battle of Savo. They were not quite sure which; there had been so many. As long as the action appeared likely to continue, it was argued, why not call it the Naval Battle of Guadalcanal?

Bull Halsey could not have cared less. He had committed himself to a fight, and by *any* name, this was only round one. It was the Bull at his best. He studied the dispositions, checked his losses, considered the options, and got ready for round two.

Injured or not, the carrier *Enterprise* had been sent up, hammers still beating out a tattoo on buckled plates, the arcs of her welders' torches lighting up the flight deck. As she steamed north at reduced speed, her forward elevators remained jammed.

Screening Kincaid's Task Force 16 were the cruisers *Northhampton* and *San Diego* and six destroyers. But the real power that supported the *Enterprise* was Task Force 64, under Rear Adm. Willis Augustus (Ching) Lee, with the battleships *Washington* and *South Dakota*.

There was only one fly in the ointment, one bit of poor staff planning. The Big E's lowered speed held up her escorts. *Washington* and *South Dakota* would not arrive off Savo until 0800 hours on November 14, Kincaid reported.

The night of November 13–14 would find Guadalcanal protected only by a few squadrons of motor torpedo boats based at Tulagi.

With new orders in his pocket, Admiral Mikawa entered upon this scene. At 0001 on the morning of November 14, his cruisers and destroyers arrived off Savo Island, having taken a lengthy detour by way of Choiseul and Santa Isabel islands to escape detection.

The cagey old fox positioned his flagships, the *Chokai*, westward of Savo to avoid the surprise that had cost Admiral Abe his command. He then sent the heavy cruisers *Suzuya* and *Maya*, the light cruiser *Tenryu*, and four destroyers eastward along the coast of Guadalcanal. Soon he heard the far-off rumble of the heavy cruisers' 8-inch batteries and the lighter staccato of 6-inch and 5-inch guns of the light cruiser and its destroyers.

For thirty-seven minutes, Henderson Field caught it. Pilots and ground crews buttoned up in foxholes, revetments, and dugouts, being joined by more than one hundred survivors from the *Atlanta*.

"Does this happen often?" a tight-lipped bluejacket asked his foxhole buddy, a veteran Cactus crew chief.

"Almost every night," the marine tech sergeant

lied. "You're lucky, pal, this is only Washing Machine Charlie. You ought to be here when the Tokyo Express comes along."

Eight-inch high explosives and invectives filled the air. Then, as suddenly as it began, the shelling ceased. "Hey," the sergeant nudged his companion with an elbow, "you lucked out again. That wasn't the feature . . . just a short subject."

Admiral Nishimura had sent a TBS communication to his chief in the *Chokai*. "Enemy patrol boats are becoming more aggressive. Adopting evasive action against torpedo attacks."

Mikawa studied the action report briefly, then made his decision: "Cease firing, reverse courses." The mosquito fleet, while not scoring any hits, had succeeded in shortening the bombardment. Even more important, the unit originally scheduled to support the advance of the troopships was now forced to leave the field, its ammunition nearly expended and its fuel tanks low. Mikawa set course back to his base in the Shortlands.

As the shelling ceased, Cactus lit up. Division wanted to assess the damage. Jeeps roared around Fighter 2 and Henderson with clipboards and staff officers. Within half an hour a pretty good picture had evolved. Not so bad—by comparison, that is, to what might have happened had the *Hiei* and *Kirishima* and their 14-inchers worked-over the field.

Louis Woods was on the phone, giving the totals to Vandegrift's chief of staff. Gerry Thomas penciled in the figures: seventeen fighters destroyed, thirty-two damaged. One bomber hit.

"How about the fields?" asked Thomas.

"The Seabee guys and our Engineers are already on the ball. They say they'll have them both patched up before first light."

Back across the International Date Line in the nation's capitol, Friday the 13th was beginning. James V. Forrestal had just given the president the morning briefing. He noted tears in the chief executive's eyes as he reported the death of Roosevelt's friend and former naval aide, Admiral Callaghan.

"What does it all mean, Jim? Have they broken through? Must we evacuate?"

Forrestal later recalled that tension and frustration hung over the oval office like a pall. He had never experienced anything quite like it. Reassurance was hard to come by as he listed the losses of the past two days, including last night's bombardment of the airfield.

And there were the reports about the Hiroshima division on its way. . . .

At 0630 hours on November 14 the battleships *Washington* and *South Dakota* were sixty miles SSW of Guadalcanal. They had missed a fight by eight hours. Limping toward the scene was the *Enterprise*, about 130 miles to their rear. Damage-control crews still hammered away at the forward elevators. Foul weather had delayed her dawn patrol, but now she had two planes aloft searching toward the north, and on her patched-up flight deck ten fighters and seventeen dive-bombers awaited the call to action. The SBDs packed thousand-pounders in their bellies.

At Henderson Field and Fighter Strip 2, true to their

promise, the guys who manned the bulldozers, Cats, blades, and scrapers had patched and filled, and stretched new Marston mats over the gaping holes left by the bombardment. The dawn search-flights got off on schedule.

They were looking for Mikawa. The old fox had thought to avoid detection by keeping out of the main Slot, directing his course far to the east of the New Georgia group. But Cactus search planes were becoming more sophisticated. By 0700 they had found him. The fix on his position crackled back to the field, and six Avengers and seven Dauntless bombers, covered by seven fighters, rose to the attack.

At 0800 the retiring Japanese column was engaged. The heavy cruiser *Kinugasa* and light cruiser *Isuzu* were hit repeatedly, leaving behind long trails of black smoke to guide other squadrons to the attack. Lieutenant Comdr. James Lee, in command of the *Enterprise* attack group, needed no second invitation. From the flight deck of the damaged carrier, his group swarmed aloft and was soon over the smoking *Kinugasa*. Two hits were registered and a near-miss ruptured the heavy cruiser's fuel tanks. A wall of flame shot into the air, the ship listed, and before the elated Big E fliers left the scene, the *Kinugasa* had gone down. Mikawa's flagship likewise suffered damage, as did the *Maya*.

The now-crippled column would be hit three more times that morning by small-squadron action before it got beyond the two-hundred-mile striking radius. Mikawa would bring his shattered force into the safety of his base in the Shortlands before night fell. But his suspected role as a decoy for the transport fleet was unmasked even as the *Kinugasa* sank beneath the waves.

And now a new excitement rippled over Henderson Field. Its shock waves reached division headquarters, bounded off the damaged flight deck of the *Enterprise*, and rebounded far south to Noumea. The transports of the Hiroshima Division had been located!

There had been unconfirmed and garbled reports of their presence as early as 0730 from a scout plane out of Henderson. The adrenalin really started pumping exactly one hour later, when lieutenants (jg.) Martin Carmody and Bill Johnson, flying SBDs off the *Enterprise*, radioed back that they had "sighted one transport through the clouds, moving south-southwest between New Georgia and Santa Isabel." They were proceeding to attack, they said.

The two navy pilots put their wings over and went down. Under the cover, they could see other transports spaced at tidy intervals and reaching to the far horizon. About them, sensing the attack, darted slim destroyers. Carmody selected the nearest transport and the SBDs went in. "We got a near-miss and a probable hit," came back the garbled report. "We also got bandits!"

Seven Zeros were on their tail. One of the scout bombers was shot down; the other made it back to the carrier with its tanks almost bone dry.

Louis Woods resisted the impulse to scramble everything flyable into a pell-mell attack. Crews were brought together and briefed. Ground crews were readied for their part in the action: they must be able to quickly rearm and refuel their birds for primary, secondary, and tertiary turnarounds, if necessary. There were to be no secondary targets, was that clearly understood? The transports and the transports alone were to be hit! Forget the destroyers. "Now, as to you fighter guys. Your job is cover, I repeat, cover!" Woods was warming to his task. "There'll be bandits up there, probably from the *Junyo* and the *Hiyo*. But I don't want you drawn away from your main job by any solo dogfights. OK, clear out!" Cactus, which had long been synonymous with hasty expedience, had at last become organized.

Woods checked with Vandegrift as his dispositions were being made. He asked that his request for coordination with Admiral Fitch in Noumea for B-17 bomber support be expedited through higher channels.

Jeeps tore through the area; heavy trucks rumbled up from ammo dumps, loaded with fat thousand-pounders. Others sped over the Marston mats, piled to the top with high-test gasoline drums, twenty-caliber ammunition belts, and thermos bottles filled with coffee. The cooks, the bakers, the headquarters personnel, and even the bluejackets of the *Atlanta* had been caught up in the excitement and had coalesced into a community with a single objective: sink the transports!

At 1130, three hours after the first alert, the first strike was mounted. Eighteen dive-bombers followed by seven torpedo bombers trundled down the runways and took off. Circling overhead were twelve F4Fs, their fighter cover. Flight Two was already standing by, its seventeen dive-bombers and fighter cover taxiing toward the runways.

It took less than half an hour for the attack wave to reach its target, one hundred miles out. They had passed over Savo Island, that grim conical pile that had been identified with so much tragedy. A little further on, the Russell Islands came into view on their left. There were only patchy clouds in the Slot. And now, up ahead, churning in symmetrical evasive-action patterns, the eleven transports and their escorts came into view.

Back at Cactus, the monitors on plane-to-plane commo began broadcasting bedlam. One voice came in more clearly than any of the others through the static. "Geronimo!" it yelled. They were going in.

The attack started at twelve thousand feet and was over in minutes. They strafed, pulled up, and headed for the barn. Looking back, they could see that several ships had been hit.

Nearing the field, they passed the second wave going out. There was much wing-wagging, and at 1245 hours the Japanese column, now in disarray and lacking cohesion, received its second blow. One transport, taking a direct hit, broke in two.

In quick debriefings held as the two strike forces were being rearmed and refueled, Woods attempted to assess the Japanese losses. In the heat of battle and its excitement, this proved a difficult task. One transport had been definitely sunk. Several others had hulled and were believed sinking. Few of the eleven had escaped damage.

As to Cactus losses, they were minimal. Antiaircraft fire from the destroyers had been ineffective. Only a few holes had been noted as planes scorched rubber, coming in. Their crew chiefs set frantically to work patching up the damage. No Zekes had been encountered.

Round three of Woods's planned offensive went to

fifteen Flying Fortresses which had taken off from Espiritu Santo at 1018 hours. They lumbered in at 1430 hours, and so did an equal number of Zeros. The Forts started their selective bomb-runs at eighteen thousand feet, dropping fifteen tons of high explosives on the squirming ships below. They scored one bulls-eye; that transport almost disintegrated upon impact.

The B-17s proved formidable in air action as well, the Japanese were to learn. With nose-, waist-, top-, and tail-guns blazing, they shot down seven Zekes. The surviving Zeros headed back with a costly lesson learned: a Flying Fortress has no blind spots.

Rear Adm. Raizo Tanaka watched the last of the B-17s disappear into the southern skies. From his tiny bridge on the *Hayashio*, the destroyer-group commander somberly reviewed the options left to him.

He had already been subjected to three devastating attacks. There would be more, he knew, and he felt both abandoned and betrayed. The cruisers he'd been promised had been taken from him. The battleships were long gone. Now the air support that was to cover his advance had proven utterly inadequate. Yet if he were to withdraw, his mission would be considered a failure, of course, and he would follow Admiral Abe into disgrace. The loss of face he would suffer was even more terrible to contemplate than the loss of the transports themselves.

Somehow, somewhere, he realized, a tragic blunder had been committed. So there were no options, really. Regardless of loss, he would have to press on, even though some of his destroyers were already packed with the survivors of the sunken or broken troopship hulks.

Orders flashed back along the line: "Form up and proceed on course."

Aboard the *Hayashio* a bosun's whistle shrilled, its notes attuned to the whine of the wind through the rigging. Together, they performed a sorrowful yet fitting requiem for a samurai.

The luckless little admiral had been correct. The air attacks continued, and supplied a classic illustration of what can happen to lightly protected ships that venture into the range of shore-based aircraft.

As the afternoon wore on, the action turned into a circus. The *Enterprise* was caught up in the excitement and Admiral Kincaid gave the word to "shoot the works."

At 1310, Fighter 10 was dispatched, arriving on the scene in time to watch two bomber groups from Cactus coming under fire from Zero fighters. Flatley's Wildcats bore in, taking on the Zekes and sending them packing. They stayed to watch another Cactus relay start a new run; then they buzzed down after them to strafe the transports at mast level.

Lieutenant Commander Thomas, commanding Bomber Ten from the Big E, took off at 1530 with seven planes and no escorts. For the moment no fighters were available. Zekes shot down three of the SBDs, damaged two, and sent the four survivors diving for the cover of the field.

At last, by 1600, it was all over. *Enterprise* had only eighteen planes left on board. The rest were settled down at Henderson and Fighter 2 with their Cactus buddies. Louis Woods sized up the situation and called it a day. Tired pilots made mistakes, the kind of mistakes that had cost those three SBDs. The order to "secure" was passed around.

Aboard the *Enterprise* that order had already gone out. She had done her bit this day, Halsey reasoned, and he ordered her back to Noumea.

It was a tired but exhilarated gaggle of flyers that shared the squadron messes on Guadalcanal that night. Carrier pilots, used to better fare, wolfed down corned beef hash with relish, little noting the absence of white napery and silver. Bottles of Scotch, half-bottles of gin, and even quarter-bottles of bourbon, all momentoes of previous 'fat cat' runs to Noumea, turned up as if by magic. There was not a man present who hadn't made at least a couple of trips on the merry-go-round. Some claimed four or five runs. The 'lies' and the jokes poured out. Bucky Lee couldn't remember how many strikes he had made. Neither could Bob Richard or Joe Sailer. Scoffer Coffin, the skipper of a torpedo squadron, was unable to recall a single detail.

At headquarters a cloudy picture had to be transmitted forward. It was firmly believed that at least five of the transports had been sunk, perhaps more. All had been hit, that much appeared certain.

In fact four transports had remained afloat. Seven had been sunk, among them the *Arizona Maru* on whose deck Lt. Masao Hirokawa had stood watching his troops "playing like small puppies." Now there were two Arizonas lying at the bottom, their holds filled with the dead. With her were her sister Marus, the *Shinanogawa*, *Nako*, *Nagaro*, *Sado*, *Brisbane*, and *Canberra*.

It was thought by the American command that the survivors would make their way north, away from the fight, during the night. They had not fully considered the tenacity of Admiral Tanaka.

As dawn broke on November 15, three of the tragic Marus were spotted on the beach off Tassafaronga Point. During the night they had been unloaded of all that was not burned or dead. A fourth vessel, unable to beach, lay off the point, dead in the water.

"Well, I'll be damned. Look at what we got here," the forward observer of the 3d Defense Battalion said to his instrument corporal. A few orders over the phone brought the muzzles of his big 155s swinging upward to maximum range. Offshore, he noted, the destroyer *Meade*'s turrets were moving, too.

Within seconds, salvos from both ship and shore artillery arched toward the Japanese ships. Huge fires erupted on their decks as the shells poured in. Columns of black smoke began drifting aloft.

A giant funeral pyre for the Hiroshima Division had been lit.

EPILOGUE

A brief sequel to the destruction of the transport fleet was played out with all the stiff formality of a Kabuki play. Admiral Kondo had been waiting offstage for his cue in the late evening hours of November 14; at 2300 he made his entrance. Leading a powerful cruiser force supported by the battleship *Kirishima*, he approached Guadalcanal in three columns by way of Savo Island.

It was to be the last time that Iron Bottom Sound would provide the theater for a major naval engagement.

The cast of characters included Rear Adm. Willis Augustus Lee, commander of Task Force 64, supported by Capt. Glenn Davis of the *Washington* and Capt. Tom Gatch on *South Dakota*. Four United States destroyers, the *Walke*, the *Benham*, the *Preston*, and the *Gwin*, had supporting roles, and only the *Gwin* would escape destruction. The other three would be sent to the bottom in an area that had claimed more ships in battle than any in the world.

Adm. Ching Lee utilized modern radar to the limit of its capacity in positioning his units for the final scene of the naval battle of Guadalcanal. In so doing, he denied Kondo's approach to Henderson Field, where the heavy cruisers *Atago* and *Takao* and the battleship *Kirishima* were to have neutralized the field and destroyed not only Cactus Air Force but the squadrons of the *Enterprise* as well. Still lurking somewhere to the north were the carriers *Junyo* and *Hiyo*. If Kondo should be successful, they might still turn the tide.

But Kondo promptly lost his major bombardment arm, the 14-inch batteries of the *Kirishima*. She sank at 0014 hours, battered by the 16-inch rifles of *Washington*, at the spot not ten miles away from the grave of the *Hiei*.

It was Kondo's final operation.

In the days and weeks that followed the annihilation of the Hiroshima Division, battle-weary marine units had been withdrawn to Australia for rest and recreation. Replacements by army troops, first a trickle, quickly moved to flood stage. And now, all that was left of the original cast that had landed four months ago were a few marine units and their commanding general.

For General Vandegrift, the last operation in the battle for Guadalcanal had come to its close. On December 9, 1942, the last phase began when command of troops on the island passed from Maj. Gen. A. A. Vandegrift, United States Marine Corps.

There was no ceremony, just a final exchange of views between two men sitting on a pile of sandbags outside the headquarters dugout. Then a handshake, and that was it. Maj. Gen. Alexander A. Patch, senior army officer present and commander of the Americal Division, had taken over.

This was a normal relief for marines who had borne

the brunt of four months' fighting against a fanatical foe. They had done their utmost and earned the gratitude of their navy and army comrades as well as that of the entire nation. Their outstanding work under their superb commander was over. Now it was their army's turn to complete the task. The 1st Marine Division would soon be ready to fight again on other invasion beaches.

As his twin-motor PBY lifted off Henderson, Vandegrift looked down for the last time. The scenery was unchanged. There was the long runway cutting through the coco palms to the ridge behind. There was Fighter 2. And off to the left, Tassafaronga Point and the unmistakable shapes of the blackened, twisted transports. A thousand memories pushed forward, and he shuddered as the altitude brought a chill to the cabin.

"There are still a lot of Japs down there!"

An aide leaned forward, "Sir?"

"We'll have to root 'em out." The moment passed and Vandegrift chuckled. "What do I mean 'we'? That's Patch's job."

Midday found the 5th Marines, tattered C-Bags hoisted on their shoulders, heading for Kukum dock. Colonel Merritt Edson's veterans of Bloody Ridge were being evacuated. Some of them had been on the line for 122 consecutive days. They were a tired but happy lot; bearded, emaciated, yellow as gourds. Fully seventy-five percent would be hospitalized for malaria the moment they docked in Australia. They had paid their dues, they felt, and they were proud that their unit rated high on the Corps' list for honors awarded.

The division had taken eight thousand combat casualties in four months, with roughly a one to four ratio of killed or missing in action. The army, still fighting, would ultimately present a comparably grim accounting. As for the navy, the ratio of killed to wounded was almost reversed; thousands of bluejackets had gone down with the ships that lined Iron Bottom Bay.

They had paid a terrible price; but that was not all that was in the minds of the "Fighting Fifth" as they stumbled past army units moving the other way from Kukum. The marines joshed their neatly dressed but equally laden replacements unmercifully. As paid-up members they had earned that right, they reasoned.

"Hey, mac, where you goin'? Ain't no USO up that-a-way!"

"Check them shaves, would ja? Hey, fellas, who's the company barber, Perry Como?"

There were instant rejoinders from the army, naturally: "Stow it, shitheads, we're going to finish up what you guys couldn't!"

"Oh yeah?"

"Yeah!"

There was one indignity that the marines failed to match. They saw it as they neared the docks, and they exploded. There, across the dusty coral road, had been stretched a hospital bedsheet. Fresh black paint still dripped from the crude banner. It read: "Through these portals passes the Queen of Battles . . . the United States Infantry!"

"Hey, do you see what I see? Get that goddamn sign down," an infuriated gunny sergeant roared. Hoots of derision moving up and down the ragged column.

Lusty cheers followed as the offending sign came down, torn to a thousand pieces by eager hands.

And just as suddenly the column was gone.

The 'Queen of Battles' sign would be put up again on Guadalcanal. In the bitter fighting ahead the army would pay its dues, and earn that right. It started as General Patch went back into the dugout to study anew the graphs and arrows on the command map. His task was as different from that of the man he relieved as day is from night. The strategic tables had been turned. As at Stalingrad, half a world away, the besiegers had become the besieged. The Seventeenth Japanese Army, isolated, cut off, and soon to be forgotten, was to become a ghost army of small but desperate men. It was Patch's job to liquidate it. He had the muscle needed to accomplish it.

Two army regiments, the 182d and the 132d, had already joined the battle-tested 164th. Now the Americal Division was fully constituted. The balance of the Marine 2d Division would soon arrive; behind them, the 25th Army Division, fleshed out by units of the 40th Division, was en route from Hawaii. Reinforcements were at full flood. There was even an outfit designated as the 3d Barrage Balloon Squadron slated to make its appearance before the year was out.

Bitter fighting still lay ahead. The surviving Sendai Division warriors under General Maruyama would see to that. So would the Kawaguchis, the Ichikis, and the pitiful remnants of the 3d Special Kure Detachment, original invaders of the island, as well as an estimated eight hundred to a thousand members of the Hiroshima Division who'd make it ashore. They were to continue the fighting for two months. The word surrender would never be considered.

On February 9, 1943, a message to General Patch came over the field telephone. Two patrols, one from the 161st Infantry, the other from the 132d Infantry, had linked up on the banks of the Umasani River. This marked the final closure of a pincer movement against organized Japanese resistance. The Army G-3 section was excited. The arrows on their situation map were repositioned quickly. Circles of command responsibility were hastily drawn in crayon on the acetate overlays.

General Patch was called in to study the updated map. The previous evening he had received intelligence reports that Japanese headquarters units had been evacuated. The signs of a hasty withdrawal were all there on the beach of Umasani, the patrols reported—abandoned trucks, weapons, ammunition, stores, and supplies. It was evident that the last section of the Tokyo Express had left the station.

Patch looked around at his staff. "We can say, gentlemen, that Guadalcanal is secure," he announced.

There was a spontaneous cheer.

The campaign had cost the Japanese 51,180 lives, but there were still Japanese in the bush—a lot of them. They were desperate men, drawn together in pathetic groups by a code that eschewed surrender and made its acceptance impossible.

There were a few with less tenacity, however.

One of those was Sgt. Matsuo Sakai. Months after the island had been declared secure by General Patch, the 1st Battalion, 160th Infantry, left its bivouac area near the Tenaru River early one sodden, rain-drenched morning for a three-day maneuver twenty-five miles east of the old perimeter.

The exercise was scheduled as part of an amphibious "dress rehearsal" for a landing on New Ireland, the next step up the ladder toward the Japanese homeland. General Homer Eaton, once the regimental executive officer for the 160th and now a member of MacArthur's staff, had predicted the landings would be a bloody affair, particularly because Kavieng, the still-mighty Japanese naval base, was located there. MacArthur himself was less than enthusiastic over the prospects. There were those on his staff who went farther, calling the operation suicidal.

The mission of the 160th Infantry was to secure a lodgement in the middle of the wasp-waisted island and to deny reinforcements up the single road which connected Kavieng with Japanese forces at the other end.

Rehearsals went on, landing craft moving the troops to the mouth of the Berendo River, where they splashed ashore under conditions which, if not approximating the landing beaches on New Ireland, did in a broad sense simulate them.

In bivouac that night near the native village of Tina, where Kawaguchi's Brigade had once bedded down, Company D, the heavy-weapons unit of the battalion, set up its field kitchens. The rain, which had poured down all day, continued during the night. The men of D-Company splashed through the mess line, pulling up their ponchos to keep the beef stew in their mess gear from being inundated.

A single Coleman lamp sputtered at the head of the shuffling line and a small tent fly protected the steaming dixies. Into this circle of light there appeared a tiny figure, between two burly machine-gun corporals. He held his plate out like the others.

But the long and the short of it caught the eye of Mess Sgt. Archie O'Quinn as he watched the company's two-hundred-odd men file past. He turned to his first cook, Lester Fruith, in amazement.

"Hell, Les," he said, "we ain't got nobody that small in this outfit."

He was right. The diminutive figure looking for a G.I. handout that night was Sergeant Sakai, formerly of the Third Special Kure Battalion, which had reinforced Tulagi one hundred days before the marines made their initial landing.

He had made his way across Sealark Channel in a small boat with a few other survivors, and had "taken to the bush" on Guadalcanal. The others, he believed, were all dead.

Later, 1st Sgt. John V. Federoff ducked his head under the tent fly which sheltered the company commander, the platoon leaders of D-Company, and a very damp session of hearts and cribbage.

Around the ammunition cases which served as tables were the dim faces of "Lee's Lieutenants:" Warren Romans, Harvey Jewett, Frank Glusenkamp, John DePotter, Bill Bartley, and George Miller. Outside the light cast by a single sputtering candle, Lawrence Becherer, the company runner, struggled to put up a newfangled contraption which had found its way to the South Pacific, a "jungle hammock." It was a lethal affair if one turned over in the middle of the night.

"Captain," Fedoroff said, pushing a much-delayed Morning Report forward, "Funny thing happened: we picked up an extra ration tonight.''

"You've got to be kidding, Top. An extra ration? Out here?''

Federoff had his tongue in his cheek. "Yes, sir. He's a transfer from the 3d Kure Special Battalion, he says.''

"Well I'll be damned! Did you feed him?''

"Fed him beans. And marked him duty.''

As it turned out, the prisoner of war had been witness to the first round fired in the American counteroffensive against the Japanese. His immediate superior back on November 7, 1942, when the cruiser *San Juan* pumped out the opening round on the Tulagi parade ground, had been Lieutenant Juntaro.

He would not be witness to the last.

Ahead were Tarawa, New Guinea, Leyte, Luzon, Iwo Jima, Okinawa . . . and Hiroshima. That was not in the minds of the men who continued at hearts and cribbage games. The sputtering candle revealed no such emotions. There was tonight to be lived through. And tomorrow yet to be embraced.

The captain signed the Morning Report, "Small world,'' he said, handing it back.

BIBLIOGRAPHY

Caidin, Martin, and Fred Saito. *Samurai!* New York: E. P. Dutton, 1957.

Casey, Robert J. *Torpedo Junction.* Indianapolis: the Bobbs-Merrill Co., 1942.

Charles, Roland W. *Troopships of World War II.* Washington, D.C.: The Army Transport Association, 1947.

Coggins, Jack. *The Campaign for Guadalcanal.* New York: Doubleday & Co., 1972.

Custer, Joe James. *Through the Perilous Night.* New York: Macmillan, 1944.

Feldt, Eric A. *The Coast Watchers.* New York: Oxford University Press, 1946.

Foster, John T. *Guadalcanal General: The Story of A. A. Vandegrift, U.S.M.C.* New York: William Morrow & Co., 1966.

Fuchida, Midsuo, and Masatake Okumiya. *Midway: The Battle That Doomed Japan.* Annapolis: Naval Institute Press, 1955.

Griffith, Samuel B. *The Battle for Guadalcanal.* Philadelphia: J. B. Lippincott Co., 1963.

Halsey, William, and J. Bryan III. *Admiral Halsey's Story.* New York: Da Capo, 1976.

Hough, Frank O., Verle E. Ludwig, and Henry I.

Shaw, Jr. *History of the United States Marine Corps in World War II*. Washington, D.C.: U.S. Marine Corps Historical Division, 1960.

Jane's Fighting Ships. Annual volumes. New York: Macmillan, 1936–41.

Japanese Aircraft Carriers and Destroyers. London: Macdonald, 1964.

Leckie, Robert. *Challenge for the Pacific*. New York: Doubleday & Co., 1965.

Lee, Clark G. *They Call It Pacific*. New York: Viking Press, 1943.

Lord, Walter. *Incredible Victory*. New York: Harper & Row, 1971.

————. *Lonely Vigil: Coastwatchers of the Solomons*. New York: Viking Press, 1977.

Merillat, Herbert L. *Island: A History of the First Marine Division on Guadalcanal, August 7–December 9, 1942*. Washington, D.C.: Zenger, 1944.

Miller, Thomas G., Jr. *The Cactus Air Force*. New York: Harper & Row, 1969.

Morison, Samuel E. *History of the United States Naval Operations in World War II, Volume 5: The Struggle for Guadalcanal, August 1942–February 1943*. New York: Little Brown, 1949.